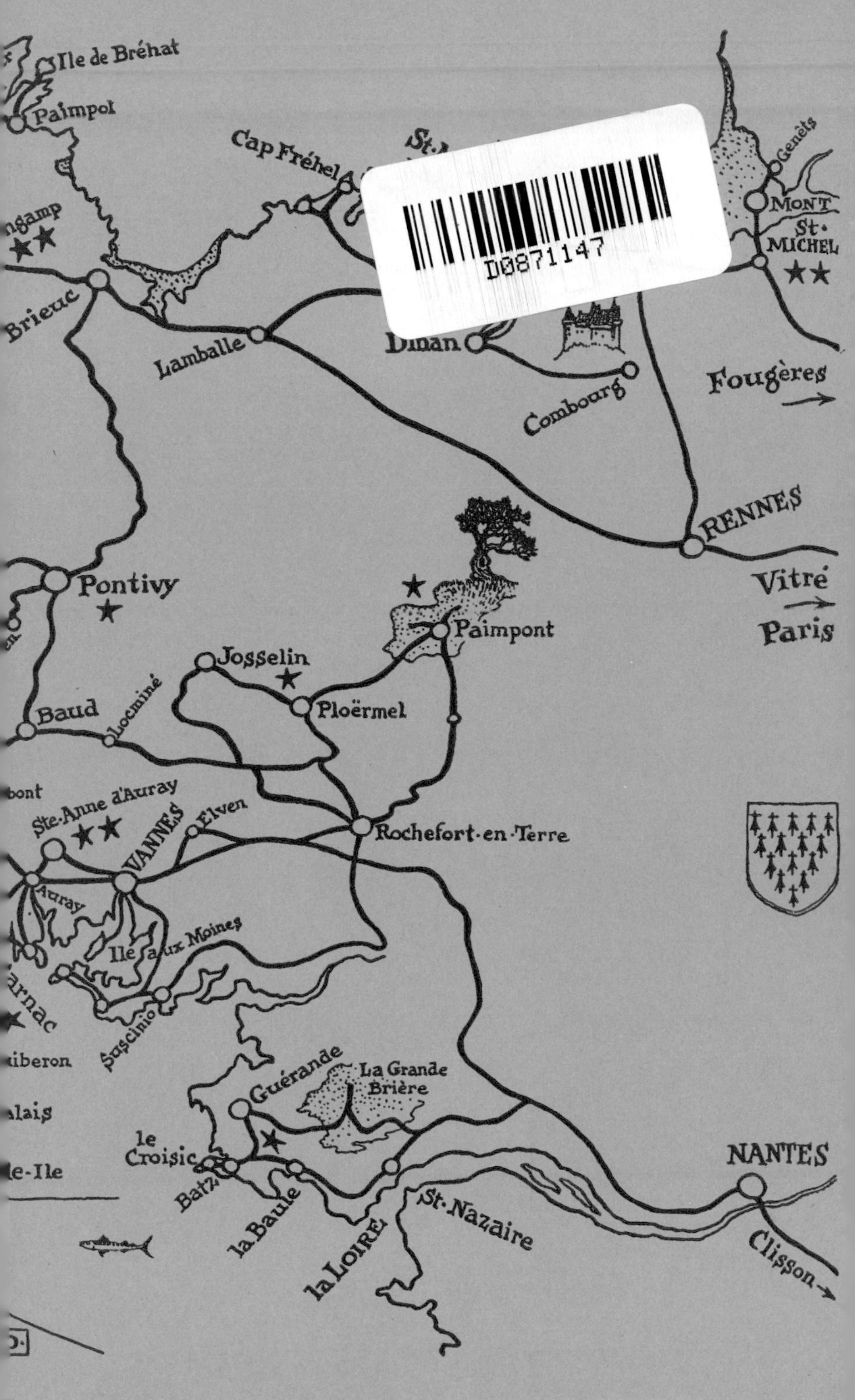

Ile de Bréhat
Paimpol
Cap Fréhel
Genêts
MONT St-MICHEL
Dinan
Lamballe
Combourg
Fougères
RENNES
Vitré
Paris
Pontivy
Paimpont
Josselin
Ploërmel
Baud
Locminé
Ste-Anne d'Auray
VANNES
Elven
Rochefort-en-Terre
Auray
Ile aux Moines
Sascinio
Guérande
La Grande Brière
le Croisic
Batz
la Baule
la LOIRE
St-Nazaire
NANTES
Clisson

Cornelia K Barden

Christmas 1930

ENCHANTED BRITTANY

Bagpipes skirl in Finistère

ENCHANTED BRITTANY

by

AMY OAKLEY

Illustrations
by
THORNTON OAKLEY

NEW YORK
The CENTURY Co.
1930

First Printing

PRINTED IN U. S. A.

To
our daughter
LANSDALE
valiant comrade
on land and sea

St. St.
Corentin Ronan

Table of CONTENTS

List of ILLUSTRATIONS

INTRODUCTION

IDEALISM is the outstanding Breton characteristic. Renan speaks of the passion of the Celts for evoking invisible things: "The poetic element essential to the life of the Celt is adventure, that is to say, the pursuit of the unknown, a never ending race after the object which flees from desire. In face of the sea they wish to know what may be found beyond; they dream of the promised land."

Love of the beautiful is evinced on every hand in Brittany, finding expression in the Gothic chapels which, like exquisite flowers, have blossomed in the most unexpected places throughout the length and breadth of the peninsula. In no less a measure do the varied and elegant costumes of the people show the Bretons' genuine delight in form and color—which is, moreover, displayed in the unconscious artistry with which they stage their local fêtes.

It is no less true in Brittany than in the Pyrenees that the climax of an orderly tour is to be found in the center. As Hautes-Pyrénées is to the mountains bordering France and Spain, so Finistère is to Brittany.

The ancient province is to-day divided into five departments. Starting from Saint-Malo, we find ourselves in Ille-et-Vilaine, with Rennes, the former capital of Brittany, its chief city . . . the châteaux its chief delights. Next we come to the Côtes-du-Nord, with Saint-Brieuc its center, distinguished is this department for its wealth of granite calvaries and for the legends of its past. Finistère, the land's end of the peninsula—its main town Quimper—is equally noted for the diverse costumes of its inhabitants and for its religious festivals or pardons. Morbihan, with Vannes its capital, no less than Finistère is noted for its wealth of costume, and, moreover, for the megalithic remains to be found at Locmariaquer and at Carnac. Loire-Inférieure boasts the medieval walled town of Guérande, isolated by peat-bogs and salt-marshes, and the principal city of the province, Nantes.

Brittany, from time immemorial, has in the popular mind been divided into Armor, the region of the coast, and Argoat, the region of the interior. The ancient name of Brittany itself—Armorica—signifies the land beside the sea. There is yet another important division of the province into two portions, Basse-Bretagne being the western half, Haute-Bretagne the eastern. Despite the charms of

Upper Brittany, it does not possess as great a fascination for the traveler as does Lower Brittany. To him who would roam at will in a realm of faëry let me recommend la Basse-Bretagne, known to the initiated as la Bretagne *bretonnante*.

Amy Oakley

Villa Nova, Pennsylvania
September 1, 1930

Enchanted forests and enchanted people exist in Brittany. The fairies still dance around the dolmen on moonlit nights, the dead walk in slow procession through the fields and along the roadways on the night of La Toussaint. The mystic vervaine of that early inhabitant—the Druid—has not lost its secret.

ANGE M. MOSHER

ENCHANTED BRITTANY

Saint-Malo
Place Chateaubriand

ENCHANTED BRITTANY

CHAPTER I
The Emerald Coast

Saint-Malo on its granite rock, its solitary spire lifted mast-like to heaven, resembles, in the fading light of even, a giant corsair anchored athwart the estuary of the Rance. Compact within encircling ramparts, the ancient town bears valiantly as any privateer the brunt of angry seas which at times, like the English foe of old, threaten its very being. Valiant in defense of their homes against the oft-repeated attacks of the traditional enemy, the Malouins, noted even among Bretons for their independence, were trained in the school of combat. To-day the unconquered city of the buccaneers, of Cartier, Duguay-Trouin, and Surcouf deigns to prosper by means of trade with the once hated

English and by the largesse of British subjects who, many thousand strong, annually invade the region of Saint-Malo, Dinan, and Dinard.

Privateers, freebooters, sea-robbers far-famed in the annals of naval warfare were the mariners of Saint-Malo. It is recorded that in the course of a single war the townsmen captured upward of fifteen hundred vessels, some of which were laden with gold and other fabulous treasure. On the strength of the prowess of its seamen Louis XIV issued orders that no sailors, officers, nor cannoneers of his admiral's fleet should be other than citizens of Saint-Malo. To this day the youngest urchin of the town is a potential sailor in whose veins pulses the eternal rhythm of the sea.

To arrive at Saint-Malo, whether by the Paris express or direct from England by the Southampton boat, is to experience a new sensation. Here one stands at the threshold of Brittany, a land as individual as if it formed no sectional part of France; but it is not France nor yet indeed Brittany that obtrudes itself at first glance, for as Brittany is a complete whole, so indeed is the capital of the Emerald Coast—the unconquerable Saint-Malo.

It is necessary to have at least a speaking acquaintance with the history of the place in order to appreciate its unique position. Jealous of the governing Dukes of Brittany, the inhabitants of Saint-Malo were, throughout the Middle Ages, rarely on a friendly footing with these rulers except when compelled jointly to combat the common enemy. Beginning with the thirteenth century, the town enjoyed communal liberty. It was the bishops who governed in the fourteenth century, and who a century later ceded their rights to the King of France, rather, so high ran the tide of jealousy, than to the Duke of Brittany. The struggle for Breton independence was virtually ended in 1491, by the marriage of the Duchess Anne to the King of France. In 1590, however, the Malouins revolted against their rulers and it was not until four years later that they finally submitted to French rule; this in the reign of Henri IV.

Anne de Bretagne represents the flower of Breton womanhood. Although twice Queen of France, she was unswerving in her loyalty to her native province, whose government was her personal concern. To the descendants of her former subjects she remains, and ever will remain, quite unalterably "la Duchesse Anne." Her career was highly picturesque from her twelfth year, when the death of her father, the reigning duke, placed the scepter in her hands. Many were the matrimonial schemes of her subjects for their liege lady, but she treated them all with scant courtesy. How she rebuffed the suit of the Prince of Orange, defying her guardian the Marshal of Nantes, who endeavored to capture her in the interest of this suitor, and how she galloped across Brittany accompanied by her faithful chancellor, has become a household word.

Realizing the impossibility of longer retaining the complete independence of Brittany, Anne gave herself in marriage to Charles VIII of France, carefully safeguarding the interests of her province. The royal trousseau contained a magnificent wedding-gown of cloth of gold, said to have cost over ten thousand pounds. The maids of honor were attired in tan velvet. One hundred and thirty-nine skins of ermine were used in trimming the bride's traveling-cloak, and her camp bedstead had a canopy and curtains of crimson festooned with gold and lined with blue taffeta. The crown of France, too large and heavy for the youthful Anne (who was twice destined to wear it), was held over her head during the ceremony at Saint-Denis, which took place on December 6, 1491, by Louis, Duc d'Orléans—who one day as king was to bestow this crown upon her.

On the death of her royal spouse Anne retired to Brittany, but her widowhood was cut short by marriage, at the age of twenty-three, to the new king, Louis XII, the former Duke of Orleans, who had long been an admirer and whose affection for her whom he was wont to call "ma petite Brette" endured to the day of her death. By the marriage of Anne's daughter Claude to François d'Angoulême (later François 1er) the last of the outlying fiefs was united to France.

The ponderous keep or Quiquengroigne of the Castle of Saint-Malo owes its origin to the Duchess Anne. In reply to the protests of insurgent citizens against the erection of this tower Queen Anne is quoted as having remarked:

> "Quic en groigne
> Ainsi sera.
> C'est mon playsir."

On the day of our visit, as we climbed the interminable flights of worn steps leading roofward, we encountered, it being a Sunday and as yet not the season of the foreign influx, an occasional sailor with his girl. The castle of the Duchess Anne now houses a Breton collection. More to the popular taste than the carefully ranged specimens of *lits-clos* (cupboard-like beds, the crux of most Breton exhibits) were fragments, nails, and spars of Cartier's vessel *La Petite Hermine,* found in Canada and presented by the Canadian Government to the native city of the discoverer of the St. Lawrence.

Stirring memories jostled in our brains, commingling like the warring factions which in ancient times had stormed the battlements. As we mounted skyward our thoughts dwelt on how the donjon had once been breached by the English under the leadership of the Duke of Lancaster, of how du Guesclin had held it against the powerful forces of the King of England (Froissart gives the enemy's strength as 4,000 men-at-arms, 8,000 archers, and 400 cannon), of how it had been attacked but not taken by the Duke of Marlborough.

Having gazed downward over the city from loopholes as we mounted the winding stair, we were to lose the vision of the distant low-lying town on entering the blackness of the topmost tower, only to regain it with lent enchantment as we emerged beneath the canopy of sky. At our feet was outspread a sea of roofs, gray, immobile, over which to windward, catching the sunlight like sails on a tranquil summer ocean, floated a galaxy of gulls. Beyond the massive towers, beyond the hoary ramparts, stretched the waters of the English Channel, rippling in sunshine. Remote, undisturbed, from this aery above the world of men we gazed seaward. Not Iseult the Fair . . . nor that other Iseult, of Brittany . . . would have been out of place atop this tower which has felt the tread of mighty warriors passionate alike in war and love. Here on occasion might the Duchess Anne have repaired whilst pondering upon affairs of state or of the heart, deriving fresh courage from the hard-gained detachment.

No rival has this tower as a view-point, unless it be the Grand-Bey with its vision of Saint-Malo. Let us descend to the street-level. We shall find ourselves immediately within the city walls, on the Place Chateaubriand—the center of the busy town's activity. A stone's throw away is the classic base for excursions, the Hôtel de France et de Chateaubriand. This hospitable mansion has been more than a haven to successive generations of travelers. It actually incorporates within its gates the birthplace of Chateaubriand, not to be conversant with whose writings is in Saint-Malo held to be a crime. In order to tempt the tourist, numerous titles—"Atala," "Voyage en Amérique," "Mémoires d'Outre-Tombe"—beckon from the window of the near-by book-shop. It is well to refresh the memory before visiting the tomb on the Grand-Bey or, as we shall do later, the Château of Combourg.

Saint-Malo is a seaman's haven. Not for a moment does the fact allow itself to be forgotten. French sailors, debonair, with wide collars and tam-o'-shanters topped with jaunty pompons, gather about the cafés. Fishermen haunt the shops where slickers, rubber top-boots, red-palmed woolen gloves wave limply without the portal. A smell of salt fish pervades the place. Let us notice Number 28 Rue du Boyer on our way to the Porte des Beys. Here, in a house worthy to be classed as a museum, may be found "Articles pour les Marins." At street corners sit fishwives with baskets in which glistening mackerel rest on beds of dripping seaweed. Gulls soar over the Hôtel de Ville. At the church door the breath of the sea mingles with wafted incense. Within the dark interior of the one-time cathedral, whose spire greets the returning mariner from far at sea, is a mosaic telling how Jacques Cartier knelt to receive the Church's blessing before setting forth on his memorable voyage destined to carry him up the St. Lawrence to the spot where to-day stands the city of Montreal.

The event of the year is the ceremony of blessing the fleet which departs in March for the Banks of Newfoundland. The narrow streets are agog before the departure. Carters are vociferous in their efforts to make headway in the perilously narrow and winding thoroughfares which form the main arteries of the town. The antique house of Duguay-Trouin, with its overhanging third floor, seems to look out on the feverish rush of springtime with naught but disdain. "What is the outfitting of a paltry fishing fleet compared with that of the men-o'-war of other days?" the spirit of the place might superciliously inquire. "Now, Duguay-Trouin—he was a man!"

Having captured an English ship and taken part in a bloody combat with English merchantmen, this Duguay-Trouin was given his own corsair at the age of eighteen. The gift launched him on a career which was to include the taking of Rio de Janeiro and the winning of the highest prize open to a seaman of the time—the rank of Admiral of the King's Fleet.

An endless promenade is the circuit of Saint-Malo's walls. Here pace, at dusk, shadowy priests telling their beads and reading well-conned words, murmuring interminable prayers. Here march by day, two by two, marshaled by vigilant gowned preceptors, blue-jacketed school-boys whose well-ordered ranks and the hum of whose voices form an ever recurrent motif. What thoughts, we wondered, stirred beneath those identical snug naval caps whose owners were so familiarly sighted in organized groups marching thrice daily through the Port Saint-Vincent. Had not these docile youths the blood of corsairs in their veins?

The castle, the town walls, the tomb of Chateaubriand—these three gems adorn the unique crown worn by Saint-Malo queen of the sea. It is at low tide that the tomb on the islet of Grand-Bey may be visited afoot, for at high tide (remember the tide rises near to fifty feet) the fishing fleet skims merrily over the causeway where at certain hours of the day you and I may cross dry-shod. On a bright spring morning Monsieur my illustrator and I turned thither, threading our way between gaily clad groups on the beach. Children dug in fine sand or clambered over slippery rocks or dabbled in sea-pools, shouting gleefully at the dis-

covery of a crab or other lively crustacean. At the entrance to the causeway a pleasant individual called our attention to warning signs.

"Some of your countrymen do not read French, it seems," he said apologetically. "Not long ago a party of Americans was caught by the tide. Rather than remain overnight on the island, as many have done, the men waded ashore, carrying their women."

Our young man proved to be the son of an admiral of France and an intimate of the explorer-owner of the *Pourquoi-Pas,* a craft whose presence in the harbor he pointed out to us. He chatted affably, telling how the scientist-explorer—whose

first wife, by the by, was a daughter of Victor Hugo—was soon to return to the arctic zone, where he was in the habit of studying the ice, flora, and fauna. We could not foresee how prominently this vessel would figure in the reports of the search for the missing *Italia*. Yet, despite its intrepid name, the *Pourquoi-Pas* was no more successful than its fellows when confronted with the problem of a clue to the lost Amundsen.

The professional classes are as underpaid in France as in the United States, according to our informant. His own fortune in government bonds had melted since the war until hardly existent.

"A relative who has emigrated to Uruguay,"

he told us, "makes fabulous sums by raising cattle on the pampas, but if I invest my money in the Americas, fifty per cent must go to taxes." Many of his friends were working as bricklayers in order to support their families. Had we heard of the new peasant deputy—perhaps a French Mussolini—who had recently been elected by all parties and sent uninstructed to Paris? "His appearance in the chamber in peasant garb will cause a sensation . . . and a year ago he was nobody. . . . Vive la Bretagne!"

A sense of adventure possessed us from the moment the causeway was reached. Land, dry land, was definitely left behind us. We had entered the kingdom of the sea. Around us, as we trod the slippery moss-grown platform—where so recently water had flowed, where so soon again water would flow—stretched wet sands strewn with glistening cobbles and rocks incrusted with barnacles and strewn with kelp. As we neared the island we gazed into the mirror of the sea and beheld there sea-meadows, a prodigal profusion of buoyant waving grasses; while now and again the current washed to our feet pink algæ and flute-edged sea-plumes, long as a man's arm, lately torn from the base of the jagged rocks. The cliffs were aglow with golden gorse.

We threaded our way to where the sole inhabitant of this isolated region, the monarch Chateaubriand, lies in state. The words of Alexander Selkirk drifted to mind: "I am monarch of all I survey; my right there is none to dispute"; but in this case solitude has its charms. Not even a name, merely a cross of granite, marks the resting-place of this known soldier and champion of the aristocratic attitude. Here, though his cause be lost, men gather in memory of the majestic style, a mantle of such rare beauty that to it we still pay our tribute although the ideas it cloaked no longer draw the breath of life.

Masses of coral-red sedum adorn the rocks, gold wallflowers shed their fragrance about the lonely tomb. Seated upon a rough-hewn semicircle of rock facing the sea, we pondered on the significance of the scene. Here indeed was a setting—chosen by this dramatic artist twenty years before he was destined to use it—from which it was meet that, according to his instructions, his voice should issue after death on the publication of his final message, a clarion voice pronouncing the "Mémoires d'Outre-Tombe," rising above the cry of gulls, the lashing of the waves, the rude blast of the tempest, heard adown the centuries. Here, on this island of death, where once, 'tis said, the druids brought their dead, rests one who bore aloft the torch of beauty, a poet-possessor of the Celtic soul, a conjurer who for a moment held ajar the doors leading to eternal mystery, a dreamer of prodigious dreams; in one word we may acclaim him: a Breton.

The tumultuous career of Chateaubriand may best be interpreted after a visit to Combourg. The château was inherited by François René Auguste, Vicomte de Chateaubriand, on the death of his elder brother who perished on the scaffold during the Revolution. It was at this somber feudal seat that the sensitive boy spent his restricted youth, virtually a prisoner in a tower dominated by the tyrannical Comte de Combourg his father. It was small wonder that the youth's thoughts were turned inward and that an egotism settled upon him which he was never to shake off. Despite dismal days which he was fated to spend there, Chateaubriand returns in later years with some wistfulness to the scene of his childhood:

CHATEAUBRIAND

Ma sœur te souvient-il encore
Du château que baignait la Dore
Et de cette tant vieille tour du More . . .

One of the poignant disappointments of our trip had been our inability to stop over at Combourg en route from Rennes to Saint-Malo. Its turrets had been barely visible, at a tantalizing distance from the railway. Our loss had at the time seemed irrevocable. It was therefore with quickened heart-beats that we discovered with what ease the run might be made from Saint-Malo. Even without knowledge of Chateaubriand the traveler would be rewarded by the trip itself, but to an admirer of the master the visit becomes an obligation. Who would not see for himself, having read the poet's description:

> In the diverse parts of the edifice were found narrow halls and secret stairways, cachots and dungeons, a labyrinth of covered and uncovered galleries, walled-in subterranean passages of which the ramifications were unknown; everywhere silence, everywhere obscurity and visage of stone! Voilà le Château de Combourg!

Now again we all but lost our opportunity of entering the château, because we had ordered a motor for a Thursday and it is only of a Wednesday, between the prescribed hours of fourteen and seventeen, that Madame la Comtesse de Durfort, née de Chateaubriand, permits the visit. A heaven-sent accident having made us aware of our error, we hastily put ourselves on the road in the very nick of time. The day was one to be found only in Brittany in the month of May. The rain had ceased, the sunlight bathed the earth, quickening it to life. Oaks unfurled the freshness of their green. In the fields masterful horses, driven tandem, plowed the furrows, plowed them deep and plowed them curved as circling waves in coves—a manner dear to the heart of the Breton.

A magpie flitted across our path, another and still a third, bringing to mind the old adage:

> One for grief,
> Two for mirth,
> Three for marriage,
> Four for birth.

A fourth greeted our entrance to the village of Combourg, where our car almost ran down the local midwife issuing hastily from her ancient domicile.

No welcome stork, however, breaks the spell of sadness which enwraps the old château.

"Alas!" exclaimed the buxom concierge, wearing cotton in both ears and, in consequence, shouting lustily, "Madame is over fifty, her nieces are the same age as herself, and there are no descendants."

Madame la Comtesse, it appeared, would not return from Paris until July and would then remain, as was her wont, at Combourg until the New Year. A magnificent magpie (who knows that it was not a fourth magpie?) dangled lifeless from a pole, a drear corpse on a gibbet, swinging, so the good dame informed us, for his misdeeds.

The formidable Château de Combourg, rising conspicuously above its lake and surrounding forest, since its construction in 1016 by a Bishop of Dol, has throughout the centuries acted with dignity its rôle of protector of the village which nestles at its feet. It was enlarged in the fourteenth and fifteenth centuries by its possessors, among whom numbered the du Guesclins. To-day, though part of the forest has been sacrificed, enough remains to preserve the stateliness and create the solitude of pre-revolutionary years. Tranquil country encircles the park, which still possesses lindens, oaks, and horse-chestnuts in keeping with the scale of the château that retains its moat and grassy mall.

Tragedy haunts the place. From a mantel the exquisite face of Françoise de Foix reminds us that her austere husband, Comte de Chateaubriand, having reluctantly taken her to court at the king's express command, wreaked his vengeance upon her for having won the favor of the pleasure-loving sovereign, François Ier, by literally starving her to death on their return to Combourg.

The restorer has not marred the apartments

sacred to the memory of the boy Chateaubriand. With emotion we may visit the narrow bed-chamber, the book-lined tower room with the master's desk and portrait of Madame Récamier, faithful friend of his last years. How must the youth have paced to and fro, wearing deeper with restless tread the worn grooves of the *chemin de ronde* as he gazed, ofttimes unseeingly, upon the familiar beauties of the immense scene. It was symbolic that he should thereafter have viewed life as one apart, from afar, from a tower.

Our departure was made amid gusts of wind. A sudden shower veiled the gray lichen-mottled château, causing it to recede until it became blurred as though seen through tears. Perhaps it was thus that Chateaubriand had beheld it upon his last visit—through a curtain of unshed tears. Haunted by memories of youth he had found it, deserted, peopled by ghosts, its dusky interior festooned with cobwebs.

To return to Saint-Malo. The birthplace of Jacques Cartier makes an interesting objective for a drive in a fiacre. The road passes through Paramé (what Dinard is to the English, Paramé is to the French) with its modern villas, its rich-foliaged pines, and comes out to open country. The scene is very typically Breton: long low cottages, slate-roofed and with moss-grown garden walls sheltering espaliered fruit-trees; hawthorn hedges, drifts of pink or white bloom in which finches dart twittering their song of springtime; laburnums, gaudy as broom or gorse; an intoxicating profusion of lilacs; then bare fields—potatoes for the English market—edged with spindling poplars; and, at last, the breath of the sea. On the Saint-Ideuc road the house of Cartier still stands near Rothéneuf and the mariners' minute chapel, Notre-Dame des Flots.

Once, long years ago, the arms of Saint-Malo were a dog gules, in honor of those ferocious mastiffs which were throughout unquiet centuries the guardians of the town. Although the ermine passant has long since replaced the dog upon Saint-Malo's escutcheon, memory of the dog still lingers. The fitting birthplace of the discoverer of the St. Lawrence—a manor-house now the property of . . . an admiral, I should like to say, but I believe it is a general of France—possesses a pair of veritable canine demons. Though they are chained by day, God knows whether or not they prowl by night. Murmuring a prayer to the Christ enshrined in the house wall, that the chains be strong to endure the tugging, I stood in the gateway and studied the almost obliterated arms of the Cartiers. Monsieur, walking a straight line between Scylla and Charybdis, plucked up the courage to obtain a nearer view of the pepper-pot tower. Frenzied barking and clanking of chains drowned all attempts at conversation with a damsel who drew water from an antique well in the courtyard, but I managed to hold my ground long enough to jot down the inscription:

A
Jacques Cartier
Hommage de la Société Historique et Archéologique
de l'Arrondissement de Saint-Malo.
24 Juillet 1905

Saint-Servan—with which the one-time island of Saint-Malo now connects by a narrow strip of land known as the Sillon—is worthy of more than one visit. Its most notable feature is the Tour Solidor, a remarkable example of feudal architecture. The tower was built here on rocks at the mouth of the Rance in 1384, by Duke John IV, who was at the time combating Josselin de Rohan the bishop for the sovereignty of Saint-Malo. Saint-Servan stands on the site of the ancient Roman-Gallic city of Aleth. The story runs that Saint Maclou or Malo, the Cambrian monk, took refuge with the hermit Aaron upon the island which bore his name. There Malo founded his monastery. In the eighth century, owing to piratical attacks and invasions by the French under Charlemagne, the citizens of Aleth migrated to the more easily guarded island, changing its name to that of the venerated Saint Malo.

Dinard, across the mouth of the Rance from Saint-Malo, should not properly be included in a

Saint-Servan ‡ The Tour Solidor

book on Brittany nor yet on France. It is to all intents and purposes an English colony. Although its luxurious hotels may be convenient stopping-places while you are making excursions, do not for an instant imagine that Dinard is Brittany any more than Paris is France. One anecdote should prove my point. A Frenchman of note engaged rooms for the season at one of the best hotels—the one at which we stayed, by the by. Our chauffeur, who told us the tale, happened to be procuring papers from the Commissaire de Police when he met the said gentleman. The Frenchman was recounting his troubles, punctuating his remarks with excited gestures. Why was it that Monsieur wished to leave the hotel?—that is, if he could do so without legal entanglement?—the commissaire inquired. Had he understood Monsieur to say the situation had become intolerable and that he must find a way in which to extricate himself or that he would suffer a nervous breakdown? What was, then, Monsieur's complaint against the management? It was this, and quite enough, too, to judge by the shrugs of sympathy with which it was received by pompous official personages: every remark he made at the hotel was answered in English—a language which he did not understand.

Dinard shares with French-speaking Paramé and la Baule the title of the most fashionable watering-place in Brittany.

Mont-Saint-Michel
The Crypt of the Abbey

CHAPTER II

THE MOUNTS OF SAINT MICHAEL

"DULL little place, Dol, well named." So quoth my illustrator as on alighting from the morning train from Saint-Malo we looked in vain for a vehicle. "Still in the era of the bicycle," he continued as we plodded along the dusty avenue leading to the center of the town, where the traffic was of this rather antediluvian nature.

Impressions of Dol are apt to grow in retrospect. Our own hopes had been raised somewhat too high by having read Mérimée's description of the place, written almost a century ago. He depicts the Grande-Rue as bordered by arched arcades supported by columns of diverse forms whose capitals represent all epochs from the flowery Romanesque to the last caprices of the Gothic. Alas! not more than three ancient mansions have survived, and it is to the cathedral alone that we must turn to find, despite the barbarous treatment meted out to it at the time of the Revolution, the true spirit of the once proud arch-episcopal metropolis.

The moment we stepped within the portals of the cathedral we realized that we had shown wisdom in putting Dol on our itinerary. Through the jewel-glass above the high altar the sunlight shone in splendor. The benign statue of the Virgin was aglow with the light of a myriad candles. The intense beauty of the whole pierced to our inner consciousness, struck a clear high note, a rhapsody of Breton idealism. Hardly a congregation in the province but plays a harmonious part in the dynamic symphony of thought arising from along the shore of Brittany and heard with the inner ear by all those possessed of a drop of Celtic blood. What if here and there a seeming discord arises from communistic industrials or dock-hands? Perhaps our ears are not attuned to appreciate the value of even dissonance to the modernity of the whole, where these trumpet blasts may form a needed balance to the long-drawn wail of wood-wind reactionaries, the resonant stringed instruments of Catholicism, the insistent rumbling of Socialistic mayors and professorial leaders of advanced thought who beat the kettledrum of progress, allowing scant measure for the pianissimo passages of their opponents.

The pendulum of fate has swung with violence

at Dol. Time was when the region was an immense forest stretching to Mont-Saint-Michel and the Isle of Chausey, wherein druids performed their mystic rites. In the sixth century came Samson the Celt, Archbishop of York, fleeing with his followers before the Saxon invaders of his native Britain, landing on these shores and founding the monastery around which sprang up the village of Dol. In his day came the floods which surrounded Mont-Saint-Michel and Mont-Dol and submerged the groves sacred to the druids; and which, 'tis said, receded from the town obedient to the prayers of Saint Samson.

In the ninth century the Breton chief Nomenoë elevated the Bishop of Dol, who was also its count, to the rank of archbishop of all Brittany—a rank which was held by his successors throughout nine centuries. These were days of glory. William the Conqueror besieged but failed to take the city. In 1203 John Lackland, King of England, having put to death Arthur of Brittany, burned the cathedral from whose ashes arose the present edifice. During the Religious Wars, Dol took the side of the League, but in 1793 it was a last stronghold of the Vendeans, who fought and won here a battle which cost fourteen thousand Republicans their lives.

In 1795 came another swing of the pendulum. The sanctity of the cathedral was violated and the building was used as a granary and stable. The bishop, Monseigneur Hercé, who had been exiled to Jersey and had returned with an army of émigrés, was taken at Quiberon and put to death at Vannes. The Collège de Dol, where Chateaubriand was once a student, was partly consumed by fire during the Terror.

So swings the fateful pendulum: the druids give place to the Christians, the aristocrats to the people, and to-day—with more than a quarter of the twentieth century already sped—dare we hail the beginning of a new era in which a truer equilibrium will assure a more rhythmically just performance of the timepiece?

Chateaubriand was in the habit of walking with his classmates to Mont-Dol. Before making this excursion, however, we motored in quite another direction to pay our respects to the menhir of Champ-Dolent. Our departure from Dol was unceremonious. The only available car was a minute Citroën, unsuitably to the spring morning still wearing its winter inclosure. Monsieur, whose frame is large, not to say bulky, was clad in the loose brown corduroys which make him so inconspicuous a part of French street life that natives have accosted him to ask their way. When confronted by the rabbit-hole door of the miniature Citroën, Monsieur was nothing daunted but, like Alice in Wonderland, lunged into the narrow burrow regardless of how he should extricate himself. When the car drew up at our destination his contortions in attempting to alight were as fantastic as those of a débutante disrobing.

Blackberry hedges lined the lane which led between flowering orchards. As we made our way on foot the only person we encountered was an octogenarian who emerged from a near-by thicket, where perchance he had his lair. In appearance he was the surviving druid of the place; what pagan rites might not his ancestors have here performed? . . . Our thoughts were cut short by his speech, which was hesitant, diffident, not that of a guide but rather of a furtive wild thing of the forest, inclined to flee, yet, urged perhaps by hunger gnawing at his vitals, lingering at the approach of man. Lifting a lean arm to heaven and indicating the lofty summit of the granite monolith of Champ-Dolent, he spoke.

"The cross has fallen," he muttered without emotion, as one to whom the cross was no more sacred than the golden bough—the druidic mistletoe.

"They put it there, the priests," he repeated, pointing aloft, "but it has fallen. They have forbidden the worship of the stone, they deny that it fell from heaven . . . but is there another to be found on all the plain? Did you ever hear tell of the battle?" His wan eyes searched our faces while a cooling breeze ruffled his unruly gray locks and whipped a tattered olive-black cloak about his lean person.

"Battle?" I said, to lead him on. "What battle?"

"It was long ago," said he, ignoring my question. "Some vow it was the Romans put the stone here and some that it was here before the birth of Christ, but this I have from those who know: it was not here before the battle. Hundreds of years ago two brothers were deadly enemies, and here they and their vassals fought a mighty battle . . . blood flowed in streams to turn the mill down-valley." His haggard eyes fixed us as though challenging contradiction. "But when the two were about to meet in single combat, then it was that this stone came between. Some say it dropped from heaven but others that it rose from the earth. The field was red with blood . . . they say it turned the mill-wheel." He rubbed his bleary eyes from which the fire had died, and unheeding what to him seemed irrelevant questions, content with our offering, shuffled from the scene.

Champ-Dolent owes its name to this lingering tradition of a Campus-Doloris, a field of battle. Some have tried to place here the famous conflict between Clotaire I, King of the Franks, against his son Chramne allied with the Count of the Bretons. The encounter probably took place nearer to Saint-Malo or, some say, to the south near Vannes. It may be, however, that Dolent is merely a corruption of Dolois—Dol signifying, in Celtic, "a fertile place."

Mont-Dol has been called by Botrel the "Mont-Saint-Michel de chez nous"—that is, of Brittany. Possessed of no architectural embellishments, Mont-Dol nevertheless, because of its isolation and the fact that it has been forgotten in the rush to the over-populous mount, has retained a well-nigh uncanny continuity with a remote past. Its seclusion remains to-day almost as undisturbed as when it rose above the primeval forest of Scissy or when ocean raged against its westernmost cliffs. The marshland around Mont-Dol has been reclaimed by means of dikes and miniature canals. From its modest summit may be seen an expanse of fertile farm lands, orchards, gardens, and villages each with its spired belfry.

A humble settlement snuggles to leeward of the mount, near the Quaternary Grotto, where Professor Sirodot of the Faculty of Sciences of Rennes discovered an immense quantity of fossilized bones and where, as late as 1913, a superb mammoth's tusk was unearthed. It is not primarily the historic but the legendary past which at Mont-Dol pours forth its timeless stream of thought, forcing the flood-gates of the mind. The very atmosphere appears to be more rare, the cuckoo's voice more haunting than its wont, as one gains the grove of chestnuts.

Centenarians these trees, superfluous to add that the gnarled giant on whose bole we rest—in whose mighty arms the birds find shelter, the mistletoe

The undisturbed seclusion of Mont-Dol ✦

foothold, where swarming bees have founded a colony—dates from 1656 when it was planted by Philippe Thoreau, brother of Monseigneur the Bishop of Dol. Like its fellows, all budding in fresh green, yet bearing the shriveled burrs of a past year, it stands as an emblem of eternal rebirth. An age-old crone, deaf to our voices, bent and hooded, her sere lips mumbling prayers or incantations, ostensibly tends a few lean cows. Yonder flap the languid sails of a solitary mill reflected in a pool which, tradition tells, fails never, because magically fed. Around us, with that intoxicating fragrance that is Brittany, riots the gorse—the paradoxical thorned plant possessing the faults and virtues of the land of which it is the living symbol.

As we looked down on the vast plain outspread at our feet we felt ourselves to belong to a world apart from that where distant orchards and pollarded willows flourished. A cuckoo called and, in the hush that followed, even the white wings of the mill ceased to stir, pausing expectant . . . as if to allow us to hear voices from the past. Sheep grazed upon the knoll where once the temple to the huntress Diana stood. On a spot where druids, Romans, early Christians have performed their rites and dreamed their dreams one comes to understand how, amid not dissimilar surroundings, tending her flocks, a Jeanne d'Arc might have seen her visions of the archangel Michael.

An intimate link connects Mont-Dol to Mont-Saint-Michel, for does not the mount on which we stand owe its very origin to the archangel? Legend tells that this spot was the scene of a conflict between the devil and Saint Michael; and the mount itself, the "giant of the marsh," is according to tradition naught else but a petrified tear which fell from the eye of the Evil One when he was compelled by Saint Michael to return to the lower regions. The tale doubtless owes its origin to the fact that here the forces of Christ were brought into conflict with the earlier pagan cults and were indeed victorious. Here for centuries a priory of Saint Michael stood, administered, as was that of Saint Michael's Mount in Cornwall, by the monks of Mont-Saint-Michel. But the mark of the cloven hoof, as well as the impress of Saint Michael's foot, has remained indelibly imprinted upon the granite rock. Let us, following the example of the archangel, leap across the intervening sands to the mount bearing his name, which is dimly visible upon the faint horizon.

Three times it has been my good fortune to behold the "Marvel of the West." Therefore at mention of its name, Mont-Saint-Michel, a vision fairer than man's fondest castle of dreams rises before me, a vision worthy to be placed beside that of the Cirque de Gavarnie or Mont-Blanc, the Cathedral of Rheims or Notre-Dame de Paris. Not without reason has the recently taken vote of Touring Club members to determine the most beautiful site of France given an overwhelming majority to Mont-Saint-Michel. Unlike the mountains, unlike the cathedrals, it combines the wonder of nature with the wondrous work of man.

No apology is needed for including the sacred mount in a book on Brittany, for any one with the least flair for nicety in such matters will feel it to be, despite its Norman-Gothic abbey, a spiritual part of Brittany. It is in truth one of the many islands of the dead famed in Celtic legend—the Mont-Tombe of ancient days. Was it not, indeed, by mere chance or, as the old song says, by the folly of the wayward river Couesnon in changing its course, that the former Breton possession came to Normandy? Both provinces having become loyal daughters of France, the dispute languishes and from the neighboring towns of Saint-Malo and Dol, as from Avranches and Pontorson, tourists pour by rail and motor in augmenting multitudes. That Mont-Saint-Michel has not lost its character, has not become commercialized, remains the wonder of wonders.

No less important than in planning the conquest of a mountain is the time chosen for a first impression if one would enjoy to the full the glories of Mont-Saint-Michel. Once in peril of the sea, of late years the mount has become—owing to the building of the dike and because of the efforts of those

Le Mont-Saint-Michel

:In Peril of the Sea

who would fill their own pockets by forcing the ocean back from the surrounding richly fertilized pastures—in peril of the land. Much has been said, with reason, in the French Senate apropos of preserving at all odds the insularity of Mont-Saint-Michel. As matters rest at present, it is the part of wisdom to visit the island at time of highest tide—that is, thirty-six hours after the new or full moon. And in order to avoid the rabble, yet to enjoy a good chance of fair weather—or, to be exact, a fair chance of good weather—let the visit be in spring or autumn. My own threefold impression has been gleaned in summer before the days of autocars, in September, and in May. Each time the sun has shone with prodigal splendor, but I have not been denied the wizardry of mist.

Two nights are all too short an allowance for the mount. Needless to say that those who make the excursion in a few snatched hours at noon miss half its charm. Let us set out upon the classic pilgrimage. To those filled with youthful enthusiasm the ideal approach is to walk, like the monks of old, from Pontorson. This method Monsieur and I followed on our first visit, and the alluring vision of the mount gained later in lurching automobile days pales beside my remembrance of what we saw that first time as we trudged along the lanes, receiving genial "bon jours" from peasants driving cattle, crossing streams where iris was in flower, getting glimpses of our goal—now seen, now lost as clumps of willows or wind-blown tamarisks came between us and the bubble of our dreams.

This last visit, however, we took the train from Saint-Malo of a spring afternoon and were prosaically deposited at the base of the mount. Engaging accommodations at the Hôtel Poulard, we climbed at once to the ramparts, passing the tawdry bazaars of the town's one street where houses of ancient tradition such as that built by du Guesclin for his wife Typhaine rub shoulders with upstart intruders. We had come at turn of the moon to see once more enacted the drama of the tide.

No water was visible save where the river Couesnon flowed between sandy banks. On its farther shore lay Brittany. Sheep grazed on marsh-pastures, pastures not submersible at the present season but at time of equinox swallowed by the sea. As we watched from the North Tower—above which loomed the formidable castle, the sole entrance to the cluster of medieval marvels which crown the mount—the shadow of the mass (mount, abbey, topmost church and spire) was thrown far out upon the sands. To our left, in Brittany, we could scarcely trace the outline of Cancale; to the right rose the shadowy cliffs of Normandy, with, in the foreground, Tombelaine, a deserted isle, once in possession of the English, who were nevertheless unable to capture the sacred mount.

The ocean, which had been lost to sight, now began to make its presence visible. Slowly, as though newborn in the firmament, the waters emerged from the azure rim where at first glance they had been indistinguishable from sky. It taxed credulity to believe that they would ever traverse the seven mystic miles which lay between. We had noticed a distant rowboat marooned upon the sands. Suddenly it came to life, lifted on the buoyant crest of the incoming wave. We had not known there were men aboard, but now we caught the flash of sunlight on wet oars as the craft made for the mouth of the river. The steady flow of water increased in rapidity after gaining the Couesnon. A tidal bore, flecking the stream with white, carried the frail craft upstream, overcoming the resistance of river-current.

Even as we watched, the tide's traditional ability to overtake fleeing horsemen became apparent. We followed with trepidation the scurrying figure of a solitary fisherman inspecting a weir. Forced to abandon the unequal struggle, the Couesnon had now been completely submerged. The hush of late afternoon was superseded by the voice of oncoming waters. The precipitous north face of the mount bore the brunt of the lapping tide. Once again was Mont-Saint-Michel "en Péril de la Mer." We could imagine ourselves aboard some princely galleon, pennants flung to the wind, about to set sail for conquest of the Seven Seas.

After a two-hour watch upon a bleak north tower we relished the welcome found *chez* Poulard. I had while yet in my teens happened upon a unique celebration at this most famous of Normandy inns. Our party had come upon it most unexpectedly—the birthday fête of Monsieur Poulard. How rotund and amiable he had looked as he stood in the quaint doorway (where welcome still awaits) receiving the congratulations of the domestics. They formed a queue that stretched away to the medieval Port du Roi which bridges the narrow street. Every one in the file bore a potted plant, geraniums if my memory holds, and the becapped bonnes were kissed soundly in French fashion. White-gowned chefs brought up the rear, and beside her husband Madame Poulard of the dusky hair beamed approval.

But the years have flown. Madame Veuve Poulard has retired to enjoy the fruits of her labor, yet, I doubt not, longs for the good old days of her activity. To-day it is Monsieur Chevalier who, with his amiable mamma, presides over the destiny of the justly famous hostelry which, as long as omelets are made at open fires, or fowls turn on spits, or *pré-salé*—the rival of Southdown mutton—causes hospitable boards to groan, will doubtless bear the nomenclature of Hôtel Poulard.

History and myth are intertwined regarding the settlement of Mont-Saint-Michel. It was a pagan sanctuary. Here druid stones were found and overthrown by early Christians. In the year 704, we are told, the archangel Michael appeared in a dream to Aubert, Bishop of Avranches, and commanded him to build an oratory on the rock then known as Mont-Tombe and in those days surrounded by primeval forest. The story runs that a delegation of brothers installed at the newly built grotto, having gone on a journey to Rome to obtain relics for the shrine, were startled upon their return to find that the ocean had encroached upon the forest and their fastness had become an island. That it was not submerged was taken as a sign that it was indeed under the powerful protection of its patron saint; and the safe return of the monks, despite the flood, was attributed to the power of the holy relics.

From this time the fame of the mount was established. Potentates of Church and State vied with one another in their devotion to the upbuilding of a fitting sanctuary. The Emperor Charlemagne, coming as a pilgrim, set the fashion for other rulers. In the days of William the Conqueror the mount was so famous that it appears in a panel of the Bayeux tapestry, where Harold is seen dramatically dragging his companions from the quicksands. Indeed, the inhabitants of the mount, villagers from the mainland who had settled there in order to find refuge from dreaded pirates, sent six vessels to aid in the conquest of England. Here Richard, Duke of Normandy, established a colony of Benedictines. In 1203, because of its Norman ownership, the monastery was burned by the army of Philip Augustus, King of France, who afterward was lavish in his gifts toward its rebuilding. In twenty-five short years la Merveille was to rise from these ashes.

In the robust days of old not a week passed, if we are to give credence to the thought expressed in the classic work on Mont-Saint-Michel by Henry Adams, but the martial strains of the Chanson de Roland resounded through the abbey's mighty halls. To-day the tourist is doomed to listen to quite another tune—the interminable chatter and banal comments of the multitude. As the visit must be made in company with a guardian, it is by all odds the wisest plan to arise betimes in order to begin the round at nine o'clock, thereby avoiding the one-day trippers. At the present moment France is utilizing the service of her *mutilés de guerre* as custodians of historic monuments. The fair-haired gentleman—for he was that indeed, wearing ribbons of many battles—who conducted us might well serve as a pattern to future generations. His knowledge of his subject was as unbounded as his enthusiasm, and his enunciation of the French tongue was so elucidating that it seemed any one short of a Hottentot must understand.

"*Escalier de dentelle,*" I can hear him say, as we climbed, amid a profusion of weathered pinnacles and gargoyles, the airy ladder of a flying buttress which bridges the way to the roof.

"And the lace of the stairs is all of granite! and of granite, madame, brought from those islands of Chausey which are now veiled in mist." He pointed in their direction with a slender mutilated hand. "How did the monks lift the material for the mammoth columns of the crypt? Could it be done to-day? It is a mystery . . . like the building of the pyramids. In fact, Victor Hugo has said that what the great pyramid is to Egypt the Mont-Saint-Michel is to France.

"Do you realize, madame, that part of our buildings go back a thousand years? Sometimes it seems to me the pioneers who delved into the living rock to plant the roots—the cellars, the crypts—of the vast conglomeration deserve as much credit as those equally unknown builders to whom we owe the chapel, fairest flower of the Gothic in France."

After an hour (in summer, parties are hustled through in half the time!) spent in roaming in cavernous regions, penetrating into ghastly cachots, shuddering at tales of the torture of political prisoners—for Mont-Saint-Michel has a notorious record in this respect and more than fourteen thousand offenders were detained here between the years 1793 and 1863—we were transported to another world when we reached that portion of the abbey known as the Merveille. This crowning glory of thirteenth-century Gothic consists of six vast halls. On the lowest floor are the cellars and the almonry; on the second floor the refectory for guests and the hall of the cavaliers. Formerly known as the Salle d'Ecriture, because it was here by the light of its many windows that the monks were wont to illuminate their manuscripts, the name of Salle des Chevaliers was given the hall at the time of the founding by Louis XI of the order of the Chevaliers de Saint-Michel. It was in this hall of many columns that the order met with medieval pomp.

In the adjoining Réfectoire des Hôtes, separated by magnificent tapestries from the roaring fires of the kitchens—alas that the gigantic chimneys are cold to-day!—what banquets have been held to the accompaniment of minstrelsy . . . the exultant strains of the Chanson. Yet the canny monks reserved the crowning section of the whole for their personal use, their own refectory from which the cloisters open. This hall, despoiled of its glory of jewel-glass, because of its unique windows still possesses an unparalleled charm. The windows are concealed, when one first enters, by deep embrasures, and yet the room is miraculously diffused in light—a clever solving by the architect of the problem of preserving the strength of an unpierced wall. Looking behind us, if we are fortunate we may obtain an alluring vision of the rose-granite cloisters in sunlight.

Confining as was the life of the celibates who dwelt here within the abbey, yet as we look backward through prismatic centuries even as we glance backward into their roseate cloister, how jewel-bright it glows! Intrenched upon their rock, wrapped in the invulnerable mantle of the archangel Michael, the monks were able to withstand attack, even presenting closed gates to the Huguenots who had won possession of the town. Again, as at Mont-Dol, the mind reverts to an age of faith with the stage set for the angelic visions of Sainte Jeanne.

Our stay at the mount was not lacking in adventure. We had been told that it was possible between Easter and September tides to obtain a cariole in which to cross the sands.

"Mont-Saint-Michel being paradise, let us follow the example of Adam and Eve," said Monsieur, holding up a post-card of the bas-relief in the chapel: *"Adam et Eve chassés du Paradis,"* under which was written, "Adam and Eve drove away from Paradise"!

"Let us," he continued, exhibiting a card of tandem carts, "try one of these 'Voitures de Genêts,' or, as the translator puts it, 'Carriages of broom,' in which to drive away."

Thus it was that we set out of an early afternoon from the *digue*. What added zest to the proceeding was the presence of a barefoot fisherman as guide, who ran ahead of the cart to test the firmness of the notoriously shifting sands. He wielded a three-pronged fork, a veritable Neptune's trident, and with its aid he marked the way with clods of wet sand. Our driver was a genial soul; a floppy béret worn askew well became his countenance, which suggested to our minds a too convivial monk—"drove," as Monsieur put it, with a broom from Paradise and settled on the farther shore. Applying his whip unmercifully, he kept his tandem horses at a gallop, for time and tide were to be reckoned with.

Regardless of the mud which was flung from the huge wheels of the cart and spattered our coats and faces, the beasts were urged onward. The exhilaration of the fresh sea-breeze, the experience of viewing the mount from across stretches of water and glistening sand keyed us up to attempt what seemed the impossible—for the season had but opened and the tides were high. Our horses plunged unwillingly knee-deep into swift-running water, urged on by the shouts of the genial teamster.

"It is near Tombelaine," the latter threw over his shoulder, indicating the island with his whip and lashing his galloping steeds, "that the worst quicksands lie"—this as we wallowed hub-deep in what appeared to us to be an unfordable lagoon.

"Ever hear of the Marquis of Tombelaine? Queer old fellow . . . dwelt all alone on the island . . . knew the sands like a book, lived the life of a fisherman; but there is no fooling with quicksands, hardly a year but some one finds it out. They got him at last . . . swallowed up in eighteen ninety-two. *Aille!*" as the lead-horse stumbled and with difficulty recovered itself; "bad place to stumble, *aille!*"

"A vivid half-hour!" I exclaimed as I relaxed my hold upon the cart, which with a final jolt brought up beside the low-lying pastures of Genêts. A pair of very woolly lambs, sucking from one ewe and wagging their minute tails simultaneously, paused and eyed us suspiciously before continuing their luncheon. Gulls flew seaward. Geese hissed their disapproval of our mud-bespattered appearance. No one seemed awake in all the somnolent village save a party of merrymakers at the inn, whence came sounds of rhythmic hand-clapping. Our homeward journey would have been an anticlimax, the tide having receded somewhat, had it not been for the increasingly marvelous views of the mount, now seen across the sheep pastures, now rising from above the weirs where fishermen foregathered, now mirrored on the tranquil surface of pools.

Ange Sauvé—bronzed as an Italian boatman, namesake doubtless of the archangel—hailed us that evening as the tide reached the portal of the mount. Would we not watch the sunset from his rowboat? That we would. Barefooted, he waded into the water to push us off, then settled to his oars.

"No one ever leaves the mount, madame," he told me; "or if they do they return to it. There is a sort of enchantment about the place. I am a fisherman. We are all fishermen and have been for generations."

"'Better a doorkeeper in the house of the Lord . . .'" I murmured.

The fiery disk of the sun dropped into a rosy cloud-bank. Our gondolier, breathing heavily from pulling against the tide, rested a while on his oars. Silently our boat drifted among floating gulls which rode, foam-white, upon the crest of the waves. Night fell as we rounded the chapel of Saint Aubert. The shadowy mount towered majestic above us—a thing intangible, holy, hallowed by time and legend, by tide and history . . . a fantasy of dreams.

Vitré: The Feudal Château

CHAPTER III

BRETON CHÂTEAUX

RENNES, the capital of the ancient province of Brittany, lies at the heart of the region of medieval châteaux. To the southward we shall later travel to Josselin and the Tours d'Elven, to Hennebont and Pontivy, already we have known Saint-Malo and Combourg; now, within a radius of, say, twenty-five miles, let us turn our steps to Fougères the magnificent, to Vitré and the neighboring Château des Rochers, to Dinan with its castle of the Duchess Anne. If we return to Rennes it will be upon a quest and not because of the attractions of the modern city which has replaced the former capital destroyed by the fire of 1720, when for seven days the flames raged. Few remnants remain of the storied Rennes of Middle Ages and Renaissance.

Six conflagrations swept the town of Fougères during the eighteenth century, but, as though by miracle, the sixteenth-century houses of the Rue de la Pinterie were spared.

"Have you seen Fougères?" writes Victor Hugo. "It is a town which should be piously visited by painters, a town which has an old château flanked by ancient towers, the most superb in the world. I have seen it in sunlight, I have seen it at dusk, I have seen it in moonlight, and I do not tire of it. It is admirable!"

Admirable indeed is Fougères, at all hours of the day, a place deserving its renown, secure in its aspect of military invulnerability. The entire enceinte should be skirted afoot. We lingered on the Place Raoul II and gazed our fill upon the grassy slopes blue with wild hyacinths, upon the ramparts and hoary watch-towers. Then we fell to wondering where Juliette Gauvain, the *amie* of Hugo, who dwelt opposite the château, had lived, and if her influence may not have caused the master to paint his picture with rose pigments.

The formidable entrance to the château is reached by crossing the river Nançon, which at this point serves as moat and, as if impatient of delay, leaps toward its tryst with the Couesnon, turning in its haste the moss-grown wheels of an historic mill. It is a challenging approach. Many a marauder has been baffled here by racing current, by sentinel's rebuff or inhospitable drawbridge. The approach forbids and yet invites. "The record of the past lies here, within your grasp," whispers the temptress spirit of the place, perchance the siren Mélusine. "Enter the court, enter." O wise man, be not deceived. Venture not to seize the rainbow's pot of gold. Forget not the adage: All that glisters is not gold . . . nor, moreover, is every walled town a Carcassonne.

Fougères is a hollow shell, a mere semblance of what was once a château-fort. Little by little the substance has been sucked by private greed. Within the court lies bareness and desolation. Too late has Government intervened. Let us turn aside to the cheery dwelling of the custodian, where the tale of the robustious days of past glory is retold with zest. It is the wife of the guardian who, ever on the alert, busies herself with the sale of books. Madame is a true Bretonne. The Duchess Anne has no warmer champion, the Church no firmer partizan, the State no more loyal patriot—yet one who sheds a tear for those citizens of Fougères loyal to their king.

"We of the border are Breton of the Bretons," she told us, "for to us fell the task, no easy one, of repulsing the Normans. The first château was destroyed by Henry II of England and this one was begun under Raoul II, Duke of Brittany. It has seen battles waged, madame. The French, under the Breton du Guesclin, stormed it in 1373, the English took possession of it in 1448, after a two-months siege. But here is the story that will interest Madame," and she held up a gay paper-backed copy of Balzac's "Les Chouans."

At this point we were interrupted by the arrival of a group of boisterous youngsters. Yves, a lad of ten, rushed to his mother for a whispered word before hurrying to Catechism. He was pressed into service and told to fetch from an inner room the photograph of his brother who, true to the military tradition of Fougères, was a student at Saint-Cyr. Recess had filled the empty square with a babel of childish voices.

"Les Chouans?" I questioned in ignorance.

"Madame knows, of course, the meaning of our Breton word? Literally, 'screech-owls.' The Chouans met at night, and, like your American redskins, they warned with a hooting cry. The name was given to the Bretons who joined the Army of the Vendée. These Bretons were country folk, loyal to Church and king. The cause of their revolt was partly the effort of the Republican Government to conscript them. We Bretons are a proud and headstrong people. The Chouans marched six thousand strong upon the town of Fougères but were repulsed by the National Guard (the Blues); later in the same year, 1793, the Chouans took the château and occupied it for five years—after which there was an end of Chouannerie.

"Have Monsieur et Dame visited the Palais

de Justice, that was the Hôtel de la Belinaye? You know it is the birthplace of the Marquis de la Rouerie—the comrade of La Fayette and friend of Washington—who fought in your war of the American Revolution."

No visit to Fougères is complete without a drive to the forest. In an ancient house on the Rue Pinterie we had been attracted especially to one dwelling, that of "Prohomme: Sabotier," who used as his inviting sign an actual red sabot. The one window on the street-level, overshadowed by the projecting second story which, with its neighbors, forms an arcade, was piled high with delectable sabots of every size, shape, and color in vogue in Brittany. "Where are they made?" we inquired, to be told, "In the forest." So to the forest we repaired.

Fougères will always be associated in my mind with my first glimpse of a Breton woodland. No longer, in all the province, is the primeval forest of ancient Armorica to be found; but the smiling well-tended French substitute, reminiscent of Fontainebleau and Corot's sylvan nymphs, is not without its charm. Foresters must needs be proud of their performance at Fougères. In the thousands of acres not a fallen twig but has been gleaned. We left our car and roamed at will where sunlight filtered through the beeches. Moss encircled their upright trunks upon which ivy crept. Moss and damp leaves formed a welcome carpet to our pavement-weary feet. A woodsy odor filled our nostrils. On and on we went, seeing no human life but here and there startling a pheasant or lesser bird, until suddenly we came upon the rustic abode of a sabot-maker.

How the centuries slipped away! We were transported into the midst of a Breton folk-tale. Around us lay the still forest, with barely enough wind stirring to set the leaves to whispering, a sound broken at rhythmic intervals by the chop of the artisan's knife. The man was short, with bristling brows, and wore a stubby black beard. He greeted our intrusion with equanimity if not with effusion and suffered us to watch the precise skill which enabled him, in a moment's time, to transform symmetrical blocks of beech wood into the semblance of foot-gear. *Click! click! click!* the blade beat on the tree stump that formed the table in this open-air workshop. In the doorway of the thatched hut appeared the man's helpmeet, a red kerchief bound gipsy-wise about her head. Her part was to wield a scoop-like instrument which hollowed the sabots; the children's, to stack them in neat pairs reaching to the low ceiling.

"They begin young," I remarked and the man replied:

"As soon as they are born."

"How long is the apprenticeship?" I asked.

"Twenty years. It goes from father to son."

The woman chewed a chip of clean white beech

A Sabot-Maker of Fougères

wood, wielding her tool deftly but taking no part in the conversation.

The sabot-maker, on the other hand, responding to our evident interest, took a log from a pile all of uniform size and, with swift strokes, chopped it into six equal parts.

"There you have six little sabots," said he, "for triplets."

"And where do you sell them?" I asked.

"To Normandy," was the answer. "Sabots in Brittany—pheuf! abundant as fish in the sea! I sell to Normandy."

The seigneurs of Vitré took part in the Norman conquest of England. Like that of Fougères, the Château of Vitré is one of the most impressive feudal survivals in Brittany, if not in France. The town of Vitré, however, unlike Fougères, has preserved its medieval aspect. Victor Hugo remarked that in all France only Avignon in the Midi might in this respect be compared to the town of Vitré. To many Anglo-Saxons the château's chief interest lies in its associations with the struggles of Protestantism in France. It was a stronghold of the Huguenots at the time of the League and resisted a five-months siege by the Duc de Mercœur, the chief of the Leaguers in Brittany. It was, moreover, by inheritance, the property of the leader of the Protestants—Coligny, Admiral of France. Therefore, as one wanders through what remains of the magnificent structure the mind reverts to Paris and the bloody night of the Massacre of St. Bartholomew, when the great Coligny was shot by a hireling of the Duc de Guise. Gayer associations are those during the period from 1655 to 1706, when the Breton parliament frequently met at Vitré, alternately presided over by the dukes of Vitré and of Rohan. From the year 1605 until the Revolution the castle was the property of the powerful family of la Trémoille.

The fame of Vitré and of its intact old Breton aspect has been so bruited abroad that when the traveler alights at the railway station the modern *place* is somewhat of a shock; but let me assure the new-comer that at Vitré nothing but the Place de la Liberté, with its pretentious station and modernized hotels, has altered in the last century. The march of progress moves here at as slow a pace as that of the snails which gamins gather in the castle's moat. We had been assured of a "reasonably comfortable" inn, so imagine our surprise when ushered into a capacious suite—did our appearance suggest opulence?—golden as to mantel mirror and clock, bedsteads, quilts, and velvet curtains, and boasting, wonder of wonders! an immaculate tub. Tea on the terrace accomplished (red-and-white awnings had been lowered by an attentive waiter to protect our eyes from the glare of the setting sun), we set out to explore the town and became immediately engulfed by the Middle Ages.

At the corner of the Rue Baudrairie and the Rue Saint-Louis a woman in a dusky room was roasting coffee over an open fire. Its pungent odor pervaded the street. We watched her from the open doorway, her only source of light, and noticed how, in the deepening shadows, she read a tattered volume, turning the handle of her roaster without lifting her eyes from the page. The persistent ting of a bell attracted attention. We soon perceived an acolyte followed by a priest, in robes of office, carrying the host to a dying parishioner. Heads were thrust from windows of houses which had appeared too ancient to be habitable. Knitters at thresholds crossed themselves as the curé and his assistant disappeared into one of the darkest of the doorways, open as if the very life of the crowded house's occupants depended upon this source of outside air. Heads were discreetly withdrawn. An increasing darkness stole upon the narrow street, a symbolic shadow, and in the ensuing silence we felt the presence of death.

In the minds of most the name "Vitré" connotes Madame de Sévigné, who dated two hundred and sixty-seven of her famous letters either from her "Tower" in Vitré or, more frequently, from the Château des Rochers. It was as much to visit this abode of the marquise as for any other reason that we had stopped over at Vitré. Which of us has not felt the irresistible charm of this *débonnaire* chatelaine who—between visits to Versailles, where she was the esteemed guest and partner in the dance of Louis XIV, or sojourns at the Hôtel Carnavalet where she held her Parisian salon—gave herself so completely to the cultivation of her actual garden as well as to the garden of her mind?

The Château des Rochers has changed not at all, one feels, since the seventeenth century when its *jardin français* was laid out according to the plan of Le Nôtre under the watchful eye of the marquise. The allées planted by her faithful Pilois have grown into avenues worthy the names she gave them: "The Solitary" . . . "The House of my Daughter" . . . "The Infinite." The ancient dial and echo wall are undisturbed, as are, to outward appearances, the château and the chapel where the uncle of Madame, the Abbé de Coulanges—the "bien bon" of the letters—officiated daily.

It was on a cloudy morning that we found ourselves pulling the bell for the concierge of les Rochers. The gray and misty weather accentuated the coldness of stone walls and slate-roofed turrets. Several pairs of sabots stood outside the portal, in cleanly Breton fashion. Hens pecked and clucked in a border of forget-me-nots. The concierge, a dour woman with her "bun" of coarse black hair covered by a still coarser hair-net, allowed us to peep into the chapel and to linger in the less chilly ground-floor room opening upon the delectable land of garden paths and forest known to the marquise as the "Cabinet Vert."

We were informed that the château still remains in a branch of the family. An air of gentility pervades the place, but it is evident that the glory of les Rochers, as of Vitré, lies in its illustrious past. Happily, we were permitted to wander through the damp grass to the forest's edge, where we could picture our exquisite marquise "half knee-deep in the dew, taking measurements," as she expressed it in an epistle to her daughter, Madame de Grignan, to whom she was wont to pour forth her soul. Through the magic of the letters the dead still live at les Rochers.

Modern Rennes is vastly more than the capital of the department of Ille-et-Vilaine. Its university, with faculties of law, sciences, and letters, is noted in the province, and more especially as being a center for the revival of the Breton tongue. The city's art galleries house important collections: its law courts are renowned—do not the walls still ring with the trial of Captain Dreyfus? It was not, however, to visit the university, the galleries, or the courts that we turned our steps toward Rennes. Our visit had one outstanding object. No lover of Brittany but should see with his own eyes the ceiling of the theater at Rennes—the masterpiece of that Breton of Bretons, that supreme artist, Jean Julien Lemordant.

Hospitable of an evening, the doors of the municipal theater are uncompromisingly shut by day. Having tried all the approaches and received discouraging answers from habitués of the café, we at last tackled the man in the tobacco shop. (In France, whether it be stamps or information wanted, try a *débit de tabac.*) The tobacconist sized up the situation at once. We had come from America to see the ceiling and the ceiling we must see.

"Go," he told us, "to the arcades behind the theater" (we had done so and found them deserted), "and midway you will see a door with a sign:

"Entrée
Réservée aux Artistes
Interdite au Public."

This was our entrance. We were to climb a steep flight of steps and to knock when we reached the sanctum of the chief mechanician.

Having carried out these explicit directions, Monsieur and I found ourselves in the presence of a sympathetic electrician, who, after all, was our man, for without the light he could literally throw on the subject our visit would have been in vain.

"In time gone by," said he, "it was quite a history to see the ceiling by day. One had to go to the *mairie* for a permit, but now I am authorized to show it to strangers."

We stumbled after him, across the deserted stage, in darkness until he turned on garish lights which illuminated the stage-drops overhead. Of the modernistic effect he seemed inordinately proud but murmured that we were perhaps not interested in stage-lighting. He then turned the ceiling switches and led us to the back of the theater. There we stationed ourselves and there we might still be stationed, heads in air, had not our necks finally reached the cracking point as we gazed at "La Danse en Bretagne."

Blazing sunlight, scintillating color, the movement and rhythm of life are all portrayed by the master's brush. The spectator throbs with the swaying figures of the dancers, who represent not Quimper, Plougastel, Pont-Aven, Pont-l'Abbé, Brest, though all are there in characteristic array, but who become personifications of the soul of Brittany. Hand in hand, rising from a foreground of blood-red poppies—tall men, small-waisted women, quizzical-faced, medieval, on and on they go to the eternal skirl of bagpipes till their leaders grow dim in distance, are lost in the clouds of heaven.

The electrician broke the silence.

"He was just one of us," he said. "I was here when Lemordant came to put it up and add finishing touches to the canvas. I was here, too, after the war, when he spoke from this stage, handsome as ever but with a bandage across his poor blinded eyes. They cheered him to the roof."

"He's handsome still," Monsieur spoke, "and, now that sight is taken from him, he rallies the idealists of the world by the power of his pen."

Bertrand du Guesclin, the hero of Brittany's wars of succession, was the antithesis of the modern knight who holds war a thing detestable. Bertrand from earliest boyhood was always engaged in a fray. He was a believer in war for war's sake. At a tender age he suffered from what to-day we should call an "inferiority complex." He was thought by his parents too homely to sit at table with the younger children, but a day dawned when he decided to claim his rights. To the forbidden board he came boldly and, calling attention to the fact that he was the eldest and that he would no longer be denied, overthrew the banqueting table, to his mother's consternation. It was a time when might made right, and Bertrand won the day.

At the age of seventeen du Guesclin was considered too young to take part in the tournament held at Rennes in honor of the marriage of Jeanne

de Penthièvre and Charles de Blois, nephew of the King of France. However, he managed to borrow a horse from a kinsman and to enter the lists, where he unhorsed sixteen seasoned knights, winning the applause of the assembled multitude and the heart of Typhaine Raguenel, his future spouse—not to mention the victor's prize, a mammoth silver swan.

When du Guesclin had reached the age of twenty, war broke out between the followers of Charles de Blois and those of Jean de Montfort, rival claimants for the dukedom of Brittany. Du Guesclin threw in his lot with Charles—who was upheld by the King of France, while Jean de Montfort was supported by the King of England, whose son, the Duke of Lancaster, was sent to command the British troops. This was in the year 1359, which is still remembered in Brittany as the year of the siege of Dinan by the English. The brother of du Guesclin was taken prisoner at time of truce, and this so infuriated the latter that he sprang to horse and galloped impetuously to the tent of Lancaster to demand amends at the hand of the offender, the Duke of Canterbury. His object was not gained, however, and Canterbury challenged him instead.

The contest was held within the walls of Dinan, in presence of the flower of chivalry of both armies, and it was agreed to abide by the result of the combat. Possession of Dinan was the stake. No odds were too great for the indomitable du Guesclin, who, to the surprise of the English, overthrew their champion and spared his life only at the request of Lancaster. A statue of the Breton warrior marks the spot on the Place du Guesclin at Dinan. It is Dinan, too, that zealously guards the urn containing the heart of its hero—his body having been interred, by a grateful sovereign, in the burial-place of the Kings of France at Saint-Denis.

The English have taken Dinan! Although not in the sense in which they attempted to do so under Lancaster. Their tongue is heard on every hand.

They have their clubs, their church. The climate, those we met assured us, is ideal. As Americans we found Dinan rather showery in springtime, but perhaps half the charm of the town, perched high above the verdant valley of the Rance, depends on the luxuriant growth of ivy, moss, and ferns which embellish its crumbling towers and bedeck its medieval gates and ramparts. As viewed from the promenade around the walls, the sea of verdure—orchards, pastures, forest patches—rivals in wealth of color the emerald ocean seen from the walls of Saint-Malo.

The most picturesque entrance to the town is through the Porte du Jersual, pierced in order that the Duchess Anne might be spared a detour on her way from the Rance to her château. The clock-tower with its powerful bell, dating from Anne's time, was the gift of the duchess. The terraced walk by which we leave the Church of Saint-Sauveur via the *jardin anglais* is known as the Promenade de la Duchesse Anne. One can visualize Brittany's duchess—who was, as well, France's queen—pacing up and down upon the ancient ramparts. Where, indeed, in all Dinan does not the valiant Anne form a necessary part of the picture?

Needless to dwell on the quaint arcades, the Romanesque porches to be found on the Place des Cordeliers, the antique houses of the Rue de l'Apport or the Rue du Petit-Fort, as we must hasten on to the château. What we know to-day as the castle of the Duchess Anne is in reality the keep or Queen's Tower of a stronghold built toward the end of the fourteenth century by Jean de Montfort when—after the death of his rival Charles de Blois and the taking of Dinan by the French under the leadership of du Guesclin—Jean deemed it expedient to fortify himself against attack by his former enemies. The castle adjoins the remaining gate of an earlier tenth-century structure and formed, with the Tour Coëtquen, a vital link in the walled defense of the town.

To-day the entrance to the château is through a flower garden and by a bridge above the abandoned moat. Although it houses a Breton collection, it is not as a museum that I think of the château. The illusion of continuity with the past holds singularly unbroken. Shall Anne not grace again with her upright little presence the stone seat from which she assisted at the mass? Shall we not see her self warming those small firm hands of hers at a roaring log fire in the massive chimney-place of her fortress bedroom while archers sit in tower alcoves, on the alert with ready bows? To-day no fires burn upon the hearth, 'tis true, and we may stand beneath the sooty chimney and gaze through the distant aperture to a far

glint of sky—comparing ourselves to the ancient Egyptians who viewed the stars by day from the Stygian depths of the great pyramid.

Among the foundations of the Castle of Dinan are despicable places deprived of every ray of light, dungeons from which a glimpse of foliage but tantalized the captive, cachots the memory of whose horrid past is not yet blotted out. What medieval contrasts! Above these secret chambers were there not scenes of revelry and endless banqueting? Nowhere in all Brittany, though the name of the duchess is ever on the tongue, did we find Anne de Bretagne and her glamorous epoch so unescapably evoked as within the Château of Dinan.

After nightfall—when came a lull in the whirring of the motors which haunt the town by day and only an occasional patter of sabots along the cobbled street broke the stillness—I caught snatches of the refrain of Brittany's most popular chanson, "C'était Anne de Bretagne. . . ." At dawn, when the alternate boom and vibration of Anne's gigantic tocsin dispelled slumber for the day, I heard upon the *place* the cooing of pigeons, and watched the swift flight of swallows darting over the lindens of the Promenade des Petits-Fossés castle-ward. Then, above the rumble of horse-carts, the crowing of far-distant cocks, once more I caught the now familiar strain:

C'était Anne de Bretagne
Avec des sabots . . .
Ah ! ah ! ah !—Vive les sabots de bois !

DINAN

Famed are the Cocks of Saint-Brieuc

CHAPTER IV

FÊTE-DAYS AT GUINGAMP

THE fame of the Rance is legendary rather than historic. The actual excursion by river boat between Dinan and Saint-Malo may pall, one fears, so oft have its praises been said and sung. Although I am not willing to admit what its partizans claim for it—that the Rance is the most beautiful river of France—yet it most certainly has no peer in Brittany. Perhaps half of its charm lies in the fact that it is to some extent a tide river, now narrowing to the form of a canal, now expanding to the proportions of a lake. Among its attractions are the modest but fabled châteaux which dot its verdant banks. Who would not, for example, linger beneath the mammoth live-oak of the château at Chêne-Vert to dream of the *belle* Alix and her loyal troubadour? Who would not sing a canticle in passing the reef of the Ile aux Moines?

The arrival at Dinan is rife with Old World associations. How tranquil is the scene! Beneath the modern aqueduct the spans of a medieval bridge form an admirable foreground to the high-perched town which from its battlemented height looks down upon the houses scattered along the quai. But, to my mind, it is from Dinan that the departure should be made in order to taste the ever fresh delight of the sudden coming upon the ocean at Saint-Malo. Of a late afternoon the emerald hue of the water is strikingly apparent as the boat nears Saint-Servan and rounds the gigantic tower known as Solidor. More like than not, if it be springtime, storm-clouds will hide the setting sun beyond extensive Dinard, while Saint-Malo, compact within walls, veiled in raindrops, will float like a phantom ship upon an enchanted sea.

Once more, for convenience' sake, let us return to Dinard but only in order to set forth on an excursion that will carry us, almost immediately, out of Ille-et-Vilaine and into the more truly Breton department of the Côtes-du-Nord. Monsieur and I paused, en route to Cap Fréhel, at Saint-Briac—a quiet family resort reached from Dinard, if no other means be available, by a ludicrously antiquated tram. At Saint-Briac, despite the intrusion of numerous villas, we found ourselves on the border of that region dear to painters, the Brittany of humble cottages, low and gray, with adjacent stone windmills and wind-blown pines, and on the clear horizon a glint of deep-blue sea.

We were not strangers to this landscape. For years we had known it through the water-colors of Florence Este. The *mairie* of Saint-Briac rivals the Luxembourg in possession of an example of her work; and the mortal remains of that valiant Este who was the life of Ker Augusta rest not in Paris but in the village churchyard where a simple inscription tells the story of her life: "Florence Este, American Artist, 1859–1926, a Painter of this Breton Country." . . . Her absence was poignantly brought home to us as we entered the garden of Ker Augusta, as we were greeted by blossoming fruit-trees along the carefully planted paths where (with true Breton democracy) pansies and clove-pinks were no less and yet no more a part of the decorative scheme than thyme, strawberries, or leeks. The Gloire de Dijon was riotously abloom, embowering the doorway, the faithful Thérèse had already welcomed us again to Saint-Briac, but Este . . . the soul of all . . . Este . . . where was she?

Cap Fréhel lies well within the confines of the Côtes-du-Nord, yet the excursion is most often made by motor from Dinard. Amédée, our sandy-haired robust chauffeur—who groomed his Renault car with the same solicitude that another man might show for his horse—clad in snug blue duster and nautical cap, drove us from the banalities of the coast resorts into what we were quick to recognize as the real Brittany, a foretaste of Finistère. It was Ascension Day. The joy of renewal and continuance of life, the eternal rebirth of springtime, was in the air. Our spirits soared on wings. The road was lined with oaks magnificent as those one expects to find in Brittany and which too rarely come to view. At other times we passed trees fagoted last year, with slender willowy profiles. Pines were in full flower, fertile as the surrounding fields of honeyed clover. They stood against the sky silhouetted as if by brush of Este.

"*Allez,*" Amédée would say at times, addressing the Renault as if it were alive; and at other times, in a tone of tenderness, he would call our attention to the car's steady performance: "Not another like her."

We whirred past blue-gray cottages roofed with slate or thatch, past wayside crosses, flower-decked, where women mumbled prayers while tending cattle. Hissing geese inevitably brought our car to a standstill before the road was cleared by means of Amédée's execrations. The *lande,* or moorland, of the cape, as we saw it in the month of May, was an expanse, a golden sea, of gorse. Later in the season it suffers a complete change and turns red-purple with the blooming of the heather.

Our arrival at the extreme tip of the rocky promontory was in a wild gust of wind and rain. With difficulty we saved our hats from being carried to the island falconries where we discovered myriads of gulls and cormorants. What power in a word! Cormorants . . . my thoughts leap hither and yon, like the waves which dash over their rocks, from Fréhel to Camaret, the Pointe du Raz, Ouessant, and Belle-Ile . . . wherever the weird outline of jagged reefs juts from a storm-bound coast. Here, where wrecks would be of more frequent occurrence were it not for the vigilant eye of the blinking or unwinking light, here we found populations of these somber birds of ominous presage who, from their chosen aeries, crane sinuous necks to gaze at man.

The keeper and Amédée being, it appeared, old friends, and the sudden shower having discouraged those holiday-makers who allow themselves to be discouraged—the unforgivable sin in a land of showers—we found ourselves in complete possession of the lighthouse. I must confess to a weakness for all lighthouses, than which there are to my mind few more romantic buildings, but in especial for the one at Cap Fréhel. It has withstood the wind and weather for two hundred years, for two centuries its light has poured forth a warning of the grave dangers that beset this entrance to the English Channel. Its office, on the first landing where we paused for breath and to sign our names in a ponderous book, is paneled in live-oak mellowed by the passage of fleeting decades. We climbed what seemed an endless spiral to behold the glittering prismatic lenses and then, in a whirlwind, we stepped to the outer platform.

Blazing sunlight had pierced the thunderclouds, the tossing channel was an intense ultramarine. In the foreground we obtained a bird's-eye view of the disused Fort de la Latte, known to history as the Château de Roche-Guyon. An infinite number of distant villages were visible from the stupendous height at which we stood. To eastward we could spy the twinkling white villas of Dinard, the solitary spire of Saint-Malo, while to seaward the isle of Jersey was distinguishable. To westward the bay of Saint-Brieuc and, not so far away as we had imagined, Paimpol—the country of "Pêcheur d'Islande"—lured us onward.

Saint-Brieuc (not to be confused with Saint-Briac) being our next objective, we conferred with Amédée as to the best plan of reaching it. He assured us that it would be advisable to motor by way of Lamballe—which, he added, with a quizzical look, would be to our liking, as it was *très rustique.* No words of mine can more adequately describe Lamballe. In a province noted for this very quality, Lamballe is rustic of the rustic. Its historic church built on a plateau dominating the plain is too often admired from no nearer than a car window. From 1134 to 1420 the town was the capital of the duchy of Penthièvre and the eldest son of the duke bore the title of Prince de Lamballe. For my own part, the place allured me because of its associations with its last princess—the beautiful, loyal, and ill-fated friend of Marie Antoinette.

Aside from the Church of Notre-Dame, the surviving chapel of the duke's castle destroyed by order of Richelieu, the Grande-Place is Lamballe's chief attraction. Here peasants congregate. Here stallions are brought from the neighboring haras—for Lamballe is famous for its breed. Around the *place* antiquated houses crowd the narrow streets, courting comparison with those of Dinan and Guingamp. The Impasse du Ha-ha leads in the direction of the church. Why the name? we asked each other. Was it because so many mistook it for a thoroughfare?—ha-ha! No one should be deterred, however, by this false attack from persevering in his quest for the approach to the elusive edifice.

Before our arrival at Saint-Brieuc I had been interested in reading of the founding of the town, now capital of the Côtes-du-Nord, by Saint Brieuc, one of the seven saints of Brittany, who had settled here with his disciples in the year 485 after his arrival from Britain. I had heard of how the saint had overthrown paganism, represented by a dragon which has been adopted in the form of a griffin on the city's coat of arms. I had read of the thorn from the crown of thorns, brought home by a devout crusader from the Holy Land and known as the Saint Bro or Briochin—from which the inhabitants take their name of Briochins—and of how the priest who, in procession, carries the reliquary containing the thorn is popularly supposed to die within the year. Never save in time of plague or other dire calamity does the relic leave the sacred precincts of the church.

The stirring history of the place had aroused my interest. Olivier de Clisson had in 1375 intrenched himself in the cathedral while waging war against the people of the town, while in 1394 the townsmen in their fortress-church were besieged by de Clisson. I had read of Jean de Malestroit who had restored the cathedral, long employed as a fortress, to its true uses; and of how Saint-Brieuc was the scene of bitter conflicts between Blues and Chouans during the Terror. I had been told of its famous granite houses, and more especially of the one on the Rue Fardel where James II of England is said to have lodged in 1689 while recruiting French forces for the invasion of Ireland. But on my arrival at Saint-Brieuc I found the pulsing life of the place so absorbing that any thoughts of its history became at once subordinate.

The center of interest in a Breton town is sure to be the market-place, and more especially if this open space be dominated by a cathedral. When we came upon the market at Saint-Brieuc, in full swing beneath the shadow of the cathedral, we knew instantly that we had found the Brittany we had come to seek; that it had not perished, as we had at first feared, during our long years of absence. Literally hundreds of white-capped women busied themselves with the sale or purchase of wares. Rusty in recognizing the costumes of the region, we were slow to distinguish the widely divergent types by which a native can as quickly place a Bretonne as a Parsee of Bombay can, for example, distinguish by his turban a Sikh from a Mahratta or a Rajput. As we mingled with the throng and observed the comely peasants, lined up with their baskets of fresh eggs and pats of golden butter, their poultry (famed are the cocks of Saint-Brieuc!) and Belgian hares or their fresh-caught lobsters, shrimps, and spider-crabs, their potted daisies, or their cherries and ripe strawberries, we began to differentiate between the homely bunchy coifs of Saint-Brieuc and those airy affairs worn at Guingamp, and to revel in the occasional mammoth head-dress—transforming each wrinkled wearer—which has been perpetuated in the statue on the promenade, the demure "Bretonne du Goëlo."

As the hour of noon approached, it was evident that there was to be a wedding at the cathedral. Through the open doors we caught glimpses of a myriad candle-flames. Already car-loads of guests had begun to arrive. A majordomo, in cocked hat and red-and-gold coat and carrying a baton of office, kept the crowd within bounds. Following the lead of the majority of those who found themselves upon the market-place, we had grouped ourselves near the portal to see the arrival of the bride. A sudden shower made the possessors of umbrellas bless their own forethought. As I was among the fortunate few, a portly peasant woman asked to share the protection of mine. I welcomed her to my nook behind the bread-seller's stand, where I was unjostled by the crowds upon the street. It was not long before the seller of loaves, a wizened individual looking for all the world like a dripping fowl, asked if he might join us. Thereafter I found myself sandwiched between the rain-drenched one and the buxom dame. Their comments were to the point.

"Madame knows the bride?" asked the bedraggled one. "A daughter of the best jeweler on the Rue Guillaume. All the wealth of Saint-

Brieuc you may see to-day, and many a one from Guingamp."

"Here come the groomsmen," said the dame, nudging me in the ribs. "Fine fellows."

I was willing to take her word for it though wondering in my Anglo-Saxon heart why dress-suits at high noon should to me appear preposterous while to her they were merely proper and fitting—as becomes a suit.

"Rain," she continued, taking a pinch of snuff between ample thumb and forefinger, "rain brings good luck to the bride. We call rain at a wedding 'the bride's tears'; they will be her last."

Cries of "There she is—the bride!" arose from the street and there indeed she was, alighting from a coupé, a radiant figure in white satin and tulle. As soon as she had entered the church the crowd surged after her in Continental fashion, knowing the cathedral to be spacious enough for all.

"You see her carriage," my dame informed me. "All the brides use it, trimmed with lilies and ferns, and in the back, you see, where you think is a window, that's a mirror . . . so love can have its day! Come, madame, come quickly; the mass will be beginning."

Apologizing to the bread-seller, unable to forsake his loaves, I scurried after my guide, who led me brazenly near the chancel where the invited guests were assembled. Therefore we had an uninterrupted view of the young couple who knelt before the golden-robed priest and who were to continue to kneel for the greater part of an hour. Organ and violin resounded through the lofty building, which was decorated with banners of Church and State, flags of the republic over the high altar alternating with the ermine banners of Brittany. Throughout the entire ceremony groups of peasant women paced to and fro—their coifs in motion hovering like mammoth butterflies beneath the gray arches—kneeling at side chapels, crossing themselves, and, childlike, stealing a look at the bride. The unbidden guests were not to go scot free. Our presence at the ceremony was actually countenanced, it appeared, for after the bridesmaids, each on the arm of a groomsman, had taken a collection from the guests, they stepped from the chancel and passed their flower-decked baskets to every member of the vast congregation, which by now included, I should say, every coif that we had seen upon the market-place.

O sleepy little town of Guingamp, how may one guess your secret? Had we not, indeed, tarried all unwittingly within your borders and never known? We had said to each other, of the Place du Centre, "What a setting for grand opera!" We had not divined that once a year, according to the sterling Breton custom, a ceremony takes place beside which the memory of such a show as "The Miracle" of Morris Gest becomes theatrical and pale. Guingamp on the Saturday preceding the first Sunday in July awakens. With open arms she welcomes her pilgrims. Ten thousand hearts and voices combine to bring into being this miracle of piety and devotion, this sacred flower sprung from the soul of a people enamoured of beauty, tradition, and romance, this fervent act—the lighting of symbolic fires in praise of the Creator. Nowhere else in all Brittany will the pagan rites now put to Christian uses be found to equal the torch-light procession of Guingamp. All the superstition of Trégor to the north, the mysticism and religious fervor of neighboring Léon, finds its culmination here in this ceremony held in what was once the capital of the Pays du Goëlo and under circumstances which enhance its every element of mystery and enchantment. There is no rival to this Breton festival, while of daytime pardons Sainte-Anne-d'Auray alone commands an equal, although not a similar, allegiance.

The allées were a seething mass of humanity on the day preceding the procession. Booths had been installed beneath the shade-trees, side-shows, a shooting gallery bearing the name "Tir Breiz Izel," merry-go-rounds; and, to cap the climax, the circus arrived with glitter and blare of drums and cymbals, with mighty wagons whence issued the roar of beasts. Pilgrims were pouring into

Guingamp ⁘ ♣♣♣
Ancient roofs and chimney-pots

town. With the arrival of every train the influx passed the terrace—for so the sidewalk was courteously called—of the Hôtel du Commerce. As we munched the inevitable *gâteau sec* offered on such occasions with tea, in lieu of the desired pastry, it amused us to enumerate the towns from which the pilgrims came.

On every woman's head perched an airy confection, stiffly starched for the occasion, of net, tulle, or lace. Those of Guingamp and thereabouts were delicate in the extreme, of hand-made net, embroidered; from Morlaix came tulle coifs of much the same form, with a little more abandon to the drooping ends that becomingly frame the face; lace mob-caps betrayed that their wearers hailed from the interior, Carhaix and Huelgoat, whose damsels vie with one another in their choice of silken shawls and aprons. Girls from Pontivy, Guémené, and Baud rivaled if they did not surpass in gaiety and color the maids of Huelgoat; lasses wearing the fly-away cap of Lorient consorted with bewitching beribboned belles from pleasure-loving Quimperlé.

Not to be outdone, the swains and husbands displayed a lavish amount of black velvet—streamers upon hats, cuffs and shirred vests—those of Pontivy not disdaining the traditional white broadcloth jacket weighted down with copper buttons. Welcoming hosts, the "Men of Guingamp" swaggered as though unforgetful of the time, long centuries ago, when, as the ballad tells, their forebears saved the imperiled city of Nantes from the clutches of the English: mindful as well, we imagined, of the days before the marriage of their Duchess Anne when three times the town of Guingamp was beleaguered by Anne's cousinly rival for the duchy of Brittany, the Duc de Rohan. Even in those days it was the *bon Dieu* who was all-powerful in the affairs of Guingamp. Did He not send the Blessed Virgin, with the Christ-child in her arms, to ring the bells of Notre-Dame and so put to flight the forces of the duke and his French allies?

It is said that in the seventeenth century there were three thousand beggars at Guingamp—about half the population. Be that as it may, one who attends the pardon knows the meaning of "the beggars have come to town." Rags, tags, velvet gowns, all are on hand. In particular they congregate in whining phalaxes about the porch of the church, where in a niche above the main portal the venerated statue of an ebony-black Virgin, gorgeously arrayed, looks over the heads of her worshipers. Here kneel, at every hour of the day, groups of the faithful; here sit priests inscribing names in veritable judgment books; here flicker in the breeze the flames of candles. Posters tell of the great doings to come. The heading, in flamboyant letters, runs:

GRAND PARDON DE GUINGAMP
Pèlerinage de Notre-Dame de Bon Secours.

The event on this thirtieth of June was to be presided over by the Bishop of Saint-Brieuc and Tréguier in the presence of Monseigneur the Bishop of Dara (Haiti), who, we heard, was a good Breton. There would be pontifical mass at ten, vespers at three, and at half-past nine the procession in which every person who would take part must carry a lighted candle. There would be the *feux de joie* (or sacred fires) on the *place,* followed by a midnight mass. The church would remain open throughout the night.

The great day dawned. Burst of sunlight pierced a cloud-banked sky. Afoot, carrying heavy lunch-baskets, or in jogging carts the peasants poured into the old gray town. Many, we could see at a glance, were extremely well-to-do, while others obviously were lowly and ignorant. Young and old, men and women were almost without exception in Breton dress, for the most part were conversing in the gruff Breton tongue. The sound of church bells filled the air, blending with the cawing of rooks and the whistles of arriving trains.

Reapers, threshing-machines, and other infernally noisy inventions had been installed in the park beneath the shade of a druidical oak. Men in beribboned hats and velvet-trimmed jackets inspected with evident interest these incongruously modern contraptions. Drovers threaded their way to the horse-fair or to the allées where cows and pigs were on sale.

Shopkeepers were reaping a harvest, to judge by the number of balloons which floated above the crowd bearing the names of rival establishments. With the pilgrims we gravitated toward the church. Within, a friendly atmosphere prevailed. There was a constant shuffling of feet, a tramping from one relic to another. We encountered many rural types. One old man, with white hair flowing to his shoulders, was carrying by its stem an enormous cabbage. Drovers had brought whips and ropes. There was much hand-shaking among them, while women embraced one another à la Bretonne—a kiss on each cheek (in French fashion) and one more for good measure.

As we entered, a group paused for holy water, rotund parents and a son, all in the costume of Lorient. The boy especially took our fancy, a lad in early teens with cherubic face, dressed like his father, in black-velvet coat, long trousers, and beribboned hat. As the hour for vespers neared, the crowd increased. Mothers with babes in arms lined the thronged aisle and, upon the dramatic entrance of the bishops, held up their children to kiss the pontifical hand as their remote ancestors had been made to kiss the divine hand of the king.

Our next emotion, after vespers and while we were awaiting the torch-light procession, was the circus. We pushed our way through the thronged allées, to the tent where a striking young athlete swathed in a crimson toga was alternately haranguing the crowd and beating a drum.

"It's the lion-tamer," a woman ejaculated, pulling her offspring toward the entrance of the tent.

Having paid a few francs, we found ourselves immediately in front of the central cage, into which the lions were already leaping. Behind us the cheaper benches were jammed, while seething masses had purchased standing room. The lion-tamer entered. A resplendent leopard-skin was wrapped about his naked body, leaving a muscular shoulder bare. A boxing match with one of the lions was interrupted by the stealthy approach of a female of the species, who advanced from the semicircle of watchful beasts, snarling and showing vengeful teeth—retreating only upon compulsion from a spiked weapon.

Once again the audience held its breath as the trainer, his head in the mouth of a mighty king of beasts, seemed unaware of imminent danger. The selfsame lioness, crouching to spring, was transfixed by the sound of a pistol fired. Shot followed shot, until the terrified creatures of the jungle, leaping over hurdles—had this, too, been planned?—bounded off-scene. Their breathless trainer meantime, pistol in hand, received an uproarious ovation.

"Some day that lioness will get him," Monsieur exclaimed.

"I don't want to see any more of it," said I.

"But wait," Monsieur persuaded. "The next are bears."

I subsided into my seat, reassured by the nonchalant appearance of a debonair youth who led into the ring a troop of performing bears. He was a Celtic type, high-cheek-boned, blue-eyed, low-shaven. He wore creased trousers of horizon blue, an immaculate white-silk shirt, and a cigarette tucked behind one ear. It was evident the man was an artist in his work, that he was a comrade of the bears. They nuzzled affectionately for tidbits, on hind legs strutting through their paces. Powerful and awkward, they stood at full height on rolling balls, laboriously propelling them. They completely won their public and bowed to the applause, solemnly repeating their tricks. Does not man, too, repeat tricks for applause?

On the day after the fête, stopping at the cleaner's for a dress, I spied at the counter a slim ex-service man whom I instantly recognized. He was inspecting a white-silk shirt and blue trousers which Madame had ready for him and I noticed that in cajoling her to lower the price he interlarded his remarks with English.

"I saw you in the circus. Your bears are extraordinary," I could not refrain from remarking. "Are you English?"

"Scotch," said he, speaking in French, "but I came to France at the age of eight, so I speak

French better. . . . Yes, I've been to Scotland—during the war I served with the British—but I wouldn't stay there to work in a mill or factory or sit at a desk adding figures. Mon dieu, what a life! I know your English workman. He drinks his tea at regular hours. He doesn't work too hard. He eats bread but no cake. In France my hours are long, but I have money to spend. My work is not work to me. I live!"

Madame had finished the careful counting of the roll of new francs the man offered her and put in her word about the fatigue that Monsieur must suffer on these fête-days.

"And are you not sometimes unnerved?" I asked, as I saw he still lingered.

"I chose bears, madame," said he, "because bears are so gentle. Sometimes they are bad, though," he admitted. "But I understand them; no two of the nine are alike . . . in which they resemble men! It is all a question of psychology. I treat every one differently and they know it. I would not be a trainer if I had to fight with my animals. . . . Have you seen the film of Michael Strogoff, madame? My bears and I take part and now I have written to Hollywood. If they could but see my bears they would want them, is it not so, madame?"

We parted with mutual assurances of the hope that our acquaintance might be renewed in America.

The Fête at Guingamp

Guingamp's famed torch-light procession transcended our greatest expectations. Thousands and thousands were participants. From our illuminated hotel we first caught the radiance emanating from the cortège reflected in windows; then the spectacle, on rounding the corner, burst upon us in reality, a sea of light, of fire. Priests directed the throngs. As they passed us came snatches of martial music, alternating with plaintive voices raised in Breton canticles, with groups chanting, in French, hymns to the Virgin. The candle-light played on lacy coifs, on banners innumerable, on sacred relics borne aloft by devotees. At last came the bishops, adorned in scarlet and gold, magnificent with staff and miter, wielding an almost hypnotic power by means of hands uplifted in rhythmic blessings.

When the final group of marchers, plowing a fiery path through the darkness, had at last been swallowed by the night, we made our way to the Place du Centre to await the procession's return and the lighting of the pyres. We had been invited to partake of ices on the balcony of the Patisserie Martinet, a point of vantage overlooking one of the three huge piles of fagots, tall as a house, flying a pennant with the naïve inscription: "Vive Jésus." The night was chill. Shivering, we declined the proffered ices. So long had been the procession that we expected to find its head already at the square, but no, the route was longer still. With impatience we waited. At last we spied the first flickering lights.

It comes! In all its other-worldly beauty the marshaled multitude marches against a background of grand-opera houses whose windows are aflare with candles, whose gables glow in the light of blowing lanterns. The crowd parts, cleft like the Red Sea, to allow passage for the bishop, who advances and sets his torch to the base of a pyre. The fagots blaze and crackle. Flames leap on high and swirl in the wind, showers of sparks rise skyward and fall like fireworks on ancient roofs and chimney-pots. Rockets soar. The procession, a sinuous river of light, is flowing uninterruptedly toward the open doorway of the church. As ours dies low the other pyres flare. The belfries of Notre-Dame are seemingly afire.

How many come to Guingamp, I wonder, and, unseeking, find not? To visit Brittany itself and not to dive below the surface into the hidden depths of Breton idealism is to miss the pearl of price—the soul of the people, where blend religion, poetry, love of beauty, and romance . . . all indivisible parts of the favored Celtic race.

Lannion: rich in timbered houses

CHAPTER V

THE LAND OF RENAN AND LE BRAZ

It is an extraordinary circumstance that in this northernmost portion of the Côtes-du-Nord and of Brittany itself, indeed—which includes the towns of Paimpol, Tréguier, and Lannion, the village of Port-Blanc—within an extremely narrow radius have dwelt some of the greatest writers whom Brittany has produced. Paimpol achieved world renown through the works of Pierre Loti (not himself a Breton) and its name has received an added popularity through the songs of the bard Théodore Botrel. At Tréguier Ernest Renan first saw the light of day; at Tréguier Anatole Le Braz sleeps his last sleep. It was at Port-Blanc that both Botrel and Le Braz lived during a long period of years; near Lannion that the poet Luzel was born, and here, too, is to be found the country home of Charles Le Goffic.

On the *place* of the Old Tower at Paimpol stands a newly erected monument to Théodore Botrel. It was our good fortune to be present on that morning of July fifteenth when this bust of the poet was unveiled. On one side of the stone are carved two women wearing the dainty coif of Paimpol, on the reverse two doughty seamen and lines from "La Paimpolaise":

> J'aime Paimpol et sa falaise,
>   Son église et son grand pardon,
> J'aime surtout la Paimpolaise
>   Qui m'attend au pays Breton.

Despite the gaiety in the air on this particular occasion, despite the historic cortège representing the entrance of the Duchess Anne into Paimpol in the year 1505, one could not but remember the dénouement of the poem, how the fisher-lad was not destined to return to wed his sweetheart but was, like full many another valiant Breton, claimed by the relentless sea.

"May God protect us, for the ocean is so great and our boats are so small," runs the sailors' prayer. With anxious hearts do the women await the return of their "Islandais."

Loti in his "Pêcheur d'Islande" has immortalized this sturdy race, cultivators of the soil throughout the mild winters, departing in their schooners with the approach of spring, to fish for cod off the dangerous coast of Iceland. Between the time of the fishing fleet's departure and the return in August or September, Paimpol, and particularly its outlying villages from which are recruited some of the finest sailors in the world, Ploubazlanec, Loguivy, Porz-Even, are conspicuously bereft of able-bodied men. It is easy to understand the thrill with which Gaud, the appealing heroine of Loti's romance, realized on her return to Paimpol in December that she would at last meet the Iceland fishermen. Yann and the boyish Sylvestre are haunting memories. Le Braz aptly described Paimpol in three words—"La mer, l'amour, la mort" . . . the theme, one might say, of "Pêcheur d'Islande."

No lover of Loti's book should fail to take the drive from Paimpol, on its sheltered bay, to Ploubazlanec by the sea; and to the Pointe de la Trinité, where, from the base of the weather-worn statue of Notre-Dame de Perros-Hamon, women watch for the first glimpse of a sail from Iceland.

Joyous as are the greetings on those often long overdue returns, yet are they not at best overshadowed by the absence of some eagerly looked for face? In the cemetery at Ploubazlanec the pitiful "wall of those who have disappeared at sea," with its mock tombs which the souls of the departed are said to inhabit on All Souls' Eve, is rarely seen without the presence of a black-cloaked widow wrapt in prayer.

A surprise was in store for us at Paimpol, in the form of the Hôtel Continental. To find in this typical Breton fishing-port, not a seaside resort,

An Icelander of Paimpol

a cuisine notable even in this land of France and almost unique in the province of Brittany, was at first inexplicable. Who, then, were its habitués? we wondered. We were to discover that Paimpol is increasingly used as a base from which to make the excursion to the Ile de Bréhat.

Of the five Breton islands known to me—the others being Ouessant, Sein, Belle-Ile, and the Ile aux Moines—I shall place Bréhat in the category of the Ile aux Moines. It does not share in the bleak and eerie characteristics of the sterner islands, despite the chain of reefs which endanger the crossing from the mainland and which, being of rose-red granite, appear ingratiatingly paintable in sunlight, across the waters; but rather, with its aloes in sheltered sunny nooks, its picturesque lanes, and the quaint head-gear of its women it resembles the island queen of the Gulf of Morbihan.

Pilgrims have for centuries poured to Tréguier. A proud episcopal city from the year 855 until the Revolution, Tréguier was built upon the site of the Monastery of Trégor, from which the region takes its name, the Pays de Trégor. Devout and idealistic, even beyond the high average of the Celt, the Trégorois, like their brothers of near-by Léon, are proverbial for their piety. The outlying village of Minihy has produced the greatest of all the galaxy of Breton saints and the only one, so I am told, canonized at Rome: Saint Yves, the incorruptible judge of Rennes who became a parish priest.

We read some of his attributes, upon the wall of the church at Minihy, the former chapel of the manor of Kermartin, where Yves, who came of a noble family, was born in 1255:

Mirror of Chastity	Refuge of Sinners
Defender of the Helpless	Father of the Poor
Protector of Soldiers	Model of Priests
Tutor of Orphans	Salvation of Mariners
Advocate of Widows	Patron of Advocates.

A popular couplet apropos of Saint Yves reflects the attitude of the Breton peasant toward the legal profession: "Advocate and not thief, thing worthy of the admiration of the people." The saint is familiarly represented, as at Minihy, standing between the prosperous man, who is richly clad and carrying a bag of gold, and the poor man, whose cause Saint Yves is customarily expected to uphold. On every hand are representations of Yves the venerated, in wood, in stone, or even in fresco. Few ancient houses at Tréguier are without a shrine to the local patron and most families include a son who bears the name of Yves.

The rite known as the adjuration of Saint Yves has, happily, fallen into disuse as a means of settling a quarrel. The aggrieved one, in times past, was wont to make a pilgrimage to a chapel of Port-Bihan since destroyed in an effort to stamp out this pagan ceremony. There, before the statue of the saint, the irate one would declare: "If the right is on his side condemn us; if on our side condemn him—cause him to die within the year." Thus, by a strange perversion, the benevolent saint became a personification of vengeance, a veritable Kali.

How different is the story which has come down to us of Yves's actual way of life! Le Braz tells in "The Pardon of the Poor," the scene of which is Minihy, of an episode in the life of Yves the Good. On a stormy night when the wind and rain beat against the venerable manor of Kermartin, the servant had gone to bed without the usual preparations for unexpected guests. Then it was there came a rap upon the door and a man entered who announced that he was a juggler by profession. He was followed by his wife, on whose merits and accomplishments he expatiated, and by his two sons, whom he described as paragons of virtue, and finally by his daughters, whose estimable qualities he was about to extol when Yves cut him short and made him welcome.

"You are at liberty to remain as long as it pleases you," said Yves.

When death overtook the saint, eleven years later, the juggler and his family had not yet departed!

Every year, on the nineteenth of May, hordes come as of old to the manor, and soup is doled out in the name of the saint, while pilgrims are given shelter in the outbuildings. Opposite, in the churchyard, is the Gothic table-like tomb of Saint Yves, beneath the arch of which his devotees feel constrained to crawl. This, in the mind of the people, is *the* tomb—not that in the cathedral at Tréguier which contains some of the sacred relics.

Brittany is especially noted for its wealth of ecclesiastical architecture, its chapels (so called with reference to their size, despite the orthodoxy of the cult), its sacred fountains, carved figures of the saints, and in particular for the beauty and originality of its many wayside crosses and elaborately carved granite calvaries. Of cathedrals

TRÉGUIER

it possesses but few, among which I should place as outstanding examples the one at Quimper, the capital of Finistère, and the one at the relatively unimportant town of Tréguier. Tourists have never been numerous at Tréguier, which fact perhaps constitutes not the least of its charms. Secure in the possession of ecclesiastical dignity, the town has endured throughout centuries of upheaval. A tranquil episcopal city it remains, despite the circumstance that its bishop now dwells at the commercially more important but far less captivating town of Saint-Brieuc. The notable quality at Tréguier is other-worldliness. Its people may be narrow in their views (note the expiatory calvary near the station by which means a group of citizens disclaimed any part in the erection of the monument to Ernest Renan), but materialistic they are not. The difference between their idealism and that of Renan (who, indeed, objected to a distinction between spirit and matter) was not perhaps as fundamental as many of them supposed. Mellowed by the passage of time, Renan, it is said, came to admire the moral beauty of the Catholic faith without in the least adhering to its principles. "Religion and knowledge," said he, "are as imperishable as the world they dignify."

A monument to the enduring faith in the soul of man, the cathedral is a priceless memorial. The youthful Renan, born within its shadow, admitted that a blighting nostalgia took possession of him when he was deprived of the atmosphere of Tréguier—toward which, throughout his long life, his thought frequently turned. It was to the cathedral that his mother brought him at a tender age, upon the death of his father, to place him under the protection of Saint Yves, guardian of the fatherless.

As we wandered at twilight through the mysterious edifice, steeped as it is in reminders of well-nigh forgotten ages, our thoughts sped first to Yves, to whom it owes the impetus for its erection in the centuries when the Gothic sprang spontaneously to flower. Passing by the Hastings Tower, remnant of a still older and more distant day, we followed the sacristan into the cloisters—the most perfect, perhaps, in all Brittany. In the center of the grassy close stands a statue of Saint Yves, lifelike in lawyer's robes. An odor of blooming things filled the dusk. There was a stir of wings, night moths hovered near, a splash of forgotten sunlight came from a bed of primroses. Around us the arched arcades spread their curved beauty above the slender gleaming columns, which to the mind's eye took on the appearance of slim angels standing with folded wings awaiting a word of command from the motionless figure of the saint. Against the hoary gray of steeply mounting roofs Gothic pinnacles arose at intervals, fantastic in the fading light. 'Tis true that monks no longer pace these sequestered pavings, but to the quickened imagination the cloisters of Tréguier are now, as in a remote medieval past, the dwelling-place of heavenly hosts.

To lovers of Brittany, much as they enjoy "The Life of Jesus" and other volumes by him whom Le Braz calls "the greatest enchanter that Brittany has produced since Merlin," it is Renan's "Souvenirs" of his childhood and youth in his native province that make the strongest appeal. The grandfather of Ernest, having amassed a competence from fishing, was the first of the family to aspire to a house in Tréguier. His son, Ernest's father, was the captain of a cutter, a Republican married to a girl of Royalist tradition from Lannion. The boy Ernest was destined for the church. Being a liberal, not at heart a democrat—although, indeed, he had faith in the gradual ascent of man—he spent his life in a series of desperate struggles in an effort to formulate his political and above all his religious beliefs.

Encouraged by his high-minded elder sister, Henriette, he broke with the Catholicism in which he had been reared. Later on he was forced to resign from the chair of Hebrew at the Collège de France, owing to the strength of the Clerical party, whose members were scandalized by his open denial of the divinity of Christ. It was rumored that Renan, famous philosopher and Orientalist that he was, would never be accorded burial at Tréguier . . . but Tréguier had no choice in the matter, for Renan is one of the few Bretons acclaimed by France and the world at large. The beloved professor of the Collège de France and member of the French Academy was given the highest posthumous honor—burial in the Panthéon at Paris. Tréguier did, however,

Tréguier : Birthplace of Renan

name her cathedral square in his honor, erecting a monument which, save for its quotations, is singularly lacking in spiritual appeal.

The modest birthplace of the master, almost beneath the shadow of the cathedral, is owned by a daughter. Here a retainer of the family, wearing the cap of the region, sold us rubber-stamped volumes. Here we were shown a case full of medals and a little worn report book.

"Look, madame," said the enthusiastic dame, "how good were Ernest's marks for studies, health, and behavior, but (was it prophetic?) look how frequently he was late for the mass!"

His grandson's picture was shown; an ardent Catholic of Catholics who lost his life in the war. The shawl of Henriette is among the treasures and a portrait of Renan's wife, who spoke no French. In answer to my inquiries as to what she did speak I was told that she was Irish.

Among Renan's favorite pupils was the Breton Anatole Le Braz. When the latter was to give his first lecture, and that at Lannion, the elderly professor made the journey from Paris in order to attend.

Anatole Le Braz! What tender memories link his name not alone with that of Renan but with the town of Tréguier and the village of Port-Blanc! Beyond the cathedral in the wooded park, formerly the grounds of the Episcopal Palace, his ashes rest beneath a fitting monument:

Je suis un fils des monts
adopté par la mer.
Anatole Le Braz
MDCCCLIX
MDCCCCXXVI

The stone is placed against a background of rocky cliff. A vista in the grove allows the eye to wander far below, to the peacefully flowing river, the tranquil country-side so typically Breton. How he loved the Breton scene! There is a spot on the road to Paimpol, about four kilometers from Tréguier, where he was always wont to stop his car and to remain wrapt in contemplation. The landscape, at this point, is as serene as one of his own masterpieces, as the idyllic "Poèmes Votifs." Across the hedges of blooming gorse, the rows of neatly trimmed oaks (without which no Breton landscape rings true to type), the fields of billowy rye ripening in the sun, prosperous thatch-topped farm-houses may be seen, and fields on fields rolling to where the distant mount, the Ménez-Bré, rises against ethereal clouds. Twice a year a horse-fair is held upon the summit of this mountain, beside the chapel to Saint Hervé, patron of bards and of all those who dwell upon the heights. Jaffrenou and other Celtic singers frequent these gatherings, and Le Braz was unflagging in the enthusiasm of his attendance.

Through a chain of untoward circumstances we arrived at Port-Blanc in time, it is true, for the unveiling of the monument to Botrel at Paimpol, but a week too late for the ceremonies in connection with the transference of Le Braz's remains from Paris to their resting-place at Tréguier. We were not aware of this mischance until, half-way to the hotel, we informed the chauffeur of the object of our visit, in asking him if he could point out to us the cottage of Le Braz. We had been attracted to the young Breton—whose litheness was revealed by trim uniform and snug puttees—by his sensitive Celtic profile. To our surprise his blue eyes brimmed with tears.

"I was his chauffeur," said he. "I was with Monsieur Le Braz for six years. His house was my home. But, monsieur et dame, is it possible that you did not hear of the change of date? The ceremony is over."

"Over?" we exclaimed, incredulous.

"Yes. It took place a week ahead of the scheduled date, changed by the mayor because of a conflict with the unveiling of the monument to Monsieur Botrel."

"And Madame Le Braz?" we queried. "Is she gone?"

"You will not see her. She spent only two nights at Tréguier. It would have been too sad for her at Port-Blanc. One of Monsieur's daughters will have the house . . . you know his son was killed in the war."

On this slender foundation our friendship for Louis was built up. On our part he was the connecting link with the family which made to us the significance of Port-Blanc. On his side, with true Breton intuition he divined the depth of our disappointment, and the fact of our having come for such a purpose was enough to establish us in his good graces. He unburdened his soul to us and told us how he was never without a letter from Monsieur Le Braz in his pocket. He drew out one and read us the finely penned script, an epistle written in cheerful vein from the Riviera, making plans for the future. This was the last of the many he had received and it had come to him in the same mail as the news of his master's death.

"It is company for me," said he with an eloquent shrug, folding the worn letter and placing it in its creased envelop.

We talked of Madame Le Braz, whom we had seen some months before in Paris, and found that because of his admiration for this gracious American lady, the godmother of the eldest of his three young children, Louis was kindly disposed toward America and the Americans. We told him, too, of the high esteem in which Monsieur Le Braz was held when he was sent by his Government to lecture in the United States and how his books were loved and cherished by the discerning. The short ride to the inn was but the first of many we were to take with Louis during our stay at Port-Blanc. It was he who took us to Tréguier, to Paimpol, to the hoary chapel of Saint Gonéry at Plougrescant, where our admiration was divided between the quaint interior with its decorations, telling the story of the creation, and the churchyard with its three-crossed gate and high stone barrier which humans may straddle but which blocks the way to the four-footed, its curious open-air pulpit, its many-centuried yew.

Had it not been for Louis, Port-Blanc might have been to us a desolate fishing village, an embryonic out-of-season resort. With Louis as our guide we were permitted to feel the glamour investing the place, to visit the house which since the father of Anatole taught school at Penvenan has been the home of the family of Le Braz. The old house is a low stone cottage wreathed in vines, to which has been added a modest wing. The yard was abloom with marguerites, to be found in every Breton garden. Its chief distinction is its view, for across the highway, beyond rocks and moorland, lies the sea. From his workroom window the master could gaze afar, reveling in sea and sails and wooded islands: the isle of Saint-Gildas with its sacred fountain (the island home of his friend the celebrated Dr. Carrel), the isle of Iliec where Ambroise Thomas, lulled by the waves, wrote the tuneful music of "Mignon."

"Kestellic," the name of the Le Braz dwelling, is a name often used for old manors, the Breton for "little castle." As we entered the gate with Louis, who had procured the keys, he pointed out a turret atop the gate-post brought from Saint-Nicholas near Guingamp. We entered a spotless kitchen, gleaming with polished brass, a dining-room rich in antique treasures, among them a carved *bahut,* or clothes-press, of blackened wood, a trophy bought for a song in Finistère, where it had been thrown outside a farm-house. On the wall a decoration of a saint, in dull red, signed Mabik Remon (the chimney-sweep who was at times inspired to paint, and only and always the figure of Saint Yves) brought poignantly to mind what we had read of him in that greatest of all books on Brittany, Le Braz's "The Land of Pardons." The study—with its books touched by his hand; its photograph of Renan, and that of Carmen Sylva on which she had written a French dedication, "He who understands the human heart and the sea, he is a master"; its fireside chair hewn from a single trunk, souvenir of his teaching days at Quimper—evoked the seer, the patient gleaner in the fields of fancy.

"Look at this picture of a fisherman, madame," Louis broke in on my reverie. "This is my wife's grandfather. It was her grandmother who told Monsieur Le Braz many of the tales he put down in 'La Légende de la Mort.' As for me, madame, I was not treated as a chauffeur in this house. Every day Monsieur would call for me to talk an hour or two in Breton."

The village of Port-Blanc may best be seen from the chapel which stands high above the patchwork of neat walled fields, the scattered cottages of the fisher-folk, the blue expanse of sea. To landward a low villa in the pines is still owned by the family of Botrel, who dwelt there for many years, fraternizing with the natives. Still they tell of how on occasions the chapel resounded to the rich melody of his song. Here, as is to be expected, may be found a side altar to Saint Yves, who is quaintly depicted between the rich and the poor.

This weather-worn granite chapel, a remarkable example of the flamboyant Gothic, is a gem of rustic fitness. It seems to have sprung miraculously to being. Its sweeping roof, perhaps in order the better to withstand the wind, actually rises from the ferns and grasses. Within the walled inclosure that surrounds the building, children gather, quite at home, playing their little games while seated upon the ancient stone base of the crucifix. The Breton is on intimate terms with his saints, who are with him in everyday life as well as at time of festival. The Virgin of this chapel is known as Celle de Port-Blanc—that is, "the One of Port-Blanc." To a humble Breton there is far more virtue in prayers addressed to the One of his own village than to a merely abstract Mother of God.

Before parting with Louis we wished to visit Saint-Servais, the birthplace of Le Braz. This was a longer excursion than the others we had been taking, and to Louis, who had for years toured Brittany with his master, a joyous liberation from the petty round. The birthplace

Anatole LE BRAZ

is situated in what are known as the Monts d'-Arrée. Curiously enough, these wild bleak moors and hills at a distance from the sea possess, perhaps as a lingering souvenir of one-time grandeur, many of the characteristics of mountains which, in ancient days of greater dignity, were rightfully their own.

The village of Saint-Servais lies near Callac, which is to be found on the highway between Guingamp and Carhaix. It is in a sparsely settled farming country where, to judge from the absence of post-cards, tourists are unknown. At Callac the name of Le Braz meant nothing to Madame at the grocery, but the fact that we were foreigners proved most intriguing. Presumably we were the first her eyes had ever lighted on.

"You speak French?" she interrogated. "How very lucky!" and she proceeded—haltingly, for

Breton was her tongue—to ply us with questions as to whence we had come and whither we were bound.

The house at Saint-Servais where the little Anatole was born and dwelt until into his teens is now used as Hôtel de Ville. Its two full stories are bereft of vines and imagination is required to fill what must once have been a walled garden with appropriate flowers. A plaque, put up before his death, reads:

Ici naquit
Le 2 avril 1859
Anatole Le Braz
L'Orphée Breton
qui ne voulut connaître
et chanter que la Bretagne

The Breton charm and flavor of this really remote and untouched neighborhood is to be found in the church. A profusion of Gothic creatures grin and leer from its lichened exterior. Its side porch, which, true to Breton tradition, is the entrance, possesses twelve stone statues of the Apostles; one, having lost his head, has the look of a Saint Denis or, as we are in Brittany, a Saint Trémeur.

Louis remarked that there were no French signs in the church and interpreted the inscription on the monument to victims of the war:

Maro vid ar vro
Doué da vean gant o ine
(Died for their country
They rest with God)

Sauntering to the back of the church, we paused to admire the baptistry with its medieval-looking font. In the profound silence of the place Louis's voice, with that same catch in it as when he read the letters, startled us with these words:

"He liked to stand beside this font. It was here that he was baptized."

Our return to Port-Blanc was in the darkness. The tide lapped hungrily against the sea-wall—for there is no beach when tides are high. A group of fishermen, with their catch, trudged, lanterns swaying, along the quay. The cry of a wild sea-bird came from afar.

"Port le Blanc, a bay in Brittany," Shakspere called the place, and it has scarcely changed since he wrote the words. To us Port-Blanc has become infinitely more . . . not only a shrine possessing precious associations with a man who was the flower of his race but also a region beloved for the wild beauty of its rugged coast and for the poetry and fraternity to be found in the hearts of the natives. To my mind it remains unparalleled by any of the more frequented resorts of the Côte Lannionaise, the coast to the north of that town of Lannion rich in timbered houses of long-gone centuries which would make its fame anywhere but in Brittany.

Ploumanac'h should be visited, with its rocks of rose granite and its shrine of Saint Guirec where maidens to this day stick pins in the nose of the long-suffering saint; to judge by the number in the soft stone when we saw it, there will be marriages a plenty within the year. Perros-Guirec must be seen, near which lies Rosmapamon, the summer home of Renan during those last years of his life when he felt a longing for his native Brittany; and Trébeurden, a haven for the newly wedded (as such I remember it); and, above all, Trégastel with its twelfth-century church and gruesome ossuary, one of the last to be still in use. Yes, above all Trégastel, if only because off its coast lies the isle of Avalon where Arthur is said to dwell . . . whether buried or alive, who can inform us? Some say he is under enchantment and lives here with Morgane, sister to Merlin, on this "blessed isle where falls not hail nor rain nor any snow." Be that as it may, we know full well that we have felt the spell of the enchanter, of those more praiseworthy successors to the wizard Merlin, in the land of Renan and Le Braz.

Morlaix :
A lofty Viaduct spans the Valley

CHAPTER VI

MORLAIX AND THEREABOUTS

KNOWLEDGE of the Breton language is the only open-sesame in Brittany, according to Anatole Le Braz; but not being possessed of this particular password, we substituted for it the mention of the name Le Braz.

"Yes, you have the right idea," the bard Emile Cueff once said to me. "You make your own observations and you understand our traditions through familiarity with the writings of Le Braz; one without the other would not be enough. You have the right idea."

Our eagerness to assist at the pardon at Saint-Jean-du-Doigt, held on the twenty-third day of June, was partly because this was one of the five pardons described by Le Braz. Our first thought, therefore, on arrival at the hospitable inn, was to mention why we had come. Madame, a widow of refinement who wore the embroidered coif of Lannion, was immediately moved to smiles and tears; for the loss of the great man is fresh in all minds.

"Monsieur Le Braz . . . how good he was to me and to my children . . . shall I ever forget his kindness to my sons. He came here, madame, but a few years ago with his American bride. He was so distingué and yet so simple and so good. It had been years since I had seen him and I did not recognize this middle-aged gentleman of so much distinction. He said to me:

" 'You do not know me?' and I said:

" 'No, monsieur,' and he said:

" 'You do not remember the fils Le Braz?'

" 'Monsieur Anatole!' I cried. 'Is it indeed you?' . . . He had known my family years ago in Lannion.

" 'Do not tell your waitress that I am a Breton,' said he. 'I shall have my little joke.'

"In a few minutes the poor girl came running to me, dumfounded.

" 'There is a French gentleman at lunch with an American lady,' said she, all out of breath, 'and he scolds me in Breton!'

" 'It isn't possible!' I said, smiling to myself at the expression of wonder on her face. It must have pleased Monsieur Anatole to see the complete success of his little ruse."

Contrary to the advice of one author, who cautions immediate flight to Morlaix when the religious ceremony is at an end, we had engaged our rooms at Saint-Jean for a week. The inn is situated at the threshold of the church and our bedroom overlooked the narrow street which would soon be packed with merrymakers. Our attentive *patronne,* Madame Philippe, in leading us up the winding stone stairway explained that the older portion of the inn dates from the reign of the Duchess Anne, and that it was here her chevaliers were entertained.

Saint-Jean-du-Doigt owes its curious name to the fact that since the fifteenth century its church has been in possession of the alleged index finger of Saint John the Baptist, brought here from Normandy by a devout Breton. Possessed of miraculous healing powers, the finger is said to be particularly efficacious in the cure of diseases of the eye. So much was this the case that when the Duchess Anne suffered from an acute eye trouble she gave orders that the sacred relic be brought to her at Nantes. Three times, the story goes, did the priest try to remove the finger of the saint, but three times it was found to have returned to the altar at Saint-Jean. The duchess consulted a hermit, who spoke after this fashion:

"Madame Anne, Monseigneur Saint Jean is so high a personage that you should make a visit to him."

Anne de Bretagne and her suite of lords and ladies immediately set forth on the pilgrimage from Nantes. Pages there were a plenty to carry her court train. With pomp and ceremony the duchess came to Saint-Jean. But, although the peasants were cured of their ills, the queen's condition was unimproved. Then once again Anne consulted the holy hermit, who said:

"Madame Anne, Monseigneur Saint Jean prefers sabots and less beribboned coifs."

Then the good duchess borrowed a dress from a peasant and, kneeling humbly with her subjects, kissed the finger of the saint . . . and was cured of her ailment.

The news of the miracle spread like wildfire throughout the nine dioceses of Brittany. The fame of Saint-Jean-du-Doigt was now established. The queen was lavish in her gifts—even to this day Saint-Jean is noted for its treasure—and, moreover, she elevated all the peasants in the neighborhood to the rank of gentlemen; if you don't believe me go and see for yourself their comfortable homesteads and the dignity of their demeanor.

The surroundings of Saint-Jean are lush green fields and wooded hills, although less than a mile away there is a sandy beach topped by a ridge of cobbles. The hedged lanes to the sea are devious and roundabout, leading past stately manors and between fields where, at times of pardon, the gay shawls of pilgrims vie with the scarlet of flaming poppies.

Few Breton parish churches are more typical of the best fifteenth-century tradition than Saint-Jean. A triumphal arch (signifying the victory of the spirit over death) forms the entrance to the graveyard. A calvary, oratory, ossuary, and fountain all are of the period, and the impressive tower of the church is itself memorable despite the fact that its spire was destroyed by lightning a few years past. Odd, was it not, that fire should destroy any part of an edifice dedicated to Saint Jean Baptiste whose fête is known as the "Pardon of the Fire"? Until recent years popular throughout the length and breadth of France, a time-honored rite older than Christianity itself and associated with pagan sun-worship at the coming of the summer solstice, the custom of lighting bonfires sacred to the saint, the fires of Saint John, has languished except in a few instances, notably in the Pyrenees and in tradition-loving Brittany.

Intense expectation was in the air. Vespers were about to let out; following which would be the procession. We had watched the arrival of the Saint Jean of the year, a toddling parishioner of the name, clad in a fleece and, with the assistance of fond parents, leading an immaculate woolly lamb . . . toy imitations of which were to be had at booths just sprung into being. At last the church doors were thrown wide. The crowd parted to

The Pardon of the Fire ‡ †

make way for the bearers of relics and flags. So massive was one banner that it required a pole "heavy as a mast," to carry which entails months of physical training on the part of the young athlete who wins the honor. On a hill above the church a towering pyre of gorse awaited the torch. As flames and smoke rose furiously, maidens jostled one another to scorch bouquets, hastening marriage, 'tis said; farmers extracted charred twigs for the well-being of crops; while blind beggars, piteous hope within their hearts, were led to garner the sacred ashes.

Impressive as was the scene, it pales in recollection before the memory of another at which we were spectators. The following day was a Sunday. At six in the morning we had been awakened by a merry carillon. Annik, the faithful bonne, had brought with undue promptness an allotment of hot water to our door. After coffee and rolls we still lingered at a window possessed of all the advantages of a grand-opera box. At the pardon there had been a certain number of strangers, but these had now departed. The women inspecting wares at the booths erected for the occasion were all coifed in the fashion of the region save a few visitors from Saint-Thégonnec, who were easily distinguished by their vivid shawls—those of Saint-Jean are heavily fringed but always black. Men of Celtic mien were in evidence—a type less frequent in Cornouaille—

among whom many were garbed after the quaint fashion of Léon, with low-cut vests and wide plaid sashes.

By craning our necks we could observe the holiday doings against a background of the churchyard in its rich setting of clipped lindens and stone walls fringed with pink valerian. In the opposite direction our windows commanded a view of the highway sweeping in from open country. Here as we watched, to the tolling of church bells, came a solemn funeral cortège . . . on foot, of course, according to the dignified French custom. We were to learn that the deceased was a man of prominence. The women mourners, thirty or forty, were enveloped in voluminous hooded cloaks embellished with velvet bands and fastened with massive silver clasps. The procession wended its way into the church, men bystanders holding hats in hands.

From a discreet distance we watched the interment. Against the neutral background of the church the women mourners formed an austere fresco. With slow steps each advanced in turn to sprinkle holy water on the corpse. Trojan women they seemed, mourning their dead with rites antedating the Christian era. Here and there among the graves other parishioners knelt at the tombs of their ancestors. Once more the bell rang, no longer tolling dolefully but clamorously, announcing the hour of mass. Mourning cloaks were hastily shed and women emerged like moths from chrysalises, endeavoring to unfurl the crumpled wings of coifs.

Thus even in the midst of what was to prove a day of uproarious merriment we had felt the shadowy presence of Ankou, the dread Reaper who lurks ever near and is not deprived of his due measure of respect among devout Bretons.

Morlaix (in Breton, Montroulez; and how a native loves to roll it on the tongue!), one of the residences of yore of the Counts of Léon—in Breton legend the Lyonesse of Arthurian romance—is one of two Breton centers in Finistère. If Quimper had a rival in all Brittany it would be Morlaix, which is to the northern portion of Finistère what the departmental town of Quimper in Cornouaille is to the southern; and Finistère, as we have already stated, is Brittany par excellence, the Brittany of painters and folklorists: in a word, Brittany Bretonnante.

Perhaps Quimper may be more overwhelming in its visual appeal, possessing more architectural wonders, a more welcoming sunlight, more brilliant and varied costumes, yet Morlaix is the traditional center of song and story in the oft-praised dialect of Léon. Dear is the Léon tongue to the bards who frequent the book-shop of Ti Breiz, kept by Francis Gourvil, one of their number, an authority on the Breton language.

Cherished, too, are the writings of the monk of Morlaix, Albert Le Grand, who in the seventeenth century recorded with such ardor the "Lives of the Saints of Brittany." Morlaix, moreover, has named one of her open squares for Souvestre, for it was at Morlaix that Emile Souvestre, best known by his "Attic Philosopher," was born. In addition to his books on the region, Souvestre performed the memorable task of translating many Breton legendary tales into French.

Although not possessing a cathedral of its own, Morlaix has in its immediate neighborhood the religious edifices at Saint-Pol-de-Léon. While many travelers passing through from Brest to Paris merely look down upon the town from the superior height of the lofty viaduct spanning the valley, the wiser ones alight and drive post-haste to that compeer of the Hôtel de l'Epée at Quimper—the Hôtel de l'Europe. It is true that the Europe has no such entrancing outlook as its fellow at Quimper, but its cuisine is equally worthy of remark.

Tradition has attached the name of Anne de Bretagne to a certain house, 33 Rue du Mur, a mansion worthy of the honor whether or no the lady in question ever numbered it among her dwellings. Perhaps she may have stopped here on her memorable entry into Morlaix in the year 1505. The house is a perfectly preserved example of fifteenth-century domestic architecture. Its half-timbered façade is richly adorned with carved grotesques and figures of the saints, while the interior with its mighty hooded fireplace and curious spiral stairway is equally reminiscent of the period. Nowadays the mansion serves as a restaurant. From the quaint latticed windows there is much coming and going to be seen if it be market-day, the prevailing head-dress being the clumsy "lobster-tail"—a strip of heavy muslin bound about the low-dressed hair, while youth and beauty has adopted more airy tulle.

In the environs of Morlaix—toward Saint-Jean-du-Doigt—lies "the valley of the fountains" with a château partly hidden from view by its luxuriant park. For many years and up to the time of his death this was the preferred summer residence of Maréchal Foch.

Morlaix is the base from which to visit the country of the *calvaires,* Saint-Pol-de-Léon, and Roscoff by the sea. Not only is Morlaix a likely center but Morlaix, as well as Port-Blanc, possesses a chauffeur notable even in the land of intelligent chauffeurs. The paragon of Morlaix, by name Le Bars, is to be found at the house where he and his wife sell Breton pottery, almost adjoining the book-shop of their friend Gourvil on the Place Thiers.

The name of Le Bars had reached me in America and on arrival at Morlaix we were told, "Every one knows Le Bars." We found him a tall, spare man in a gray duster, austere at first glance, melting at mention of his offspring, Annaïk, Marie-Thérèse, Michel . . . I wonder if the list has grown. We caused much merriment by our open preference for Annaïk, not only because of her more friendly ways, the twins being still in babyhood, but because of her good Breton name.

"Yes," chimed in an old fellow we took for the children's grandfather, "the next should be Mônik, Yann, or Yves—not Joséphine, Jacqueline, Framboisine, nor yet Albert nor Robert, names the peasants think distinguished. Breton names are good enough for Bretons."

The only drawback to motoring with Le Bars was the peculiar make of his automobile, which, although an open car, interposed a solid barrier of glass between himself and his would-be questioners. Stating, with a wry look, that all patrons were not so inquisitive as ourselves, he yet admitted we had reason on our side and assured us that he would order a different model.

Like Rouen in Normandy, Saint-Pol-de-Léon possesses not only a cathedral but a second church of equal fame. We had no sooner set foot in Brittany than we began to hear all other spires compared with that of the Creisker of Saint-Pol-de-Léon. "If an angel came from heaven to earth," the saying goes, "it is on the point of the steeple of the Creisker that he would first set foot." The fact that the delicate lace-like effect

of this soaring spire is entirely a creation of granite caused Vauban to call it the most daring use of stone ever undertaken by man. The flatness of the surrounding country makes the Creisker visible from afar . . . a beacon alike to devout pilgrims of the faith or to those who come to worship at the shrine of beauty. The story goes that the original building was a thank-offering of her house, given by a maiden who was paralyzed because she worked on a fête-day and who subsequently was miraculously cured by the bishop, Saint Guirec. This episode took place in the sixth century, while the present tower, a model for many others in the province of

Brittany, dates from the first half of the fifteenth century.

The charm of the cathedral (no longer used as such, Saint-Pol not having fulfilled its promise of becoming a prosperous town) had, as far as we were concerned, remained unsung. Perhaps it was in part owing to this very fact that we were carried away by the discovery of its merit. It also possesses a spire, two in fact, of the first order—one, as I remember, in the Norman style, the other, with a characteristic exterior gallery, more typically Breton. As we entered the main door we discovered that a thorough spring cleaning was taking place, something we had never associated with Old World cathedrals. In different parts of the huge building a small army of men was employed with brushes and ladders, scouring lofty columns and scrubbing time-worn pavings. We offered thanks, though cleanliness be next to godliness, that the odor of soapsuds and the sound of the scrubbing-brush had not as yet invaded the vast choir where in unbroken silence the stony forms of prelates lay in state. Of singularly touching and overcoming beauty we found them, these prostrate bishops of long ago, resting from their labor; their feet cushioned upon the conquered dragon of Saint Pol; content, it seemed, to remain in effigy within these sacred walls until the trump of doom.

No one should leave the town of Saint-Pol without having heard the legend of its saint. Not Saint Michel nor yet Saint George had such a way with dragons. Saint Pol, you must know, was a Welshman who settled on the Ile de Batz in the year 530 and who later became bishop of the region of Léon. On his departure from his native shores he had asked the parting gift of a certain bell from King Mark, but the latter, hoping that refusal would defer Pol's departure, left his wish ungratified. On Pol's arrival on foreign shores, the story goes, a salmon was captured and brought to his presence and inside it was the identical bell. This circumstance and the sanctity of his life soon brought him the rank of bishop.

Now, there was on the island of Batz a formidable dragon. One really feels a sympathy for the beast. At a word of command it allowed the prelate to put his stole around its neck and to lead it to the brink of the sea, where it obediently threw itself into the waves. The place is known as the abyss of the serpent, and here the creature is said to writhe and bellow to this day. Then there is the Coat-ar-Sarpant. Saint Pol's nephew, who had vainly endeavored to convert the pagans in this region, had been forced to retreat to Brasparts. At last he called upon his uncle for assistance. It was, as you might guess, the question of a dragon. This one proved as subservient to the saint's wishes as the one of the Ile de Batz. In fact, when the people complained that in a few years the dragon's offspring would prove a like source of terror, the parent trotted off to round up its young.

Swirling wind and sand in the eyes detracted somewhat from our enjoyment of the short ride from Saint-Pol to Roscoff by the sea. Flat treeless fields where early vegetables are grown for the English markets were lacking in attraction, unless for the novelty of observing tree-cabbages with stalks attaining the height of a man. An admirable setting they formed for a troop of school-children chasing butterflies. Monsieur started to sing:

"Savez-vous planter les choux à la mode, à la mode?" and they were quick to chime in:

"Savez-vous planter les choux à la mode de chez-nous?"

Our appetite for *primeurs* was all on edge by the time we arrived at the inn opposite the church on the walls of which the arms of Roscoff, a boat, are repeatedly sculptured. There are but two sights at Roscoff, though the town is popular with the English. The second is a gigantic fig-tree with enough leaves to safeguard the modesty of every inhabitant. When I tell you that it has flourished and borne fruit in proportion to its size ever since its planting, around 1600, and that nowadays it bears from four to five hundred kilos a year, you will realize that to see it is in itself worth a trip across the Channel.

It was at Roscoff that "Bonnie Prince Charlie," fleeing after Culloden, was permitted to disembark, having evaded his would-be captors with the assistance of a corsair of Saint-Malo. Scotland, in centuries gone, frequently at odds with England, became Brittany's most natural ally. It is said that the ring found on the finger of James IV after Flodden was that of Anne de Bretagne, who had incited him to rise against the common enemy. Still cherished in this part of the world are memories of Mary, Queen of Scots. The house of "Marie Stuart" is the first sight of Roscoff. As it happened to have a for-sale sign displayed on the day of our visit, it offered a sore temptation. Its Renaissance exterior, the arcades of its courtyard, the romantic tower on the shore, reached by traversing a tiny garden all abloom, enticed us. It was near this tower that the winsome Queen of Scots landed; she was at the time aged five years, eight months. After a solemn entry into Morlaix—the year was 1548—she continued on her triumphant way to Paris, where with much ceremony she was affianced to the Dauphin, the short-lived François II. Our thoughts sped across the Channel to haunting Holyrood.

Rich are the Costumes of Plougastel

CHAPTER VII

GRANITE SHRINES

"The Versailles of Brittany!" the guardian remarked as he preceded us into the courtyard of the Château of Kerjean.

"Its proportions are more homelike!" I exclaimed and, "What amazing flowers!" as my eye caught sight of tree-fuchsias trained against the château wall, spangling it with a myriad blood-red blossoms.

"I do my best, madame. The hydrangeas aren't bad, though I say it; hortensias we call them, for Queen Hortense. But this makes me a poor horticulturist." The man tapped a leg obviously wooden, though it did not prevent him from wearing the customary sabots.

Monsieur and I had come that afternoon by motor from Morlaix, not, indeed, with any preconceived enthusiasm; but our interest had grown apace as our car traversed the domain of Kerjean.

The park has preserved the cachet of a Breton forest. Mammoth beeches, whose fantastic branches were encrusted with mossy green, created the illusion of a romantic age. We passed the ancient pigeonry, a veritable citadel of birds, while at the axis of a grass-grown allée, arresting even at a distance, three stark posts demanded explanation. Our inquiries led up to the disclosure that these were the rigid supports of former gibbets—conveniently near to the castle gate and not, I suppose, considered unsightly nor of ill repute by the lord and builder of Kerjean, the Seigneur Louis Barbier, or by his gentle lady, Jeanne de Gouzillon. The moat once crossed, despite the feudal aspect of its outer fortifications Kerjean smiles a welcome with all the grace inherent in the architecture of the Renaissance.

"One could be happy here," I said to Monsieur. "This is no haunted Combourg—that is, if one could enjoy merrymaking so close to the lowering gallows."

"Aye, men have loved at Kerjean, madame," said the guardian, "and they have hated. What would you? It is life. Do we not all love and hate? As for me, do I love the Germans?" and he slapped his game leg as he spoke. "There is the tale of the lady Françoise de Quélen, the ever faithful spouse of René Barbier. Come, I will show you the vaulted chamber where she bolted the door, imprisoning three neighboring seigneurs who had made a cold-blooded bet to seduce her during the absence of her lord at court.'' With a barely perceptible halt in his gait the guardian traversed the spacious yard and led us down a winding stair to the kitchens and adjacent subterranean chambers.

''This,'' said he, pointing to an unsavory retreat, ''is the hiding-place used by the last in line of the descendants of the Barbiers, the Marquise de Coatanscour. Poor lady . . . she and her sister took refuge here during the Revolution. They were avowed Royalists and organized the opposition to the Blues. Yes, they were taken to Brest and executed.''

Fire and the violence of revolutionsts have played havoc with one wing of Kerjean, as a ruined wall bears testimony, but the remaining portion appears to be safe from further molestation or neglect. Purchased by the State a few years before the war, the château was made the depository of numerous examples of Breton rustic art. One of the Le Braz family was chosen as curator. Impoverished conditions since the war have retarded the restoration of the place. However, like the valiant ex-soldier its caretaker, Kerjean rises above disabilities. A spiritual witness to the survival of beauty, partially ruined, scantily restored, not as yet rich in acquisitions, the château-museum occupies a unique position. The rare charm of its floral setting, the background of its forest, the intrinsic merit of its architecture unite to cast around it a glamour difficult to analyze.

Not far from the gallows, where some of their remote ancestors like as not may have swung, a family of peasants dwell, friends of our chauffeur; friends to all the world, one would guess. The robust housewife was not a motherly type without reason, being, she told us, the parent of eleven sons. Presentable examples of her skill in this direction, all grown to manhood, were gathered about the hearth where, on the open fire, pancakes were browning. The savory odor filled the little room, mingling with that of fresh-drawn cider.

"Join us, monsieur et dame, you have arrived just at the moment. This is our supper, madame." The woman caught my admiring glances: "Upstairs we have iron bedsteads, but some still prefer the lit-clos. It is practical." She rose and opened the lattice of one of the built-in beds that lined the walls, giving the kitchen the appearance of a state-room.

"You see, madame, how snug one is," said she, with pride displaying the lace counterpane and fluffy red coverlet. "And you have privacy: close the door and there you are!"

Between the double-decker beds a grandfather's clock with mighty pendulum of shining brass ticked loudly, as though to remind us of the lateness of the hour. We were not allowed to depart, however, before visiting a new-born colt in the adjoining stable, and I was given all the full-blown roses that bedecked the cottage wall. In bidding our adieus we remembered the words of Le Braz to the effect that in Brittany the surest way to be an aristocrat is to be born of the people.

In all Brittany, land of granite though it be, old and gray as to cliffs and grottoes, menhirs and dolmens, cathedrals and châteaux, there is no more characteristic expression than the calvaries of the district of Léon. Hardly a *carrefour* but has its humble cross or crucifix of chiseled stone, but I allude in especial to the more famous conglomerations, of which the best examples are to be found at Guimiliau, Saint-Thégonnec, and Plougastel. Like Kerjean, these shrines lie in the neighborhood of Landivisiau, where, at the ancient fountain, strangers are eyed with suspicion, their intrusion arousing perturbation among the washers of linen at the pool.

Lampaul-Guimiliau is first encountered if the traveler comes from the direction of Kerjean, and the magnificently sculptured *poutres,* or crossbeams, of the church—the ends held in the jaws of a dragon of Saint Pol which might have had its inception in Cathay—form an interesting comparison with those in the chapel of Kerjean. Yet it is to Guimiliau proper that we must hasten.

The assemblage of buildings at Guimiliau conforms to accepted Breton tradition. Graves cluster around the church—of necessity, so devout are the habits of the people, situated in the heart of the village. Therefore space in the graveyard is at a premium and the concessions are not by any means in perpetuity. At the end of a few months or years, as the case may be, the bones of the deceased find their way to the ossuary, according to a custom still prevalent in Brittany.

The ossuary or bone-house, being a place where relatives frequently repair to offer a prayer before the box containing the remains of their ancestors, is as elaborate in design as the church itself. The graveyard is surrounded with a wall the opening in which forms a portal symbolic of the triumphant entry of the dead into God's kingdom. Guimiliau is the wonder of wonders, the holy of holies, the most astounding efflorescence of sculptured granite in all the province.

The calvary at Guimiliau, erected in 1581–88, obviously inspired the one at Plougastel. The central cross rises above the platform ornamented with statues and a frieze depicting scenes for the most part from the life and passion of Christ. From the open-air pulpit, an integral part of the *calvaire,* the preacher of long ago was wont to deliver his exhortations, indicating with a wand the personages of whom he spoke. The Abbé Le Roux, it is said, never failed to impress his audience.

When he came to the representation of Catell-Gollett (the dissolute servant who was condemned to eternal flames) he would first tuck up his gown and mimic Catherine's departure for the ball—much to the delectation of listeners—but when the dénouement was reached and he impersonated the Evil One in his seizure of the hussy, such a bellowing resounded near and far as to cause the congregation to flee, imagining the devil in pursuit. Here was an abbé worth his salt!

The calvary of Saint-Thégonnec, begun in 1610, with its sacred surroundings still intact, is in two senses Guimiliau's closest rival. On the day of our visit we collided at the Arch of Triumph with a blushing white-robed nun in sabots, followed by a clattering flock of school-girls likewise shod after the fashion of Anne de Bretagne. To what extent, we asked each other, would these young lives be overshadowed by rigid adherence to the outworn Breton fetish, the Cult of the Dead?

"Weddings and baptisms—those are the times to see the Breton off guard and arrayed in his ancestral costume. Go to Plougastel-Daoulas—the little village near Brest where marriages take place but once a year. I was there this spring; all Brittany was aflame with gorse, from Brest to Saint-Malo . . . and yet men lingered in Paris! Brides! You should have seen them at Plougastel: a dozen in their stiff starched caps with wings framing their honest bronzed faces; and bridegrooms with wide-streamered hats and gay blue jackets. Mon dieu, what figures! Go see for yourself in sunlight. You will worship the madonnas of Plougastel." So spoke our friend, the painter whose masterpieces France acclaims.

June 30: the fête at Guingamp; July 1: the pardon at Plougastel-Daoulas . . . so read the uncompromising dates. Finding choice impossible, Monsieur and I made the momentous decision to try for both! The story of the fête has been told. On the following morning we were up with the lark in order to take the 7:28 from Guingamp to Morlaix, where the faithful Le Bars was to be in waiting. I remember with amusement a party of jolly young people whom we singled out among the departing throngs. A sunburned bourgeoise insisted to brother and friends that the diminutive train on a far track was not for them.

"Read for yourself: 'Direction Paimpol.'" She pointed to the track nearest the platform.

But brother, knowing the characteristics of the cars and engine which ply to Paimpol, was unconvinced.

"Ask the guard." Sister was emphatic.

The ball of their argument was tossed to and fro until it hit a passing guard. The official assured the girl that their train would start from the near track. She was triumphant. Meanwhile other travelers piled into the miniature train and settled their worldly goods. It put on steam and with pompous puffing pulled out . . . to back onto its proper track! With consternation the brother rounded up his party, their bundles, their innumerable boxes and hampers. Again the moot question was bandied from one to other. With French logic the brother admitted the guard was in the right. The train did start from the near track. The outcome, with its element of surprise, gave ample source of conversation to both sides. Their animated chatter was borne to us until the train officially departed, "Direction Paimpol."

Our own express pulled in from Paris, stuffy and littered, and occupied by yawning gentlemen of the road. Pillows which had eased the night journey were tossed from windows on arrival at Morlaix, to return that night to Paris; fat and dusty they looked, connoting the fat and dusty forms of commercial travelers whose heads they had cushioned. Alighting at Morlaix, we found Le Bars in readiness.

The air was fresh, the sky blue, larks sang on the wing. Heaven seemed near at hand as we sped between hedged fields of undulating rye, through high wild reaches, moorland golden with broom. From the church at Sizun rose the mournful cadence of the Catholic creed. The arch of Sizun, a particularly pleasing example of this Breton specialty, is topped with a calvary. The Virgin and Saint Anne are at their traditional posts, the two thieves hang upon their respective crosses—for they play a prominent part in the more elaborate representations of the scene at Golgotha—but the Christ is missing.

The absence of the central figure was brought about by a feat of a young daredevil. Climbing to the top of the arched gateway, he mounted upon the crumbling stone of the crucifix itself. Hapless youth! No one was able to tell us whether he was hurled to instant death on the distant pavement. Surely, in the popular mind, the suitable punishment would have been no less than eternal damnation. I found myself weaving a tale of how, ostracized on every hand, the heedless one would have been forced to leave his native land and, begging his bread, make his way to the nearest seaport. Or would his conscience have tormented him, forcing him to study for holy orders? But the fate of him who mutilated the calvary of Sizun remained an engima.

At Daoulas the Romanesque cloisters, now the property of a Parisian chemist, detained us long enough for us to voice our admiration.

"Lucky you did not come in autocar," the concierge told us. "Such tourists are not admitted to disturb our seclusion."

Should we reach Plougastel by noon in time to see the letting out of the congregation after mass? Luck was indeed with us. Although the procession was not till three, yet not for all the rewards of men would we have missed that godsent first hour of afternoon.

In time! We congratulated each other and the chauffeur as we alighted. The few minutes we had to wait were spent in studying the calvary, which lacks, however, the setting of the one at Guimiliau. Carved stone, although replete with humanity (Christ's entry into Jerusalem is to the accompaniment of Breton bagpipes), was forgotten as the church doors burst open and the entire population of Plougastel poured forth. The women came first, medieval in garb and features. The starched folds of their caps, their high-bosomed bodices transformed them into the type we sought . . . humble, more bronzed, perchance, but nevertheless here they were, the sought-for Bretonnes, every one an Anne de Bretagne! Of a higher type than other Bretons we had seen, the men were tall and lithe, genial in manner, worthy descendants of Celtic forebears. We were swallowed up in a seething merry throng—all, as we noted, in the costume of the place. Breathlessly we remarked babes and toddlers in vivid shades of blue, for all the world, with their bronzed faces, like little Cantonese.

A brass band stationed outside the porch added to the din of voices. Above the blare of drum and trumpet arose the clangor of church bells. We watched the antics of the ringers, leaping as they tolled. The excitement grew more and more intense. Color and sound, warp and woof, were woven into a pattern of fantastic, barbaric beauty. Volleys of rifle-shots rent the air, rending likewise our equanimity.

"What is it?" I gasped to a Breton neighbor. "What victory are they celebrating?"

Her answer completely nonplussed me:

"It is a baptism, madame."

I remembered the advice we had been given: "Weddings and baptisms . . . those are the times to see the Breton off guard."

Taking refuge from the throngs which were

disbanding for luncheon, we stepped into a shop. Madame, herself a picture of a Plougastel matron, spread before us embroidered aprons, gaudy neckerchiefs, and the striking blue prints worn by adults. Into the shop as we made our purchases who should come but the newly christened babe. Safe in the arms of Grandmother, the wee lad swathed in white became the center of an admiring circle. Sugar-coated almonds (de rigeur at French baptisms) were handed by a smiling relative who with courtesy included us. The hero was carried in state to an inner room where it was evident other festivities were about to begin. The owner of the shop found time, however, to serve her customers.

"Sunday is a busy day," she told us. It was hard to hold her attention amid the coming and going of purchasers with whom she exchanged greetings in Breton. One child must have its costume, which had been made to order; another, scarlet ribbons for its brocade bonnet, and of course Madame must sew them. Black velvet and broadcloth were measured for ample dames and immaculate coifs were produced from innermost recesses of ancestral chests.

Would we return after luncheon to view the procession from her windows? Madame inquired. We acquiesced with alacrity, noting the jostling crowds already assembling on the thoroughfare. A scent of ripe strawberries was in the air. Many

The Procession at Plougastel

had bought closed boxes to carry home; even in London epicures relish the famed strawberries of Plougastel.

After the excitement of the preceding evening at Guingamp, our journey, and the tumultuous nature of our reception at Plougastel, we were thankful to find a quiet field in which to picnic before returning to that climax of all Breton pardons, the religious procession held—this was no exception to the rule—after vespers.

All the country-side poured, that afternoon, into the narrow street along which the cortège would pass. Sailors from Brest (bearing on their caps the name of a battle-ship or simply the band of the training corps) had re-joined their families for the afternoon . . . seamen of one's dreams, young and bronzed and stalwart, overgrown boys

Kaleidoscopic in Medieval Splendor

whose earnest gray eyes gazed fearlessly from life's threshold, seeking to fathom the unknown as man may fathom ocean's depths.

A welcome as to old friends was vouchsafed us as we entered the crowded shop and were led to a point of vantage, a second-story window. As the procession approached, Madame, leaving her garrulous intimates below-stairs, joined us a while with innate courtesy. In her genial presence we felt ourselves a part of Plougastel. We laughed with our hostess at the jog-trotting of some of the sacred images borne by small boys eager to overtake the band. The desperate efforts of the priests to establish order likewise brought smiles to many faces in the street below. Flags fluttered in the breeze. With brazen instruments and robust Breton voices lifted to a man, with tumultuous ringing of church bells, with the solemn passage of banner-bearers in costumes worn in daily life, yet reminiscent of the Middle Ages, the newly wedded, mothers, widows, radiant maidens, blue-coated sons of Plougastel bearing relics, sailors, novices, and priests—all the population passed before us in kaleidoscopic splendor. What man can tell us that we have not known provincial France . . . pre-revolutionary, medieval? He who has seen Plougastel before the completion of the bridge to Brest knows that the gods have indeed been kind.

Daoulas

The Whirling Mills of Ouessant

CHAPTER VIII

FROM BREST TO THE ISLE OF OUESSANT

BREST is a sailors' town. It is not possible to think of Brest except in connection with the sea. French town though it be, Brest is, surprisingly, a center for some of the most Breton excursions in all Brittany. The peninsula on whose southern shore the city lies is the westernmost extremity of Finistère, the Land's End of Europe. Between the Pointe de Corsen and the western hemisphere stretches a No Man's Land of water. As the province is divided into Lower Brittany on the west from Upper Brittany on the east, so may the lesser peninsula be divided. As we have come to expect, the more characteristically Breton of the two divisions lies to the west: a land of high seas and ships; of reefs and flashing lights; of toilers armed with rakes harvesting the fruits of ocean—the whole blurred in obliterating smoke from seaweed pyres. I speak of le Conquet, Porspoder, Aberwrach.

"He is not Duke of Brittany who is not lord of Brest," were the words of Jean de Montfort, who won the title of Jean V when his ancient rival, Charles de Blois, fell in the decisive battle of Auray. Richelieu realized the strategic position of Brest and the natural advantages of its almost landlocked bay. At the instigation of the cardinal a dockyard was begun in 1631. Vauban, distinguished engineer and Marshal of France, paid a visit to Brest in 1680 to superintend the erection of fortifications. As a naval port and arsenal Brest has no rival in France. Indeed, the insular Baring-Gould admits that the harbor is perhaps the finest in Europe.

Brest bears the reputation of being the rainiest town in France. Some detractors go so far as to compare it to Singapore, where rain falls every day in the year. The American soldiers, whose chief port of debarkation it was during the World War, were inclined to take this view. Little trace of their passage remains in the city, nor yet in the suburb of Pontanézen—that sea of mud converted into a model camp by General Smedley D. Butler.

A sailors' boulevard is the Rue de Siam, named for the Siamese ambassadors who traversed it in 1686. Its name carries us beyond the boundaries of Brest, to the limitless paths of ocean, to the torrid harbors of Siam, to the uttermost poles. Officers, men of the fleet, eager youths of training dépôts lend it animation. On a summer afternoon Brest is gay as a dress parade, but readers of Loti's masterly "Mon Frère Yves" cannot fail to recall Brest's seamy side. Vice lifts its evil head. The Celtic love for strong drink too often prevails.

Eastward from Brest rise the architectural wonder of the church at le Folgoët and the lofty menhir at the watering-place of Brignogan—the Pierre du Miracle with its superimposed cross welded upon the druid stone even as the Christian faith in

Brittany rests upon an undisguised pagan foundation. The circuit of le Folgoët (including Brignogan and Aberwrach) is an afternoon's drive in autocar, while another afternoon is needed for the circuit of le Conquet. These trips should unquestionably be taken, whether or not one ventures to the farthest Breton island, dread Ouessant.

Aberwrach! . . . Even the salt breath of ocean is lost in the all-pervading acrid odor of burning seaweed. White smoke arises at intervals along the rock-bound shore. A desolate, forsaken land, this coast of the seaweed-burners. Yet they give it a certain fame; painters, sitting to windward, revel in these stalwart figures raking, bending, struggling to the smoldering fires like demons of the pit. Tossed by the sea upon the shore or drawn from the watery depths with rakes, the seaweed is first spread out to dry in odoriferous rufous masses. Then comes the process of burning and from the remaining ash is extracted the product of iodine.

Blear-eyed and parched, a motley crew (for we had come on a Car Armoricain), we gathered in the courtyard of the Hôtel des Anges to refresh ourselves with that mildest of beverages, *limonade gazeuse*. Once the Convent of the Angels, this was—like the porch at le Folgoët, one of Anne de Bretagne's benefactions. The ruined chapel was to our minds of less interest than a bedroom opening onto the garden where we found *lits-clos* in use by the rising generation. Children's socks and sandals were kept atop the beds, whose doors gleamed with polished brass. It was thanks to our admiration for a snow-white kitten that we were bidden to cross this, to us, captivating threshold. I noted the crucifix on the wall; yet into this very room, filled with the tang of the sea, I doubt not that to the credulous the moaning winds still waft other than human voices crooning other than Christian lays.

After Aberwrach I place Porspoder as a seaweed-burning center. They are, or so it seemed to me, two of the most desolate and melancholy villages to be found on this most lonely and denuded portion of the coast. Our second day's excursion from Brest, in a motor procured for the afternoon, was to what might be called the lighthouse zone . . . where, after dark, may be seen the flashing lights of the Pointe de Saint-Mathieu, the isles of Ouessant and du Four, and that mightiest giant on the Ile Vierge (near Aberwrach), higher than the towers of Notre-Dame in Paris and casting its warning ray full forty miles to sea.

My thoughts recur with especial fondness to the hour spent in the district of Porspoder, at the village of Aberildut. How suggestive of immolations were these funereal-looking pyres! We paused beside a wagon-load of dried kelp with which the fires were replenished. It was a surprise to be greeted in English by a satanic figure brandish-

ing a poker, who told us, as he emerged from smoke, that during mobilization he had been on a war-ship to New York.

"Money is easier to gain in the States," said he, rolling his trousers higher above the knee. "We sell the *soude* [ash containing iodine] for eighteen hundred francs the ton. It is necessary to keep it in these bricks," he went on, kicking one as he spoke, "or it would be too heavy to handle."

We drew back because of the scorching heat and the almost suffocating fumes. Wiping the sweat from his brow, the man assured us that the natives did not mind the smoke.

"This little girl will show you," said he, calling to a wide-eyed hanger-on who had been suck-

ing her thumb during our conversation. Perhaps it was the hope of a possible sou at the finish that caused the bedraggled child to plunge into the thickest curtain of smoke. She emerged, as if from the enemy's lines, rubbing her eyes from which tears streamed and violently blowing her stubby nose.

Before reaching Saint-Renan, that most medieval of Breton towns, whose market square with Gothic houses would make it noteworthy even if it were not for its associations with Ronan, the Celtic saint whose pardon is held at Locronan, we made a detour to what I believe is the tallest and assuredly the most impressive menhir in Finistère.

The menhir of Kerloas is placed to perfection. It is off the main highway; no commercial signs nor guides mar its solitude. In fact, it would be somewhat of a puzzle to find at all, were it not for the knowledge which old men and wives of Brittany possess on such matters, and will impart if you or your chauffeur accost them in the Breton tongue. In this case it was the road-menders, breaking stones by the roadside in the primitive European way, who pointed out how far our car could carry us. We took the old route from Plouarzel to Saint-Renan and turned right where the road branches. We drew aside for creaking loads of clover, we slackened our pace for cows driven by men in beribboned shade hats. On foot we crossed a field carpeted with daisies. Moles had tossed the earth into piles like giant ant-hills. No sound was there but the drone of bees.

The menhir stands alone on a ridge overlooking distant cottages, pasture-land where cattle graze. Hedged about with gorse and bracken, the stone commands admiration if not adoration. Its mighty finger points skyward, majestic, symbolic. Sphinx-like the mystery of its past enwraps it. What rites have men practised here at the base of this colossal monument reared by the hand of man countless centuries ago? Do the newly wedded come, even now, to practise superstitious survivals in which their fathers had implicit faith? The grass about the colossus is well-trodden, yet the tourists who find Kerloas are comparatively few. Do the dead perhaps return? In Brittany one senses the nearness of unseen presences. Are these grasses pressed by ghostly feet? Do druids come, as 'tis said they do at Carnac, to hold their rites by the cold light of the midnight moon?

On Friday the thirteenth, at 7 : 30 A. M., we found ourselves about to embark on the *Enez-Eussaff* for the island of Ouessant. No power on earth could deter us now. After long debate Ouessant had won the day, despite the oft-repeated adage, "He who sees Ouessant sees his blood." Its very name, Ouessant, had had a strange fascination for us ever since we first heard it when eastward bound from London on the P. and O. liner *Egypt*. "Yonder's Ushant," the quartermaster had pointed out; "the sailors' dread."

The *Enez-Eussaff* (Breton for *Isle of Ouessant* or "farthest island") is not a boat for summer tourists. The very sight of her is enough to turn their stomachs. She was alarmingly low in the water. Cinders belched from her one battered stack, which might have been black by intention or might have been blackened by soot. Prepared though we were for general untidiness, we had not by any means expected to fare twelve miles from shore in so insignificant a craft. The fact that owing to the lowness of the tide the passengers on the dock looked down upon her smokestack, exaggerated, perhaps, her many shortcomings.

Sailors in patched salmon jeans formed the crew. Uniform was unknown even to the captain, an unimpressive drab figure, whose one distinguishing mark was a vizored cap. Gesticulating with a thumb swathed in crude bandages, he directed the embarkation. The first to go aboard were four lean cows quivering beneath the whips of drovers. A half-dozen daughters of Ouessant had gathered at the dock. Their striking costumes were in themselves enough to repay an early morning visit. All wore white caps and dark hair falling loose over shawl-draped shoulders. Several of the older women were swarthy as gipsies, with deep-set blue eyes and the unmistakable features of the Celt. They were joined by a group of boyish sailors—in training at Brest, we conjectured from the ribbons on their tam-o'-shanters, *2e Dépôt des Equipages.*

There was a general hand-shaking and conversation in uncouth Breton. "Ça change un peu," a woman remarked to a bystander, pointing out the uniform of a dark-eyed lad who would have been a beauty had he not disclosed the absence of front teeth. We counted on having the entire group as fellow-passengers, but when the time came, only two of the women went aboard—to retire to the cabin and not to reappear. The occasional sailings of the *Encz-Eussaff* are apparently an opportunity for seeing friends, giving and receiving news of the island.

Cattle occupied the stern. The upper deck at the bow we had entirely to ourselves. The captain shared the bridge with a beautiful Ouessantine who had been a late arrival and the center of interest on the dock; a girl of sixteen or thereabouts; a bride, to judge by her appearance and wedding-ring. Her sturdy hands and ankles betrayed the peasant, but her charming face and winsome smile instantly won hearts. She wore a lace cap over vivid-blue ribbon which also trimmed the front of her carefully pinned bodice. A huge bow, tied coquettishly to the left of her chin, held her coif and gave her the demure aspect of a school-girl. She carried a fragrant nosegay which on coming aboard she handed to the captain, who to our amazement buried his wizened features in its rosy depths, uttering exclamations of delight.

Slowly our boat slipped its moorings and we set forth into the unknown. The Rade de Brest, or inland sea, was all animation. Ferry-boats plied their way; red-sailed fishing-smacks and white-sailed pleasure yachts skimmed over the blue waters. A tiny catboat, bobbing like a gigantic wooden shoe, had painted on its bow the name *Mon Sabot*. An elephant balloon strained at restricting cables. Submarines crossed our path, graceful as porpoises. As we passed into the open sea we could discern the cliffs of Camaret and a clear-cut row of cottages perched on the headland of the Pointe des Pois. Four cruisers steamed proudly by, single file. We were rounding the Pointe de Saint-Mathieu now, with its forsaken abbey and monumental light.

The *Enez-Eussaff* never docks except at Brest. Six crowded rowboats put forth from le Conquet, our only call on the mainland. In one stood two raven-black-bearded friars with shovel hats, and a curé with gold-rimmed spectacles. The three crossed themselves on embarking. The friars, perhaps exhausted by a long journey, fell into heavy slumber near us on the deck. The priest entered into animated conversation with a bony Ouessantine who had just come aboard and whose flowing white locks and piercing eyes made her look less like an ordinary mortal than like our conception of the witch of Endor. At intervals she raised a lean arm and her face became tense with emotion. Was she denoucing some tribal enemy, in her brutal Breton tongue?

One rowboat contained half-grown pigs. There was a moment of comic diversion among the passengers—some of whom had found the deck, while most were crowded in the cabin—when a porker escaped from his brethren and trotted, grunting, into the engine-room. According to the seaman who made the rescue, pulling the shrieking animal to safety, "He went to the kitchen to have himself cooked."

Every way we looked were red-winged sloops of Douarnenez, le Conquet, and the islands: lobster boats, thick-set and stocky, in naught resembling the svelte sardine boats of Concarneau. The coast, with its semaphores and lighthouses stately as obelisks, its myriad burning mounds, was definitely receding now as we steamed westward. Reefs and islands—many deserted, others showing signs of life by the curling smoke of their fires whose acrid odor drifted to us, so near were we to their jagged shores—broke somewhat the vigorous swell of the Atlantic.

The island of Molène, like the Ile de Sein, is almost level with the sea, fringed with rocks to which the algæ cling. Molène is still remembered as the scene of the wreck of the British liner *Drummond Castle,* bound from South Africa for "home." The passengers in evening dress were celebrating the last night of their voyage, already anticipating the greetings awaiting them at Plymouth. The vessel struck the reef of Pierres Vertes and immediately foundered. Of all the company—there were forty passengers—but three were saved alive. Twenty-nine bodies were recovered by intrepid coast-guards of Molène. With the characteristic veneration shown by the Breton to the dead the corpses of the women were dressed by the natives in their own most cherished garments, the mass was said and burial made . . . the graves may be seen in the cemetery. In recognition of the devotion of the islanders the British people presented a clock for the church tower and a modern cistern, though 'tis said some inhabitants still prefer the salt taste of their polluted well-water.

Turning from the shelter of the harbor of Molène, we faced the open sea. On and on into the unknown, Ouessant-bound, we plunged. The morning was gray and chill, the wind pierced through our warmest garments. One by one our fellow-passengers, livid-faced, retreated to the cabin, till only the two drowsy friars remained. On the bridge the captain paced unceasingly, glancing from time to time at his beautiful companion, who, with closed eyes, drooped heavy-headed as a wilting flower. The wind, barely perceptible at Brest, had risen to an amazing velocity. It buffeted our faces, and tugged at our garments as if it would drag them from our bodies. Above the chorus of the battling sea it howled like a banshee. On a rising tide, we had been told, death comes to the Breton. In a storm at sea the peasants hear the despairing voices of the drowned who are floating seaward, far from the blessed shore where they would rest at peace.

The boom of cannon fired at Brest barely reached us now. Lightning seared the heavens.

BREST ⁂ Le Port de Guerre

Above the roar of wind and waters thunder crashed. The sky grew leaden. A blackness as of descending night settled upon us. Spray dashed in our faces. Rain swept the deck and blotted out the many islets; yet, as with uncanny precision the *Enez-Eussaff* plowed its way, we caught glints of riotous surf lashing bared reefs. When at last the storm abated the sky brightened, an auspicious omen for the last stretch of our journey—the crossing of the Gulf Stream. Caught in the long swell of the Grand Courant, our frail craft tossed like a cockle-shell, but fear, by now, had left our hearts. Our insignificant captain loomed with a larger importance in our eyes. Considering his exhibition of seamanship, we, as passengers, could give ourselves up to the enjoyment of the moment. What fools we had been to doubt the seaworthiness of a Breton boat. As for the captain, these men were born to the sea . . . life is safe in their keeping.

As we disengaged ourselves from drenched wrappings our eyes sought the island. Because of the difficulty of the approach Ouessant remains remote from the mainland. We felt as if on a liner skirting a foreign shore. Gulf-weed scurried by, swirling in eddies. We passed a rock with an isolated light, the Phare du Jument. The coast of Ouessant is undoubtedly forbidding. For the whole seven miles of its length, unlike Molène and the Ile de Sein, the island consists of a mighty plateau, presenting on all sides formidable cliffs. A less resisting formation would long since have succumbed to the thundering assault of the Atlantic. The entrance to the one harbor at Lampaul (otherwise known as "the bourg") is guarded by an enormous rock seemingly crouched like a mythical monster. On its flank waves dash and fly incessantly, while gulls circle around its head, uttering discordant cries.

On arrival at Lampaul, we had the feeling of the completion of a long voyage. Greetings were ecstatic, as at Brest farewells had been as if for irreparable partings. We anchored at a distance from the dock. Pigs and cows were without ceremony thrown into the water, swimming, each after its fashion, to the shore. For the passengers, however, rowboats were provided. One of the first to go ashore was the captain's protégée, who, exquisite flower that she was, finding herself no longer tossed by the storm, had completely revived. On the dock she became at once the center of an animated group of lads and lasses, and we asked the seaman who rowed us to point out her husband.

"You mean Marik?" he questioned, surprised at our ignorance. "She is the captain's bride."

Half the population of the village was lined up on the embankment to watch the debarkation. A Breton frieze from the hand of a master was formed by the women in white or austere everyday bonnets, their gay shawls and voluminous skirts outlined against the somber background of a leaden sky. To one who has worshiped at the shrine of Cottet's triptych in the Luxembourg, Ouessant is a canvas come to life.

Women predominate on the island, where the cultivation of the soil is entirely in their hands. If wheat and rye are to be planted, cultivated, winnowed, theirs is the task. In opposition to the usual Breton custom the men are rarely fishermen, for even the sturdy lobster boats cannot be assured of a safe haven at this island swept by the wind and waves of the Atlantic. Ouessantins are mostly sailors, in the mercantile marine or in the navy. Until within recent years a proposal of marriage was woman's prerogative. A custom still obtains that during the engagement the girl dwells with the family of her fiancé. In case of a dissimilarity of tastes, no stigma attaches to a broken troth. One of the most curious observances is the burial of a waxen cross, or *broella,* in lieu of the body of a person lost at sea. The churchyard of Lampaul lies in a sheltered oasis where flourish some of the few trees on the wind-swept island. Christianity was brought to Ouessant as early as the sixth century by Saint Pol de Léon, who founded a chapel here on his way from England.

Ouessant still remembers having been ravaged by the English in 1388 and the fact that in these waters in 1778 the French fleet won a glorious victory over the hereditary enemy is not forgotten. For years the property of the Governor of Brest, Ouessant was sold in 1764 to the French Crown. The island occupies a strategic position as an outpost of French territory and guardian of one of the most important maritime routes of the world.

Two lighthouses of the first order illuminate this entrance to the British Channel, their names almost as formidable as their stark selves—Creac'h and Stiff. It was to the former that we made our way afoot. The peasants we passed gave us hearty "good mornings," but retreated as hastily as frightened animals if they caught sight of our kodak. Cottages along the way were surprisingly neat (as to exteriors!), with shutters of bright blue or green. Bent tamarisks waved in the wind, while fuchsias and vivid marigolds enlivened dooryards.

Passing the chapel of Notre-Dame des Bon Voyages, we came upon clustered windmills whirling eerily and shepherd lasses blowing after vagrant sheep. One girl, whose habitual shyness was evidently overcome by the unprecedented experience of actually conversing with Americans, told us that the mills themselves, flimsy wooden affairs, were sometimes blown into the Atlantic, leaving naught but the ruined stone foundations. The sheep, it appeared, were saved from a like fate by low stone walls, built crisscross, behind which they could crouch to windward. Had we heard how the winds came to Ouessant? Stretched out beside our Ouessantine on the close-cropped sward, we were all eagerness to hear. Before us spread the vast Atlantic, hurling wave after wave against the island's rocky bulwarks. The horizon was streaked with the smoke of ocean liners; wide berth they gave to "seaman's dread"!

"It was like this," the daughter of the guardian of the light—for so she called herself—shouted above the roar of wind and breakers. "In those days there was no wind in this region and men had no sails to their boats. The ocean was a vast pond and sailors were bent to their oars like slaves. Now, a captain journeyed to a far country to seek the home of the winds, and found it. After consultation with the wise ones of that land he learned how to secure the winds, and that he did with the aid of magic. With much difficulty he tied them into eight vast sacks and cast them into the hold of his vessel. Now, the captain's plan was, once out to sea, to drown the unruly winds but to keep those which could be of use to man. Men say that women are curious, but the men, too, are curious, are they not, madame? There was on that boat a sailor lad, no more than a boy, who thought he should like to see for himself what it was that the captain prized so much. He crept into the hold when no one was looking and picked up one of the sacks.

"'Light as air,' said he to himself. 'Now, what can it be? No harm in looking,' he thought and punched a hole with his pocket-knife.

"'Poof! Whew!' blew the wind, for he had released the so'wester. The vessel was blown sky-high and the winds were scattered north, east, south, and west. . . . That happened near Ouessant, the old folks say . . . we have no reason to doubt it, madame."

The fear of missing the *Enez-Eussaff* and having to remain for an indefinite period on the island made us hasten our return to Lampaul. Leisurely as though time did not exist was the departure of that trusted vessel. Had it been our private yacht the deck could not have been more completely our own. Although rays from the setting sun pierced the clouds, we were not over-confident as to what weather lay ahead. As Ouessant faded, however, with it disappeared the boisterous seas, the unruly winds that had buffeted our approach.

Threading its way among the reefs, the *Enez-Eussaff* came at twilight to Molène, isle of mystery, wreathed in vaporous smoke, burial-ground of ancient druids. Le Conquet was a flaming beacon, Ouessant a far-distant gleam as we glided in darkness toward the lights of Brest.

A Spinner of Morgat

CHAPTER IX

CAMARET-SUR-MER

THE Crozon peninsula seen on a map resembles a gaunt right arm reaching out to sea. The gigantic thumb of the outstretched hand is tipped by the Cap de la Chèvre, the little finger by the Pointe des Espagnols. The central digits, compressed and stubby, form the points of Gouin, Toulinguet, and Pen-Hir—popularly known as the Pointe des Pois. Coming as it does between the Pays de Léon and Cornouaille, the rock-veined arm is bounded on the north by the roadstead of Brest, on the south by the bay of Douarnenez, while to the west its clenched fingers defy the power of the Atlantic. The little finger, pointing toward Brest, bristles with protective forts. The fourth and third fingers are likewise armed. Our concern is, therefore, with the index, the thumb, and the curve between fourth and fifth, the cove where Camaret lies hidden.

Camaret possesses two outstanding features. It

is the first lobster port of France. It is the place most closely associated with Charles Cottet. Had we not known of Cottet's predilection for the region, we might, like many another, have passed by the entire peninsula of Crozon, but we were irresistibly drawn thither by memories of the canvas, "Fishing-boats at Camaret."

From Camaret to Quiberon the coast of Brittany is studded with fishing ports, some of prime importance, while others are mere hamlets scattered near a cove. To lovers of the picturesque there are four ports on the mainland which I can, without qualification, recommend: Camaret, with its snub-nosed lobster boats, dingy and brown-sailed, its red-clad mariners; Douarnenez, with its communistic population oddly contrasted with the idyllic beauty of its site, comparable only to the Bay of Naples; Audierne, where, as at Douarnenez, red sails vie with the blue of sardine-nets, where seamen swagger alike in coarse jeans of blue or red; Concarneau (a phantasmagoria of color, with blue predominant), whose sardine boats, elegant in line, fleet in the wind, have made her fame . . . a walled town seen with a foreground of a myriad masts and partially veiled by fluttering nets.

Tourists who come to Camaret would prefer to stay at the annex of the Hôtel de France should they remain at all; but painters choose the unmodernized Hôtel Moderne. It is essential to the

traveler to lodge upon the quay, to enjoy the port at all hours of the day and night. There is frequent coming and going of lobster boats at hours varying with the tide; there is an inconstant sky, leaden and lowering for the most part—for we are still in the neighborhood of Brest—with clouds hanging ominously low and heavy as if threatening to crush the abrupt headlands which guard the entrance to the port. Against this background of boats, headlands, and lowering sky the drama of the fisherman ashore is enacted. In Brittany, life runs with the tide.

High water was at break of day when we first saw the departure of the fishing fleet, which took place with much creaking of cordage and flapping of sail, as of gigantic birds testing their powers. Gulls swooped and skimmed over the glassy water; men in brilliant red or faded-to-salmon jeans called to their comrades as they hoisted lobster-pots. Their going left Camaret forsaken.

I remember an occasion at a later hour when the dock was a jostling throng come to bid on a catch of a hundred or more skates laid out in pallid comeliness. Low tide should be passed over rapidly: a time when boats are stranded, moored in mud and slime, when a sickening stench pervades the port, penetrating into bedrooms despite the precaution of closed windows.

The contrast between low and high tide is no more striking than between the low life of a Saturday afternoon and the high note struck of a Sunday. On Saturdays old salts gather with their pipes along the quays; the fishing-smacks return, landing their crews with clatter of wooden shoes and inarticulate jargon. The catch is unloaded, men come ashore bent beneath floats and lobster-pots which they pile on the dock before making for the nearest cabaret—A l'Abri de la Tempête, A la Descente des Pêcheurs, Au Retour de la Rade. Guffaws are heard, and the ring of glasses. The sun has set and the long Breton evening—it is light till ten—tempts men from home. Weathered faces are flushed now; songs are boisterous, men reel as they swagger along the quay; many are quarrelsome; the mirth becomes ribald. Girls are rarely to be seen on this dock, but now and again a haggard woman in black, with gaunt face framed by the bonnet of the peninsula (similar to that worn by *sardi-*

nières all along the coast) ventures from her kitchen to remonstrate with her man. Sometimes she wins the day and he shuffles off, an unwilling victim. More often the wife is shoved away, and the maudlin chorus breaks out anew. Sailors from Brest, with brazen-faced hussies on their arms, form roisterous groups. It is on Saturday night that the menace of the week, the culmination of foreboding days, reaches its sinister conclusion.

Sunday, on the contrary, is a day of resolution. The brutish have slunken to their lairs or furbished themselves in a way to be no longer recognizable. Not a costume of red sail-cloth is to be seen. Earthly manners have been laid aside with workaday apparel. Behavior is as seemly as the rough cloth costumes of the men, whose scrubbed faces shine beneath mammoth bérets. Chimes summon to the mass.

We breakfasted of a Sunday in the café of our hotel, regaling ourselves with the sketches of Camaret left by former visitors—two by Sauvaige, the friend of Cottet. A poster caught our eye, a law on the repression of drunkenness, giving the penalties of fines and imprisonment and signed by Poincaré, when President of the republic. Another, applicable to Finistère and signed by the préfet at Quimper, gave rules for the closing of establishments open to the public, decree of September 30, 1920:

1 Chief towns of the arrondissement at 12 o'clock.
2 Chief towns of the canton at 11 o'clock (and in communes of more than 5,000 inhabitants).
3 Other communes of more than 5,000 inhabitants at 10 o'clock.

All dances were included save family reunions.

Our host, noticing our interest, assured us that drunkenness was less prevalent than before the war, partly owing to stricter regulations and the high cost of liquor and partly to the augmented activities of temperance societies.

"Drink is the curse of the Breton," said he. "It is the hydra to be fought if we would save our children and the race. If you care to come with me, monsieur et dame, I'll show you what the Catholics are doing. They have established clubs known as Abris-du-Marin. Ours is on the terrace above the hotel."

Following our host, we mounted the steep steps from the wharf to the modest mariners' shelter. Over four thousand seamen had made use of its facilities during the year, while those at Guilvinec and at Douarnenez had each accommodated over one hundred thousand. The society, our host informed us, had been in existence for thirty years and, in addition to furnishing reading-rooms, lectures, radio concerts, in many of its shelters it provides carpenter shops and apparatus for the tanning of nets and sails. It also publishes an excellent "Almanach du Marin Breton." We did not wonder at the latter's popularity, combining as it does wit and humor with useful information of tides and lights. I was particularly intrigued by a sketch of a typical Breton fishing port with sail-boats riding at anchor. A fisherman has just landed with a catch of mackerel. An elderly gentleman, straw-hatted and carrying a bulging umbrella, accosts him.

Tourist: "That must be very amusing—your mackerel-fishing. But how do you catch so many fish, since your boat is always anchored in the port?"

Mariner: "Always in the port!!! Every morning you are still snoring in your bed when we return, worn out after having passed the night hauling immense nets in darkness and often in the pouring rain!!!"

A procession was to be held in honor of the Sacré Cœur. At the Place Saint-Thomas a baker's wife carried candlesticks to deck the open-air altar.

"You should come," said she, "on the second Sunday in July, for the Benediction of the Sea. The relics are carried to the chapel on the mole—Notre-Dame de Rocamadeur. The sea is blessed, that it may give its produce in abundance and that it may not engulf our mariners. One sees many in tears that day, I assure you, madame, the women who have lost their men. When you see crêpe worn at Camaret it is often for those who will never return from the fog-bound coast of England."

As the crowd broke up after the ceremony we watched a group of seamen with their families who made their way to the port and boarded a fishing-sloop, the *Avance,* flying a pennant and the French flag. The curé, accompanied by an acolyte, was welcomed aboard. We were informed that this was a new boat and was about to be blessed. We caught the sound of intoned prayers and of responses. The fragrance of incense reached us. Holy water was sprinkled by the priest. The benediction given, the latter removed his surplice, putting on his shovel hat. The ship-owner then produced a bottle, wine-glasses, and cigarettes. Without sail but with much puffing of motor the *Avance* set out for a cruise, riding rough-shod over the moorings of a near-by rowboat, which was dragged in its wake. To the amusement of those aboard, the acolyte (become an ordinary small boy) sprang into this dory, attached it as a tender, and so rode forth to sea.

The harbor of Camaret is almost closed by a natural breakwater known as the "Sillon." On this narrow spit of land stand Camaret's most picturesque monuments, the little fort constructed by order of Vauban and the seafarers' chapel of Notre-Dame de Rocamadeur. Throughout the centuries these two historical monuments have withstood the wind and weather, but, probably owing to its proximity to the fort, the spire of the chapel was decapitated by an English bullet—this in 1694, at the time when the Anglo-Dutch fleet was repulsed from the neighborhood of Brest.

The key to Notre-Dame, we discovered, after various fruitless inquiries, was to be had at the *buvette* of Madame Le Fur Cornec, on the left as one approaches the mole. We were granted the privilege, rare indeed in rural France, of taking the key in our own hands and, unaccompanied by a concierge, unlocking the resisting door. The exterior adjacent to ways where lobster boats were building, the approach cluttered with lobster-pots and drying nets, gave us the impression of a place rarely visited, if not actually neglected. Imagine, therefore, our surprise, when we had opened the door, to find ourselves confronted by a most kempt and evidently well-beloved chapel. Votive offerings in the form of ships hung before the altar; one model with white sails set bore on its bow the name *Camaret,* on its stern the one word, "Souvenir." Life-savers with crossed oars decorated the walls, commemorative of the ships *Notre-Dame de Lourdes* of Ouessant, the *Rouanez ar Rosera,* of Audierne, the *Saint-Christophe* of Camaret. Incorporated in the altar was the model of a four-masted ship. The benches, on which congregations assemble monthly, bore good Breton names scored with pocket-knives: Le Hir, Le Moal, Le Garrec.

On the left wall of the chancel hung a painting, dark, one might suppose with age, at first glance an old master. But as our eyes grew accustomed to the somber tones we recognized the characteristics of Cottet. The picture represented the assembling of the women of Camaret about their burnt chapel. Against a leaden sky where ominous storm-clouds foregathered the gutted church stood stark, the headlines beyond seen through the remainder of bare arched windows. Roofless, its shattered spire apparently impervious to fire, the church with its background of ragged sky would have been a desolate subject even without the congregated women of Camaret, shrouded in voluminous hooded cloaks, huddled together to voice their lamentations. Yet in the very fervor

of their despair might be sensed the faith, the power that had in this instance been able to recreate from its bare skeleton the solid form of the edifice in which we stood.

Next to the sea with its boats the fame of the Crozon peninsula rests with its moors, sparsely sprinkled with groups of low cottages, an occasional windmill, a dolmen or other druidical remains. (The one hundred and forty-three menhirs in the alignment on the plateau of Lagatjar, mostly overthrown by an earthquake before our era, have recently been erected on their original foundations.) My illustrator and I remember two strikingly similar walks, the one from Audierne to the Pointe du Raz, the other from Camaret to the Pointe des Pois. In 1910, the time of my

first visit to Brittany, I preferred the former, but to-day, because of the raft of holiday-makers who overrun the neighborhood of Audierne, my preference leans toward that from Camaret.

It was late June, the heather formed a haze of purple bloom, the gorse, close-cropped, was prickly to the tread as we followed a sheep-path along the margin of the cliffs. It was at the cove of Toulinguet that we came upon them—Henri and Henriette. During our stay at Camaret they had been a source of constant diversion, this Parisian bride and groom who, from their looks, should still have been at school. Henriette was ensconced with her inevitable turquoise parasol . . . there was so little to the piquant Henriette that the sunshade almost eclipsed her. Henri, who, regardless of the freshness of the early morning, wore flapping white ducks on his lanky young legs and a shirt revealing his sun-tanned throat and arms, was in the act of gathering orchids (of the purple-fringed variety) that mingled their fragrance with the breath of the sea. Stepping cautiously, he descended lower and lower on the cliff until his foot dislodged a stone, which fell crashing to the rocks below, startling perched cormorants who circled overhead with raucous cries.

Abandoning her parasol, the bride ran swiftly along the cliff path calling, "Henri, come back, you will be killed!"

But Henri, nonchalant, continued his rock-climbing, evidently enjoying the charming frenzy of his companion. All in due time the orchids were laid at her feet, and as we tactfully hastened on our way we noted the embrace of the united pair, who, their flimsy garments fluttering in the wind, stood silhouetted against the waters of the Atlantic.

High on the margin of the cliffs which bear the full impetus of an unwearying ocean stand five houses, the same that had been pointed out to us from the deck of the *Enez-Eussaff*. The first, a manor of some pretension, belongs to the poet Saint-Pol Roux; two of the three humble cottages of the cape belong respectively to the widow of Cottet's friend Sauvaige (it was here that Cottet stayed and painted) and to the novelist Toudouze, for whom the quay in Camaret is named, and the third, with its larger neighbor, to Antoine, ex-director of the Odéon theater at Paris.

Highway terminates with the hotel overlooking the sheltered beach of Veryhac'h, but following our wind-swept trail to land's end, we come upon the point of Pen-Hir. As we gaze from the semaphore or, perilously, from a perch upon rocks, we are stunned by the abyss between us and the waves that surge around the base of the headland, dashing as if with murderous intent, falling back foaming, only to renew the charge with added fury. The rocky islets, or "Tas-de-Pois," carry the eye in the direction of the Pointe du Raz, the mystic Isle of Sein floating in haze; toward Brest the Pointe Saint-Mathieu, Molène, and even Oues-sant are clearly visible. Our guide-book informs us that this view has been "classified." One is inclined to grant the paternal French Government the quality of omniscience, so all-seeing are its agents, so infallible their judgments.

To windward of the point the cove of Pen-Hir gives nightly shelter to a myriad sardine boats of Douarnenez which fly before the wind like frightened birds hastening to roost. Clouds, hawk-like, hover in pursuit. At dusk, as stars shine faintly in the heavens, lights twinkle forth and smoke spirals rise from decks, to float on the tranquil air like incense to the gods.

The hotel of the Pointe des Pois, overlooking

beach and cove, forms a comfortable base for trampers. It was our pleasure to arise before the families of French bourgeoisie there installed; to dip in the waves while yet there were no tracks upon the immaculate sand save those of gulls; to visit the dripping grottoes as the tide ebbed, revealing walls shaggy with seaweed, soft to the touch as the coat of a collie.

The farther rocks were covered with bladder-weed, mussels, and barnacles, and, as ocean receded, shrimps innumerable might be taken from surrounding sea-pools. Later in the day the stout actress would disport upon the beach with her attentive English husband and yapping Pekinese; here, too, the stocky Dutch couple—she of the pendant earrings and Spanish shawl and her companion—would gambol in scantiest of bathing-suits; here the sun-browned twins would frisk, pursued by a Chinese amah; and young people with rolled pajamas would wade deep, garnering with long-handled nets a crop of lively shrimps. Morgat outstrips the Pointe des Pois in fashion but not in rustic charm.

Our visit to the Cap de la Chèvre included lunch at one of Morgat's Grand-Hôtels, set in a bower of palms and roses; and although chiefly in pursuit of rural color, we were impressed, as who could fail to be, by the vision of the Bay of Douarnenez, blue as the Bay of Naples—the Ménez-Hom its Vesuvius. From the extreme point of the cape the view was still more striking, although Douarnenez lies hidden. As we stood upon the mighty headland, bevies of little red-winged boats scurried homeward. Impressive as were the stupendous rock walls bitten by the Atlantic and known as the "Château" of Dinant, enchanting as may be the grottoes—above all that of the Corrigans, or Breton fairies, which but twice a month is visible for a few short days to man, at time of full and new moons, famed for its profusion of orange starfish and blue anemones drenched with sea-water—to me the essential beauty of the peninsula consisted in the primitive villages replete with human life that cluster at intervals from Crozon to the tip of the Cap de la Chèvre.

On this windy promontory innumerable stone mills with thatched tops and buoyant sails ground untiringly. Bulging bags of wheat or rye awaited their turn at mill doors. At every village veritable sibyls employed the traditional distaff. Newly washed wool hung dripping in the sun. Cows, returning, as the day waned, to dark hovels, startled by the unfamiliar sound of a motor horn, bolted into hedges—one, with board on face, turning its head inquisitively to see the monster pass.

I remember that we wandered afoot through the lanes where larks were singing on the wing, where poppies glowed, where, well used to wonders, we perceived trees endowed with the power of locomotion . . . trees that proved to be old men bent beneath mountains of gorse.

I remember lines of connected cottages with magpies chattering on their uneven roofs, windmills that people knolls, the tang of the sea, and, above all, at dusk, that our path led us to a monument which gives its name to the place—the Point of the Dolmen. A solitary reminder of a bygone age, the dolmen stands upon an isolated moor . . . a fitting place for reverie. I remember that mist blowing from the ocean had already engulfed the pines upon the ridge when, as daylight faded, our thoughts were abruptly brought back to the present by the whirring of an aëroplane in homeward flight toward Brest.

MORGAT: THE DOLMEN

The regal velvets of Carhaix

CHAPTER X

THE BLACK HILLS OF FINISTÈRE

Turning our backs upon the sea, we are about to penetrate into the heart of the hills. Our most natural means of approach is Châteaulin, where converge the ranges of Monts d'Arrée and the Montagnes Noires. Following the roadstead of Brest to where it narrows into the river of Châteaulin, we come to the town itself, whose chief charm is its situation upon the Aulne, canalized to form a part of the waterway from Brest to Nantes. In long-gone ages a mountainous country, central Finistère still looms above the surrounding plain. Although the Ménez-Hom of the Montagnes Noires, rising as it does from the coast rather than from the plateau of the interior, presents the appearance of a superior altitude, yet Mont-Saint-Michel-d'Arrée (in the direction of Huelgoat), which rises to a height of only 1,282 feet above the level of the sea, is the culminating pinnacle not alone of the Monts d'Arrée but of all Brittany. One quarter of the department of Finistère is given over to moorland, and so much so is this true in the neighborhood of the hills, that, because of these wild heaths, the mountain brooks and tarns, the wooded slopes, the resemblance to the highlands of Wales or Scotland is at times striking.

A favorite walk from Châteaulin is by way of the ivy-clad remnants of the château of a long-forgotten Count of Cornouaille. From the hotel on the Quai de Brest we cross the river, and, skirting rocky cliffs, mount steeply to where a fifteenth-century chapel has survived the destruction of the still older fastness. At the turn of the road a sabot-maker has set up a rustic booth and is constantly at work, an apprentice following every motion. Opposite the ancient chapel a road invites the passer-by to try his luck inland . . . the road that leads past the farm of the spreading moss-grown walnuts, the road that eventually divides into enticing lanes whence, trespassing in high places, welcomed by peasants tilling steep fields, we may behold the distant gray-roofed town with its verdant setting, the puffing train to Quimper which passes over a lofty viaduct.

It is doubtful whether we should ever have come to Châteaulin save to attend the pardon at Rumengol—Le Braz's "Pardon of the Singers."

With this end in view we had engaged our rooms at Châteaulin for the week of Trinity Sunday. The day dawned radiant. We had arisen betimes —had, indeed, caught in the act the woman who cleans the café, kneeling in a wooden box and scrubbing with a will. We noted the hobnails in the soles of her sabots (a sure sign of near-by hills), and also that she spoke no French but called in Breton to announce our arrival.

A dubious-looking car arrived at last, long after the hour stipulated. Laden with note-books, crayons, and camera, we motored along the canal road as far as the next village, and then, with the hour of mass at Rumengol nearing, the car stopped. Our nonplussed and absurdly young chauffeur proceeded to disembowel the motor's internal workings. Minutes, quarter-hours passed. Exasperated, we plead with the driver of a truck drawn up beside a mill to take us, but he refused, saying that our chauffeur would be displeased. He would come, however, to inspect the motor. We had been there an hour? Too bad!

A stream of automobiles flowed in the direction of Rumengol. As they rolled past us we caught sight of costumes of Quimper and Quimperlé, of Bigoudens from Pont l'Abbé, with fluttering ribbons and cap-strings, crowded into trucks, camions, autocars with never an empty seat. A limousine passed with his Eminence the Bishop of Quimper.

"Is there a train to Rumengol?" I inquired of a man in the crowd which had gathered to proffer advice.

"Oh yes, madame, there is a train." Hope

stirred in our breasts, only to be stilled as the man continued: "But it has gone."

"Then there isn't a train," said I, with pent-up impatience . . . but this he would not admit.

The man from the mill had at last located the trouble—a stoppage in the tube that fed the carburetor. He asked a coifed by-stander to lend a hair-pin, whereupon she drew forth a monster which obviously would not fit. I then offered a choice of medium or "invisible"; the latter did the trick!

"Had you had bobbed hair," Monsieur remarked, as the car once more got into motion, "we should still be dawdling like yonder fisherman on the bank of the canal."

The legend of Rumengol has to do with the most famous tale of the golden sheaf of legendary lore dealing with ancient Armorica. In the fifth century of our Christian era Gradlon was King of Cornouaille and held his court at Quimper. The royal widower was growing old . . . his vast possessions were as naught to him in comparison with the love which he bore for his only child, a daughter, Dahut, the apple of his eye. The princess Dahut was the most bewitching of women and her voice was of a sweetness to lure all men to her. Yet, in spite of the love lavished upon her, Dahut grew pale and discontented. She could not live, so she told her father, away from the sea.

Therefore the king bestowed upon her the gift of his regal city of Ys, washed by the waves of the Atlantic. Now Corentin, the Bishop of Quimper, heard tales of the behavior of Dahut in her palace beside the sea . . . yet Gradlon would not give ear to the tale of his daughter's lapses from the path of virtue.

Now, according to the record, Ys was a city of fabulous splendor, but it was built beneath the level of the ocean. Gradlon, having turned over the administration of Quimper to the bishop, came to dwell at Ys. One evening as the king nodded in his apartments Dahut came to him by stealth and, at the instigation of a domineering lover (none other than the devil incarnate, who had gained power over her because of her evil ways), stole from the king's neck the chain with the silver keys to the gates of the dike. "The princess of the keys," the Bretons call Dahut—that is, Alc'huèz or Ahès.

The sleeping monarch was awakened by the voice of Guénolé, the Abbot of Landévennec.

"Flee for your life, O King," he commanded. "The flood-gates are ajar."

As he spoke the angry roar of the waves drowned his words. It was indeed true: the city was rapidly being submerged with all its trapped inhabitants. As the king mounted his charger he called for his daughter, and Ahès, distraught at her deed, clung to her father, pleading to be saved.

The saintly Guénolé led the way, but, for all his prayers, the fugitives made no progress in their flight from the onrushing waters.

"It is because of the harlot who rides behind you." Guénolé spoke sternly. Some say that at a word of command the king himself thrust his daughter from him, others that the abbot did the deed, while still others say that no sooner were the words spoken than Ahès herself released her hold and sank into the raging and relentless sea. Immediately the tempest ceased and the king and his companion found themselves washed upon the shore where the church of Poul-Dahut now stands near to Douarnenez.

For a while Gradlon dwelt with Guénolé at his abbey of Landévennec, at the mouth of the river of Châteaulin, within sight of the sea. But the sound of the waves drove him to distraction. On moonlit nights he would rise and pace to and fro, and from his chamber window he had visions of his beloved daughter Dahut rising from the sea. She had become a siren beautiful beyond compare and every lover who swam to win her kiss was thereby doomed. Therefore the world-weary Gradlon left the abbey and dwelt as a hermit in the wilds of the forest of Kranou. It is said that when he came to Rou-ven-goulon, the Red Stone of the Dawn, he beheld a fire, for the druids were offering a sacrifice. Here he determined that a Christian church should arise, sacred to the Virgin. On the site of the oak under which Gradlon died—in the presence of Guénolé and the last of the druids, who clasped hands over his body—arose, according to Gradlon's command, the primitive church of Rumengol.

The story goes that when at last Gradlon came to the heavenly gate he was welcomed by the blessed Virgin, who congratulated him on the beauty of the edifice built in her honor and offered to grant a request.

"May it please you to lead my daughter, Dahut, once more to the paths of purity."

The Virgin shook her head sadly; that was beyond her power. Then, at least, would she deprive Dahut of her musical voice by which she lured men to their doom?

Again the Virgin shook her head, but, pondering, she spoke at length.

"Have no fear, Gradlon," said she. "Such a race of sweet singers shall arise at my shrine of Rumengol that none shall listen to Dahut." . . . Some say that thus the first bard was created.

The mass was almost at an end as, after parking our car, we marched up the dusty road with other belated pilgrims to Rumengol. The congregation, of proportions entirely out of keeping with the capacity of the church, was assembled in the open air around a stone oratory. The devout knelt, stood, or sat on the hard ground. The majority of the women wore black broadcloth lavishly trimmed with velvet. Silken aprons vied with one another in color and richness of embroidery. Coifs there were from every district of Finistère: lacy ones from Quimper and Audierne; beribboned ones from Quimperlé and Pont-l'Abbé; net of Saint-Pol de Léon and Morlaix; elegant black hoods from Ile de Sein, and bonnets of shaggy-locked Ouessantines. Numerous and upstanding were the women of Plougastel with their tight bodices and plaid neckerchiefs, their nunlike starched head-dresses framing placid faces, the growing girls bedecked in caps and shawls of glistening brocade. Commonplace hats are virtually unknown at Rumengol, for even the men, shepherds of the mountains in rough homespuns, Plougastels in vivid-blue or purple coats, *glaziks* (wearers of sky-blue jackets from the neighborhood of Quimper), affect floppy bérets or beavers with buckled streamers.

In the babel of Breton that arose as the crowd surged, after mass, toward the church the tone of our voices caused perhaps less remark than if we had spoken in French. One sailor, who had been to England, pointed us out to a group of women; while an old man remarked, rather doubtfully, to his neighbor:

"It seems to me they are not of this part of the country." . . . Monsieur in his corduroys and Madame in her extinguisher hat preferred to pass for natives.

promised a change of weather. Cloud-shadows floated over hills and fields, over green hedges and dusky woodlands, over the arm of the sea stretching inland to le Faou. At Rumengol the priests and choristers eyed the clouds with inquietude. Rain fell at last . . . fine and steady, increasing to a deluge.

Throngs poured auto-ward, those without umbrellas scurrying to save their silks and velvets, carrying or dragging countless children. So many remained, however, that the departure of the others left no space unfilled. The Bishop of Quimper—who, to our satisfaction, preached in French—continued his sermon in the open air without undue haste or change of manner. His refined and spiritual features framed by flowing white locks, his delicate hands used in many gestures, the modulated cadence of his voice, the earnestness of his message, held his audience despite the increasing downpour. To-day France celebrates her mothers, he told the people, and we at Rumengol extol the model for human mothers. Does not the fate of Brittany, of France, depend upon the mothers of the race?

Without banners, which might have been marred by the rain, a faithful group of bishop, priests, and choristers, followed by a rabble of coifs, set out on the traditional procession. Sheltered by evergreens, we awaited their return, but soon word was passed from mouth to mouth: "They will not come by the fields; it is too wet."

Following an old woman who throughout the service had held a mammoth burning taper with flame blowing and wick guttering but never extinguished, we made our way churchward as the sweet-toned bell announced the procession's entrance. The edifice was again packed with a surging, ever changing throng. Melodious voices were raised, chanting praises to the Virgin. The faces of young and old, uplifted toward the gleaming candles of the high altar, seemed transfigured. Could it have been the play of light and shadow, the mellowing haze of incense, the power of song which so transformed them, or did these people, one and all, feel themselves miraculously refreshed? Did not their eyes shine with a mysterious inner light? No false note was apparent, unless it were ourselves . . . but truly our sympathy was unfeigned. Were we not verily in harmony? . . . seekers, ourselves, after the underlying spiritual truths for which these people sought?

Huelgoat, literally "wooded height," stands on the road from Châteaulin to Morlaix. It should if possible be visited on a fête-day, as the costumes of its women are among the most beautiful in Brittany. Our first stop in the hill-country is the town of Brasparts, a rendezvous for hunters; otherwise uninteresting save for its fascinating church which, with its curious ossuary and its calvary depicting Saint Michel's victory over a most archaic dragon, well repays a visit. After Brasparts our interest centers in vistas of Mont-Saint-Michel d'Arrée with its tiny chapel to the saint—the highest point in Brittany.

As Kerjean is the Versailles of Brittany, so is Huelgoat its Fontainebleau; a châteauless Fontainebleau, however, but bearing a resemblance nevertheless as to sun-flecked forest paths, moss-grown rocks, and gurgling brooks. Huelgoat forms perhaps the most appropriate center for a sojourn in Argoat—inland Brittany. But, despite Huelgoat's rustic charm, my own preference lies with Armor, the country of the sea. Callac, paradise of trout-fishermen, is not far distant, nor is Saint-Servais, birthplace of that "son of the hills adopted by the sea," Anatole Le Braz.

Herdsmen of the hills may be seen in the highlands around Huelgoat. It is a mysterious cloud-capped region cleft by ravines—one in the forest of Huelgoat known as the Gouffre d'Ahès, for here, 'tis said, were cast the bodies of Ahès's lovers. Dangerous bogs have engulfed the too adventurous; a country haunted to-day and through long yesterdays by Ankou stalking with his scythe of death.

Saint Herbot, most popular saint in the neighborhood, like Saint Cornély, is the patron of horned cattle. The church bearing his name is the Mecca of herdsmen; and all oxen are allowed to rest on the day of this saint's pardon. A native youth poured forth a description of that day of days:

"There were, monsieur et dame, not a few beasts—bulls, cows, and calves—driven around the church this year. The grounds were packed with cattle-owners and visitors from Huelgoat. Have you seen the hair from the tails? It will lie before the altar for a twelvemonth and then be sold for brushes. There was a year of epizoöty when so many herds were driven to Saint-Herbot that the sale of hair brought three thousand francs."

The chapel of Saint-Herbot stands against a background of ancient trees. Beneath their shade a moss-grown calvary, medieval in expression, replete with meaning, guards the entrance to the portico of the Apostles, who stand in painted dignity within their niches, having somehow survived the vandalism of revolutionists. Stepping inside, we were cut off from the present by mysterious time-blackened walls that spoke to us of an age of faith like a sun long set in a sea of doubt, yet lighting still with its afterglow the heaven-aspiring land of Brittany. Standing between colossal columns at the entrance to the bell-tower, we were confronted by the radiance of a luminous rose-window through which light streamed upon altar and tomb, statues fashioned with loving hand, a rood-screen masterly in execution.

Before the Revolution there were in Brittany over a thousand chapels dedicated to the Virgin, but not one of the thousand, I wager, excelled in beauty the resting-place of Saint Herbot. Perfection is a dangerous word, but how the chapel of Saint-Herbot near Huelgoat could be altered to approach more nearly an ideal I know not. For my part, I am convinced that it embodies all the endearing qualities essential to Breton architecture.

Seven Roman roads radiated from Carhaix. To-day the town has little to attract the tourist if we except a few antique houses, one the birthplace of La Tour d'Auvergne, who was named by Napoleon the "first grenadier of France." It is recorded that in his youth La Tour d'Auvergne wished to join four hundred men of his regiment who were following La Fayette and Rochambeau to fight for America's freedom, but the king could not grant leave to his officers to take part in a combat against a friendly nation.

The pleasantest episode of our short stay at Carhaix was falling in with an elderly cultivator of the soil who volunteered to show us the insignificant remains of the Roman aqueduct, considered entirely beneath our notice by our contemptuous chauffeur, and which we were endeavoring to find afoot. The old man, wearing a wide straw hat with flowing velvet streamers, was returning to his farm, an unwrapped loaf of bread tucked under one arm. He peered through gold-rimmed spectacles with interest when told that we were Americans with Celtic blood and that we admired the singing of Breton bards.

Had we heard Jaffrenou, a resident of Carhaix?

Yes, we had had that pleasure.

We should see the crowds that gather to hear him when a Gorsedd (song-festival) is held on the Ménez-Bré . . . his bard name is Taldir. It appears that Great Britain, like ancient Gaul, is divided into three parts: England, Scotland, and Wales, and that in Wales and Scotland, not to mention Ireland, the Celtic tongue is often heard to-day. When Jaffrenou traveled in these lands he found that he could converse with their people and understand their speech.

And had our friend known Le Braz? The kind old face beamed upon us. Indeed he had, and did he not read Le Braz's books by the fire of a winter's night? Those dealing with the past history of Armorica interested the country man the most. To him it was inspiring to remember that the Romans had trod these selfsame roads before the dawn of the Christian era. . . . When tilling his fields he had even turned up several of their coins.

Although we preferred the old fellow's company, it was necessary to return to our cantankerous chauffeur. I had asked the latter whether he had lost the fingers of one hand during the war and, stepping on the gas, he had replied:

"No, an accident when speeding."

Monsieur had inquired how that could be, as we had noticed that the car bore a plaque with the image of Saint Christophe. The man looked so absurdly crestfallen that I hastened to put in a word that, although his hand had been injured, did he not think it was owing to Saint Christophe that his life had been spared? . . . at which his rotund face regained its former complacency.

Speed being the idol of this particular driver, the long ridge of the Montagnes Noires, as we approached Châteauneuf-du-Faou, is blurred in memory. I recall, however, that we paused in the town to admire the costumes of a wedding party and, as Americans, were warmly greeted.

The old man we accosted had been a miner in Arkansas and had worked his way to Birmingham via New Orleans.

"All these men you see here," said he, waving a lean arm toward the spirited dancers of the gavotte, "have been to America, working in the Michelin tire factories or in the silk-mills at Paterson, New Jersey. That is where the bride and groom, with the costumes you so much admire, will live . . . in Paterson, New Jersey."

At Pleyben, too, memories of dancers on the sunlit *place* share the honors with my remembrances of "the latest in date of the great Breton Calvaries" . . . comparable to the calvaries of Saint-Thégonnec and Guimiliau. Highways cross at Pleyben, which stands on the route from Morlaix to Quimper and that on which we traveled from Carhaix to Châteaulin.

The Sardine Port of Douarnenez

CHAPTER XI

THE BAY OF DOUARNENEZ

Zola in comparing the Bay of Douarnenez to the Bay of Naples has stolen the thunder of all who follow him. The thought springs spontaneously to being, especially if your first glimpse of the bay be from the beach of Morgat, whence, seen across blue waters, the cloud-capped Ménez-Hom does indeed suggest a smoke-crowned Mount Vesuvius. Proud of having found the apt comparison, on putting it in words you are irritated by being told, "Yes, as Zola has well said."

On crossing the bay one is surprised to find that the inhabitants of the tiers of whitewashed houses rising so delectably above the shipping of the harbor of Douarnenez do in some respects resemble the Neapolitans. Here, as in Naples, an impasse has been reached between the ardent adherents of the Catholic Church and the Communistically inclined. Nowhere else in Brittany are faces ravished by poverty and drink more apparent. In their despair at ill luck many fishermen, finding life unendurable, have turned to rioting and talk of revolution. That all well-being—health, wealth, and happiness as opposed to starvation and disease, untold misery—should depend upon so fickle a creature as the sardine . . . is this not enough to turn men, hungering for the good things of life, into scoffers?

Douarnenez, it must be known, is the chief sardine-fishing port of France, not even excepting Concarneau. Its docks are enlivened with red-clad fishermen, flaming as the flags of Socialism. Roisterous are they with song and robust oaths. Seen against the intense blue of the waters, the subtler blue of the sardine-nets that dry from mastheads blowing in the breeze, the population of Douarnenez—men reckless and swaggering as pirates of old; women aging early, it is true, but one and all transfigured by captivating bonnets—intoxicates the artist. Like bees to honey, painters wing their way from far and near, unheeding Communistic strikes, unsavory odors at low tide, the all-penetrating smell of sun-dried fish. Has not the sardine brought Douarnenez into being? All homage to the shimmering creatures which are shaken by myriads from nets! The women who wear the bonnet of Douarnenez (whether Douarnenistes or no) are called *têtes de sardine,* for they are the workers in sardine factories where, swifter than guillotines, their knives decapitate their palpitating victims.

The fishing fleet numbers almost a thousand boats. Remember that sails are ruddy in hue and that every craft carries sea-blue nets. The delicate filets give an added grace to the boats of Douarnenez and Concarneau not to be found in lobster-fishing ports such as Camaret, for example, or the Ile de Sein. Dock walls as well as mastheads are festooned with nets; nets hang limply from second-story windows or flutter from poles beneath the dormers of the Rue Sainte-Hélène. The return of the fleet, often in early morning, is the event of the day. Women, commissioned by the sardine canneries, vie with one another in shouting bids for the catch as the boats near port. The gleaming fishes are poured into awaiting baskets. The sabots of the *sardinières* are heard on the cobbled ascent to the town as their laden owners trudge to packing-rooms. Do not, O fastidious housekeeper, be put off with Portuguese sardines but demand the choicer variety from the coast of Brittany.

While Monsieur busied himself unnoticed with sketch-books—artists are tolerated as harmless cranks, at Douarnenez—I caused more remark, owing to my apparent lack of occupation. I felt tempted to set up an easel and so to pass unobserved. The women felt sure that I wished to see the sardines split, dried, plunged in oil, or boiled in tins, though nothing was farther from my thoughts. The old salts sitting on stanchions or on coils of rope surmised I was looking for a boat. One old codger in a dory caught my eye by a fancied resemblance to old Father Neptune rising from the sea; exchange for a trident the oar which he held upright and the picture would have been complete. So insistent was he that I was to go with him to the Isle of Tristan that I yielded . . . putting myself completely in the power of this fiercely bearded Poseidon and trusting that he had complete command of his element.

"For fifty years," said he, gruffly, running bronzed fingers through bushy locks, "I've cheated Ankou, so you needn't fear to step into my boat."

As I seated myself at the bow he took a minute béret from his pocket. Worn over his shaggy hair it resembled a coronet. Installed at the stern, he began to waggle a solitary oar after the manner of Breton fishermen, who maintain that it is sheer madness not to see where you are going.

"Hauling nets is for the young," said he. "I had my share of it, fifty seasons come New Year's. I leave it to my sons and their boys; there are enough of 'em."

Asked whether his were a rewarding calling, he gave me a searching look with eyes still penetrating enough to discover a distant sail.

"It's a hard life," said he, "the life of the

seafaring man. First I served my time in the navy. Many's the year that's gone since I first crossed the line and got my ducking; old Neptune's no easy master and yet I'd change him for no other. If you mean money . . . on a good year we'd clear around four thousand francs for the three months of the season. The sardines come north about June and sometimes linger in these parts till December. But there's more than the sardine to reckon with . . . and they're fickle as hussies . . . there's the porpoises, the dirty beasts, plow clean through your nets and ruin 'em."

"And the storms?" I suggested.

"Oh yes," the old fellow admitted, "we get our share. If there's a God, it must make him sick to hear some men pray when they think their last hour's come. There's nothing they wouldn't promise then."

"And you," I said, "do you not pray?"

"I'm a Mason," he responded. "Ask the Catholics what that is," drawing his beard to a Mephistophelian point, "and they'll tell you it's the devil's own child."

"In my country," I said, "being a Mason implies belief in a Creator."

"Pshaw!" said he, "not so with us of the Grand Orient de France."

I remembered the words of an elderly Breton priest who had said:

"On this point we share the opinion of our

enemies—namely, that the struggle between Catholicism and Freemasonry is a struggle to death, without truce or mercy."

Launched on the sea of controversy, we had come in reality, almost unawares, to our desired goal, the island of Tristan.

"It is a tale for old wives," my skeptic announced. "What's more, you can read it all in books; but I'll tell you this: there was once a Saint Tutuarn, a Welshman, who lived here. Tutuarn-Enez, the place was called or, as we say now, Douarnenez."

After parting from my ancient mariner I took the old pagan's advice and read what I could find "in books" about the Ile Tristan. Legend has it that here dwelt Sir Tristan of Lyonesse, lover of the fair Iseult. As though to substantiate the case, near by, at Plomarc'h, certain remains are said to be those of King Mark's palace. Known in Breton as Marc'h, the unfortunate monarch is said to have had horse's ears. So eager was he to guard his secret that his barbers were invariably put to death. What was the life of a plebeian in those days compared with the pleasure of the king? But one barber plead to be spared and pledged himself to keep the secret. Yet so intolerable did the knowledge become that to relieve his torment he cried aloud to the sands beside the sea:

"Marc'h, the King of Plomarc'h, has horse's ears!"

Immediately a couple of reeds cut and left in that place by a passing bard echoed: "Marc'h, the King of Plomarc'h, has horse's ears!"

Saint Ronan, one of the most picturesque of the Celtic saints, came to Brittany at the end of the fifth century and settled in Cornouaille. He tarried first near Brest (the town bears the French version of his name, Saint-Renan) and later came to dwell as a hermit in the neighborhood of Douarnenez. So dynamic was he throughout his life, and far from easy to satisfy, that after his death it was a problem to know where he would wish to be buried. The bishops of three dioceses—Vannes, Léon, and Cornouaille—who coveted the honor of possessing his tomb, decided to let the saint himself indicate his choice. Therefore they had the body placed on a cart drawn by oxen and decided to abide by the stopping-place thus revealed. The oxen, turning away from the coast, bore their sacred burden to the dense forest which at that time mantled the "mountain" of Locronan. Trees crashed miraculously to let them pass and when at last the oxen came to the site of the present-day Locronan, the place of Ronan, they stopped. Here, it is said, the interlacing branches became arches of granite and the body of the

saint was likewise changed to stone as well as the bier on which it rested.

Ronan, far from being a likable individual, was feared more than beloved during his lifetime. His power over the elements seems to have been supreme. A virago by the name of Kébèn was his chief reviler. She even went to the point of slaying her own child in order to accuse the hermit of the deed: but Ronan, taking the maiden by the hand, brought her back from the jaws of death—to the amazement of the spectators and the confusion of Kébèn. So virulent was the woman's hatred that when the body of the saint, drawn by the team of oxen, passed by her dwelling, with muttered maledictions she struck the lifeless upturned face. As was to be expected,

ORA PRO NOBIS ✠

vengeance was swift. The earth opened where Kébèn stood and engulfed her struggling form. To this day, therefore, the women of the neighborhood show their devotion to Ronan's memory in touching fashion. On days of pardon, young and old alike stoop to kiss the left cheek as they pass the recumbent effigy on the tomb . . . seeking thus to obliterate the scar caused by the act of Kébèn. This tale was in our minds as we gazed upon the strange ceremony in the chapel erected in Ronan's honor by command of Anne de Bretagne.

Locronan's square, with its massive fifteenth-century church and Renaissance houses of the sixteenth century, its antique well with iron mountings, is perhaps the most remarkable setting to be found at a Breton pardon. No modern note jars the harmony of the ensemble. The whole is enhanced by the background of the hill of Locronan, fringed with rugged pines. Into this typical Breton *place* every year, on the second Sunday of July, crowds pour. Every seven years comes the Grande-Troménie in which all Cornouaille shares. Our visit was on the day of the more local gathering.

As we approached the village, men and women, girls and boys wearing the costume of the environs of Quimper (Saint Ronan does not seem to appeal to the *sardinières* of near-by Douarnenez) were approaching afoot, by the green lanes—hedged paths between fields where ripe rye and scarlet poppies glowed. Along the highway they gathered in laughing groups, singing and calling as they came, or rode in carts driven by men in pale-blue jackets and velvet hats, the women's minute caps and fluttering cap-strings enlivening their more somber costumes; tiny maidens dressed like their mammas were doll-like and demure. Likewise by motor and even by bicycle they continually came.

Once a year this sleeping town—in centuries now fled famous as the home of skilful weavers, whose prosperity dated from the fabrication of sail-cloth in demand all along the Breton coast—stirs and, waking from somnolence, comes to life. Let no man judge Locronan unless he has seen issue from the portico of its weathered church resplendent prelates, banners of red and gold, parishioners in all the splendor of their surviving medieval fine array. The hill of Locronan sings that day with color as the cortège wends its way, mounting steeply between crazy-quilts of fields to a point overlooking the Ménez-Hom and the vast sweep of the Bay of Douarnenez.

No narrow literalism should prevent the enjoyment of the tales told everywhere in Brittany . . . the land where imagination runs riot to the confounding of the practical-minded. Once, and there is a notary's testimony that this is true, the priests decided to postpone the customary procession, owing to the rain. At the appointed hour—this scene was witnessed by many reputable citizens—the doors, locked by the verger, were thrown open and the velvet banners, upheld by an invisible host, issued forth into the raging storm; as the ghostly marchers tramped mountainward a hole of blue sky hovered overhead, and never a drop of rain fell along the route where the sun-tipped pennants were borne aloft.

Continuing our journey around the bay beyond Locronan we come to Saint-Nic—named, I surmise, for the good Saint Nicholas in his rôle of protector of seafaring men and not as the children's patron—the kind bishop who, so runs the tale, on three successive nights tossed a purse of gold in at an open window as dower for three

penniless maidens of noble birth . . . whence grew the legend of Santa Claus.

Guide-books are rather terse when speaking of Saint-Nic, which is merely mentioned as being a "sixteenth century church and calvary with personages." Remembering the neglected cemetery of Plogonnec, recently seen, we were attracted by the contrasting charm of the blossoming churchyard and well-kept chapel at Saint-Nic. Although the road had been inundated with tar, we found a way to enter. Picking our steps, we approached by an allée of cypresses, pausing to admire the primitive "calvary with personages" and the Gothic side porch, and finally reaching the main portal at the end of the nave.

The door stood open. Looking from daylight into the dim candle-lit interior, we saw a white-robed nun, in exaggerated coif, carrying tall branched flowers wrought to resemble gold. We watched her genuflections as she stepped from the chancel with her golden sheaf. Her face was still unseen, veiled in shadow, but her every motion suggested harmony with her surroundings, peace. Saint-Nic was otherwise deserted. Outside, in the churchyard, doves were cooing.

Ménez (the Breton word for mountain) appears frequently upon these tombstones: Ménez-Stum, Ménez-Damoy, Marie Anne Ménez. So rooted are the inhabitants of the region to their hills that they seem even to have taken the mountain's name. Our drive led us to the hamlet of Sainte-Marie de Ménez-Hom, situated in a high rural district. A herd of cows had been admitted to the welcome shade around the church and was grazing while their guardian told her beads as she knelt at the foot of the calvary, motionless as one of the stone figures. Shortly after Sainte-Marie we left our car by the roadside and started to trudge to the top of the Ménez-Hom. The insignificant altitude of this hill is forgotten because of the magnificence of its position, rising like Fujiyama from the sea. Partly, perhaps, because of the remembrance of the days of yore, the hills of Brittany are still known

locally as mountains, even as titles still serve as a mark of respect when one addresses the ancient nobility of France.

The twenty-first of July, which it happened to be, was one of those heaven-sent days when the atmosphere is clear enough to make the horizon plainly visible, yet with suggestions of clouds in the blue haze of distance. As we trod over the prickly close-cropped gorse toward the central and highest mound of the three rounded knolls that crown the mountain we met tandem carts, gorse-laden, careening like prairie-schooners. As we neared the top the land was abloom with heather. A cairn has been set up, in Celtic fashion, and from this viewpoint, incontestably the finest in all Brittany, a bit breathlessly we surveyed the landscape.

On one side rose the rolling hills—Mont-Saint-Michel the highest, with its suggestion of a peak—the rounded hilltops of the ranges of the Monts d'Arrée and Montagnes Noires. Hills and the

sea! At our feet the intense blue of the Bay of Douarnenez, dotted with tiny winged craft, stretched from the headland of the Cap de la Chèvre beyond which rose high whitish cliffs and, yes, the Tas-de-Pois! The roadstead of Brest glimmered in sunlight, there lay the peninsula of Plougastel and far-distant Brest. We spied the top of the new bridge from the headland of Crozon to Châteaulin; and beyond, the woodland of Landerneau with its enchanted oaks, still known as Arthur's forest.

As we faced the sea, where nestles Douarnenez, we were astounded by the numberless patches of the fields; never before had we seen such variety of color, rye, wheat, and oats, all golden on this summer's afternoon, the peach-bloom pink of clover, plowed earth, the vivid green of grass, and, at our feet, the unforgettable purple heather from which arose the drone of bees. The spire of Ploaré was lifted in austere grandeur, the curtains

The Menhir

of pines that screen Locronan contrasted with the gleaming wheat-fields.

Aloof, above the world, we lingered, dreaming dreams, saturated with the unearthly beauty of sky and sea, the illusive unreality of earth itself. Permeated with the peace and tranquillity of the place, we had no concern with the strife of Catholic or Freemason. Pilgrims to Ménez-Hom, seekers after truth, we cried, do you not lay hold of a mystery older and more far-reaching in its appeal than Christianity itself: the spiritual oneness of man and his Creator? The uplifted hills, the reflecting waters of the Bay of Douarnenez, blue as the Mediterranean, spoke the answer with the voice of silence.

L'Ilienne

CHAPTER XII

THE ISLE OF THE ENCHANTER

A LITTLE jogging train on what the English call a "light" railway carries the traveler from Douarnenez to Audierne. The platform at Douarnenez, on the eve of our departure, was cluttered with baskets of fish packed in wet bracken. A fishy odor pervaded the waiting-room and we noticed that a *sardinière,* pushing ahead of us as we impatiently anticipated the opening of the ticket office, was bespattered with fish-scales. Between Douarnenez and Audierne there is little to choose; each, like Concarneau, is renowned for its fishing fleet. A school of mackerel off the Pointe du Raz, swimming from the nets of fishermen of the one, only to come upon fishermen of the other, would find it a choice between frying-pan and fire.

A short run through a country golden in July with ripe grain and animated by industrious harvesters separates the two towns. At Audierne railway ends within a stone's throw of the harbor. Standing upon the dock—crowded, this day and hour, with fisher-folk, men in scarlet, women in caps of the *sardinières*—we were inclined to place Audierne even ahead of Douarnenez, so serried were its red-sailed sloops, so glistening the sunlight on plaster house walls mounting from the waterside to the hilltop crowned with twisted pines. He who has beheld this scene knows all Audierne has to offer—unless, indeed, he may be so fortunate as to happen upon a market.

My memory carries me back almost a score of years, when this was our good fortune. Brittany was new to us in those days. It was incredible as a fairy-tale to see the piles of witches' brooms, the hand-hewn sabots, wooden rakes tossed haphazard as jackstraws along the dock, to watch the purchasers, dames in medieval guise in the starched caps of the cape, gaffers hobbling with age, garbed in the voluminous knee-breeches of the region, the *bragou-braz*. One old fellow—I see him yet, poking a woolen-stockinged leg into a boat-like sabot—was the mayor of the neighboring village of Comfort.

Audierne glories in its boats. Chief among these may I place the boat to Brest which with consistent irregularity connects the continent with the Ile de Sein. Before leaving the mainland, however, we must explore the peninsula, the near-by Saint-Tugean, the more distant extremity known as the Pointe du Raz.

The Church of Saint-Tugean is one of the astonishments of this astounding land of Brittany. Shaded by sheltering trees which flourish in an inclosure walled against cattle, this architectural gem is out of keeping with the squalor of the surrounding village. The explanation was furnished by Monsieur l'Abbé, an affable Celt who has written a brochure on the origin of this chapel, dedicated to Saint Tugean or Eoghan, once Bishop of Derry in Ireland, and at the time of his death in the year 618 rector of Brasparts and abbot of the monastery of Daoulas.

Finding the chapel locked, we were about to knock at the door of the priest's house when our chauffeur summoned Monsieur l'Abbé in the peremptory manner common to Breton drivers, who if they wish to ask their way, toot horns at house doors. Monsieur l'Abbé beamed reassuringly, however. Anticipating our need, like a good follower of the saint he bore a key. He proved to have spent many years in Haiti and had "assisted" at two revolutions. On growing old he had decided to return to Saint-Tugean. His great-grandfather had bought the edifice after the Revolution, in order that it should not be destroyed, and now he in turn intended to save it from decay. His regret in learning that we were of the Protestant fold was extreme—accentuated, perhaps, by the dread that therefore we might fail to loosen our purse-strings.

"Before Luther and Calvin," said he, "we

The Quay at Audierne

were all of one church . . . had it not been for Calvin and Luther . . . You have pictures of your parents in your house? Very good. We have pictures of our God, the Holy Virgin, and the saints—that is all. The difference between us is so slight, so very slight, m'sieu et dame."

Entering by a low and narrow gate, which symbolized the humility of the true Christian, we were confronted by a barbaric interior. The wooden heads of dragons supporting the cross-beams—seen in so many Breton chapels and representing the serpent or demon—were daring enough in color and design to grace a Chinese temple.

The abbé led us to the highly colored statue of Saint Tugean, portrayed between a comical small boy whose face is swollen with toothache and a no less comical mad dog. It is the saint's prerogative, it appears, to cure the one and the victims of the other. There was a time when a pope's highest gift to a potentate was a golden key in the making of which had been mixed metal from the chains of Peter and Paul. These were known as the keys of Saint Peter. Perhaps there was a connection between these keys and those of Saint Tugean. At his pardon, keys used to be distributed the wearing of which insured immunity against the bites of mad dogs, while the bread blessed on this occasion was used throughout the year as a cure for toothache.

"Is there no dentist in the region?" Monsieur flippantly inquired, but he was told that the people preferred to keep their own teeth, made whole by the intercession of the saint. To which response Monsieur murmured words of regret that he did not reside in the parish.

Saint-Tugean was erected by the sister of François 1er in fulfilment of a vow. When her brother was taken prisoner in 1525, after the Battle of Pavia, Marguerite, then Duchess of Alençon, determined to raise the ransom required by Charles Quint. She traveled throughout the provinces to accomplish her purpose, and at last was ready to sail from the "Point of Finistère," probably Audierne, where she was advised by the natives to put herself under the protection of Saint Tugean. This she did, vowing that if her mission were successful she would transform the lowly chapel near by into a church. After becoming Queen of Navarre, Marguerite erected her thank-offering to Saint Tugean.

Plogoff—whose church is dedicated to the Welsh bishop Saint Kenan, spiritual adviser to Queen Guinevere—stands on the road to the extreme point of Finistère, land's end. Nine miles from Audierne, the rocky headland of the Pointe du Raz is one of the famous sites in Brittany. Hundreds visit it daily in summer, whether by private motor or by autocar, from Audierne or direct from Quimper. At midday in midsummer, with tourists crawling like inquisitive flies over the jagged cliffs, performing a bit of rock-climbing with the aid of sturdy-limbed guides, the point becomes almost banal. Yet it is not necessary to wait until the storms of autumn create a tempestuous atmosphere. All that is important is to stay a while at the point, at the Hôtel du Raz de Sein, and the wonder of the place will grow upon you. Familiarity not only does not breed contempt but fills the mind with wonder at the inherent poetry latent in the soul of man.

Where on earth, I ask it of you, should Merlin have been born if not on the Isle of Sein, which floats like a lustrous water-lily beyond the treacherous and sinister channel? Where indeed if not on the Isle of Sein should druidesses, nine in number, have guarded the mystic brew three drops of which enabled man to read the future? Where else but on this frequently mist-veiled islet should druids have interred their dead? and from what port should they have set out but from the forsaken harbor which once, 'tis said, served the fabled city of Ys, and where, on days of calm, fishermen still claim to hear the church bells ringing in Ahès' submerged capital? Where indeed but from the deserted shore of this Bay of the Dead should barges put forth at dusk, freighted with the souls of the departed, invisible passengers who nevertheless toss golden coin in payment to their human boatmen on arrival at the Ile de Sein, the Island of the Dead?

Come, muster your courage and wander with me afoot over miles of lonely wind-swept moorland to the shores of this selfsame bay. Tread briskly, for the air is fresh and salt with the tang of the sea. As we tramp along the cliff's edge on a cow-path leading toward the commanding

A Gaffer
garbed in Bragou-braz

Pointe du Van, there is no sign of humanity—save, perhaps, guarding her cattle, a solitary daughter of the cape, taciturn, garbed in black, with stiff-winged head-dress. In the distance, it is true, may be seen, on the crest of the ridge where villages lie, little far-off mills which raise beckoning arms in the breeze as if entreating to be allowed a respite from perpetual motion. But in this land of death the wind dies not; whether or no it be one of the spells of Merlin, who can tell?

Hastening, for the sun has set now and we are far from the dwelling of man, we come upon the desolate rock-strewn shore of the bay, which doubly deserves its name of Trépassés from the traditional ferrying of souls and from the fact that, as an aftermath of storm, the corpses of the shipwrecked are not infrequently washed ashore. Turning away from the waves which, to our ears attuned to lesser vehemence, seem to threaten thunderously, to raise a ghoulish pæan, we trudge toward the lagoon, or Etang of Laouël. This, too, we have been told, this stagnant pool, shunned alike by man and beast, covers the site of Dahut's iniquitous city. A solitary heron, sensing our approach, rises out of the mists that partially veil the water. Wild ducks, skimming low, depart in formation, rending the dampness of approaching night with penetrating cries. In the fading light the chaotic rocks barring our homeward path assume the shape of phantoms.

"Ile de Sein, possessing few attractions for tourists, is interesting as a druidic burial-place and as the 'Enez-Sizun' or 'isle of the seven sleepers' of Breton legend." . . . "There is not a more desolate place to be found in France." . . . So much for the Blue Guides. Having read that the island was the legendary birthplace of Merlin, the enchanter of Arthurian romance, that it was here this antichrist, offspring of the union of woman and devil, was instructed by sinister fairies, we could not be blamed for wishing to see the region. As if this were not enough, the island, like Ouessant, Mont-Saint-Michel, and the Grand-Bey at Saint-Malo, is one of those traditional burial-places of the druid dead to which the Bag-Noz (Boat of the Dead), commanded by the first to die in the year, is said still to ply . . . its lights are reported by fishermen to twinkle luminously at dusk. Moreover, the island was an Ultima Thule of the ancient world and is even linked with Ulysses's Isle of Circe.

It became a veritable passion with us, this desire to set foot on the island, as day after day we gazed westward across Europe's most treacherous channel to where the dim isle, almost level with the tide, its distant houses glimmering in sunlight, floated like a barge of dreams. At night, too, we were tantalized, even on looking from our bedroom window, as a new star took its place among the constellations—the flashing star that shone from the island.

Inquiring of Monsieur Keradennec, our helpful host, we gave up all thought of connecting with the boat said on paper to ply weekly from Audierne to Brest. Our hope lay, it appeared, in another direction. It was possible to signal from the semaphore and a fishing-bark would be sent, in which one could, in from three to five hours, make crossing—five miles by actual measurement.

"It is all a question of wind and tide," our host informed us. "We never know when we go to the island at what time we shall be able to return."

"'Or if you will ever arrive,'" Monsieur chimed in, quoting the book he was reading. "'No stranger may buy land there. The island was the Sena of the Romans.' Mark this: 'According to Pomponius Mela, writing in the first century, the nine druidesses had power to unchain winds and waves, to metamorphosize themselves into animal forms, to cure the incurable, to predict the future . . . but only the brave received their prophecies, as to hear them it was necessary to go to their island. After the death of the last druid, when monks had brought Christianity to the Ile de Sein, it is said the surviving druidesses found shelter in the rocks of Minconoc and eked out a living by selling' . . . what do you think? . . . 'good weather to sailors.'"

"For centuries the island was deserted," our host took up the tale. "It had a bad name. Finally a few fishermen moved there, although the place was said to be haunted. Knowing the superstitions of the people, a desperate lot of pillagers settled on the island, wreckers, 'demons of the sea.' They took good care to have it known that those drowned without sepulcher were abroad on stormy nights; then all decent folk would stay within doors, and, take my word for it, blood-curdling shrieks were actually heard . . . whether from evil spirits or their impersonators, who can say? Above the sobbing of the wind would rise the dying groans of those who crawled from wreckage only to be murdered in cold blood.

"Sein was notorious, a few years back, for the fights to the death held there. Seamen from the continent would go to the island for the purpose of settling feuds, knowing the absence of police and the indifference of the population to what did not concern them. Government has changed all that by stationing two gendarmes there. Since establishment of a modern life-saving station Sein has more than redeemed her former notorious reputation."

The first Sunday in August dawning auspiciously, we decided to make our excursion. We were assured that a sail-boat equipped with a motor would put forth at an early hour from Sein and we should be notified when to repair to the fishermen's cove of Bestrée. After a delay the summons came. We climbed as skilfully as we might, it being low tide, down the slippery flight of steps leading to the water's edge where a waiting rowboat took us to our bark. We had as fellow-passengers four Iliennes, whose delicately chiseled profiles were somberly framed by voluminous broadcloth head-dresses. It was evident from the first that our boat was "en panne." An hour passed, but not one of the six men aboard—three is the usual crew—nor yet the four small boys, presumably learning their future métier, could get even a momentary spark of life from the ominously silent motor. Another hour and a boat, a lobster-fishing craft like our own, passing with noisy chuggings from the direction of Audierne, was hailed. Would it take passengers? Our fate hung in the balance until the bark obligingly pulled alongside. There was much scrambling as five petticoats, myself included, got aboard, Monsieur being the only man to make the transfer.

The wind was high, flecking the waves with whitecaps. Free-winged as a bird, our boat, skimming seaward, drove before her flocks of black-mantled gulls. We skirted the Raz de Sein, churning in treacherous whirlpools, path of ocean liners which plow their way between the rock-bound Pointe du Raz and the reef-surrounded island. Here, by night, gleams the sparkling eye of little Vieille and also that of hoary Gorlébella—scene of Le Braz's gruesome tragedy "Le Gardien du Feu."

As we plunged onward, now rising on the crest of the wave, now almost engulfed in the trough of the sea, a gigantic shark cut across our bow; his course like our own carried him far into the Bay of Audierne, avoiding the more troubled waters. A swift tide was running, and wave after wave, sweeping the deck, would have drenched us save for borrowed oilskins.

Miraculously short the transit seemed, yet as we had left the Bestrée cove at three we were surprised to hear three striking (it proved to be sun time) as we neared the mystic island. The houses gleamed like mosques of pearl in the unearthly atmosphere of this Breton isle, this unpricked bubble resting ever so lightly (would it not vanish from our sight?) as though afloat twixt sky and sea.

The rocks of Gador, those of oracular fame, came into view, the reef-sheltered southern harbor filled with boats from Paimpol, the farther harbor of the Iliens, glowing with ruddy sails. The island is not more than a mile in length, a half-mile at its widest point. Standing amid raging seas—three hundred reefs may be seen at low tide from the platform of its lighthouse—and affording no invulnerable refuge from the fury of uproarious waves, the island had presented an enigma. It had been beyond our understanding that men should be willing to live there. No, it is not the advantageous lobster-fishing alone, as we had been told, which holds them. We know better now, having seen with our own eyes. It is the enchantment of the place. Be not deceived by partizans of Ouessant, Bréhat, Groix, Belle-Ile; there is no island comparable to Sein. The Breton mysticism finds here its adequate expression. Here the mariner, son of Celtic sires, casts his moorings between adventurous voyagings; here, as on high seas, he feels no limitations, is bounded by wide horizons, by the dome of heaven to which his aspirations lead. Here beauty dwells.

A row of plastered dwellings overlooks the two ports; the breakwater forms the boundary of the one promenade of the town, which has no other name than the "bourg" or borough. Beyond these fairly imposing domiciles is a network of narrow ways just wide enough in which to roll a barrel, recalling foot-paths of Venice. Houses are solid-walled and huddled against the wind and wave. Hotels bear no signs; would signs perhaps blow menacingly in winter gales or is it that no one stops here overnight save an occasional commercial traveler or mad painter? Yet there are inns, two of them—Hôtel Valin and Hôtel des Touristes, both plain but clean.

A seaman directed us *chez* Valin and here we presented to Madame Veuve Valin the trump card which was to be our open-sesame . . . for

the natives stand aloof and are not easily won. This card was no less than a letter from Henri Royer, the distinguished French painter, far-famed for his delineation of Breton character. It was addressed to Mademoiselle Catherine Milliner.

"Mademoiselle," Monsieur Royer had told us one April day beneath the horse-chestnuts of Paris, "is the daughter of a late mayor of the Ile de Sein and although her brother lives here in Paris, she is faithful to the home of her ancestors. Indeed, she is the Providence of the island."

Madame Valin exclaimed on hearing from

whom the letter came, "But he is here, Monsieur Royer; he is stopping on the island!"

Whereupon Madame provided us with a demure young Ilienne to guide us through a labyrinth of alleys to the farther quay on which stood the house of Milliner. Finding that Mademoiselle was at vespers, we decided to follow her thither. The church was situated beyond the precincts of the village on a *place* guarded by two menhirs familiarly called "the gossips." It was packed to the doors. The men, massed to the front, were hidden from us by a sea of black-hooded women until the latter turned their chairs to kneel. As the wearer of a hat I was unique. At a given moment the congregation issued from the church door in procession, filing in somber state before the menhirs and against a background of low white cottages and poetic Breton sky and sea. Such is the custom, it appears, on first Sundays. Entranced, we gave thanks for having come to Sein, and resolved, contrary to our expectations, to stay at least overnight.

After the service we repaired once more to pay our respects to Mademoiselle Milliner. This time we found her and could well imagine the sensation she must have caused upon a Paris boulevard when she visited her brother, a wholesale importer of lobsters. We wondered that Mademoiselle, exquisite though not in her first youth, was content to remain on the island, until we discovered that the women of the Ile de Sein are perhaps the most charming (I am tempted to say the most elegant) to be found in Brittany and, like the women of Plougastel, of an unexpected refinement.

"There are times," Mademoiselle told us, "when I am afraid. I dare not look at the barometer when the winter storms rage and we must barricade our houses and are forced to listen to the howling of the wind. But this is my home. I am the last to live here, and we were once nine."

In answer to our questions, she told, quite as a matter of course, how in the winter of 1896–97 the islet was covered by the sea for several days, the lamp in the lighthouse extinguished; how there have been times when the people were saved only by clinging onto the housetops. Once, she had heard her mother say, at a time of imminent peril the curé, who had taken refuge in the spire of the old church, had actually given the people absolution.

"But it is home," she told us, smilingly; "it is home."

Monsieur Royer was astounded when we came upon him that evening, indulging in a game of cards at his inn door. He introduced his three companions—youths with bronzed faces and wearing the garb of lobster-fishermen but who, he assured us, were merely bankers from Paris, although good fishermen, as we should see.

"Ce n'est pas banal!" he kept murmuring at intervals and seemed fully as much amused at this unexpected encounter as we were delighted at our own good fortune.

It was arranged that we should all dine together—a tax on the capacity of the round table at the tiny inn. Shall I ever forget the meal? Royer, the presiding genius of the place, recounted anecdotes covering the twenty summers that he had painted on the island, reminiscences of Cottet, of Le Braz. One of the party proved to be a wit, another a tomboy who delighted in teasing the blushing bonne. We helped to eat the three kilos of shrimps and the lobsters which were the result of the morning's fishing expedition. Living samples were brought from the kitchen to show us the difference between the *homard* with formidable claw and blue tail and the *langouste* of reddish hue and with Mephistophelian antennæ.

"Yes, my friends are lobster-fishermen as well as bankers, real amateurs in the French meaning —lovers of the sport—not mere mackerel-fishers, whom the people of the island scorn."

Imagine us, with nine o'clock striking, still gathered about the festive board, our sunburnt faces illuminated by the light of a lamp hanging over the table as it might have hung in the saloon of a ship at sea. The two fishermen forming the crew of our friends' boat had come in to share biscuits and wine and, as nine o'clock is the time limit when drinks may be served to non-diners, the shutters had been closed in order that our conviviality should not be interrupted by a vigilant gendarme.

Before turning in for the night we strolled along the quay to count the flashing lights . . . there were sixteen or more, as I remember, dominated by mighty Ar-Men, standing on the westernmost reef, guarding, as our friends put it, the route to America. It was twenty-two miles northwest of Ar-Men, they told us, that on May 20, 1922, the P. & O. liner *Egypt* sank, rammed in a fog by a coastwise steamer, with 334 souls aboard, of whom

232 were saved. The tale was more poignant to us than they knew, for we had once spent three blissful weeks upon the *Egypt,* voyaging from London to Bombay.

They told us, too, that the French have been pioneers in the "science" of construction of lighthouses, and that of all the achievements of the engineers perhaps none is more noteworthy than the building of Ar-Men, begun in 1867 but not finished for fourteen years. The first year there were only eight hours when work was possible, the next year eighteen hours, and the time increased as the structure rose above the level of the waves. Between the island and Ar-Men, a distance of over five miles, extend the notorious reefs, hidden at high tide, known as the "Pont de Sein."

White are the blinding flashes of Ar-Men; white, too, the flashes from Sein which, with undeviating regularity, lighted the house walls seen from our window. Opposite, across the distant Raz de Sein, shone the green eye of Vieille, red or white when seen from shore; other lights pricked the sky like fixed stars. As I watched, there arose from behind the breakwater, beyond the sleeping harbor, a gibbous moon, orange as a Breton sail. In its train, at respectful distance, Venus followed, and still later I observed (for who would sleep on such a night?) the faintly gleaming Pleiades.

A silvery path lit by the moon led temptingly

to anchored ships. Only the house walls and the shimmering water were turned to catch the full glare of Sein's glassy eye. Ghost-like figures lurked in the shadows. Could Ankou be abroad?

Dawn and high tide brought with them a frieze of fishermen against a background of sky and masts and swirling gulls. Clad in the subtler blue, never in scarlet, the fishermen, each with solitary oar on shoulder, laden with lobster-pots or cork floats, tramped in succession along the dike. Swift were departures with the wind. Sloops slipped from their moorings, jibs straining, topsails raised with creaking cordage. One by one the boats passed from sight into the mysterious haze of early morning. Seaweed fires smoldered along the shore, the smoke curling skyward. Women hurried by, carrying flails, bound for the tiny stone-walled fields where rye was to be winnowed. Breaking through barriers of mist, the newly risen sun proclaimed another day.

Ar-Men Light.

Quimper The populous and ancient Rue Kéréon

CHAPTER XIII

QUIMPER THE PROVINCIAL

WHAT Paris is to France, Quimper is to Brittany. True, there are larger cities in the province—in order of importance first Nantes, then Rennes, and Brest, but they are French rather than Breton, and with the exception of Brest they are not situated in la Bretagne *bretonnante* . . . nor yet are Saint-Brieuc, Lorient, or Saint-Nazaire. It falls, then, to the share of Quimper, with its scant twenty thousand inhabitants, a population slightly larger than that of Morlaix and somewhat smaller than that of Vannes, to rank not alone as capital of Finistère but as the key to our understanding, the key (comparable only to the silver one that hung from the neck of Gradlon, the founder of Quimper) which, despite all barriers of race or language unlocks the flood-gates of the mind—the gates erected by human limitations against the sea of knowledge—and we are inundated with clairvoyance to divine the meaning of this Celtic kingdom of Cornouaille.

It is recorded that a Sire de Landerneau, homesick for his native Brittany, remained unmoved by the splendors of the court at Versailles. In fact, he remarked, to the amusement of courtiers, that the moon at Landerneau was larger by far than that of Versailles. Thus the moon of Landerneau has become a byword in France. Like Landerneau, Quimper shares the distinction of being one of the places cited by Parisians when they wish to denote a narrow provincialism. It is this very quality, which Quimper undoubtedly possesses in high degree, that so endears the town to amateurs of the picturesque, of the individual.

Quimper takes its name from the Breton word "Kemper," that is to say confluence—in this case of the rivers Steir and Odet. Situated at a distance of some eleven miles from the sea, Quimper is nevertheless a considerable port. The exuberance of native life to be seen along the quays of the Odet rivals although it does not surpass that on the equally populous and far more ancient Rue Kéréon by which the traveler threads his way to the cathedral. To say that Quimper possesses the finest markets in Brittany, the most beautiful and beloved cathedral, is only to emphasize the fact that no town in all the province of Brittany is to-day comparable to this capital of ancient Cornouaille. Perhaps this is as it should be, for is not Quimper the metropolis founded by Gradlon, the legendary fifth-century monarch come from Britain—naming his kingdom for the older Cornwall? Was it not given by him into the especial keeping of that most saintly Breton Corentin and was it not indeed known up to the Revolution by the name of Kemper-Corentin? Thus virtue triumphs and Ker-Ys (from which some say Paris took its name, the peer or equal of Ys), has become naught but a name.

The vicissitudes of Quimper have been many since the time that Gradlon, hunting with his retainers in the wood of Nevet near Plomodiern, was welcomed by the hermit Corentin and the entire party fed upon a solitary fish which, when halved by the hermit and one part returned to its native pool, had the uncanny habit of becoming whole. This miraculous occurrence was the means of Gradlon's conversion to Christianity.

The kingdom or countship of Cornouaille was united to Brittany in 1066 by the marriage of Hoël, Count of Cornouaille, to the sister and heiress of Conan, Duke of Brittany; as, in like fashion at a later date, the duchy of Brittany was united to France by the marriage of the Duchess Anne, twice the bride of a King of France.

Quimper, fortified in the thirteenth century, suffered severely in the war of the Breton succession. In 1344 it was pillaged by Charles de Blois, and the following year refused an entrance to Jean de Montfort. In the sixteenth century it took the part of the League against the heretical Henri IV.

Profitable as it might be to linger on the history of the place, yet it is my preference to describe Quimper as we found it on a recent visit, Quimper in the act of celebrating the Fête-Dieu. To my mind, headquarters should be made at the truly admirable Hôtel de l'Epée on the quay here known, probably because of its luxuriant horse-chestnuts and the proximity of the Champ de Bataille, as the Rue du Parc. Its close rival, the Hôtel du Parc, has an equally effective outlook on this frequented thoroughfare skirting the Odet. Foot-bridges lead across the meager stream to the prefecture silhouetted against the abrupt wooded hill of Mont-Frugy. Yet there are sojourners who prefer rooms in the rear, quieter save for chimes, with windows overlooking a jumble of ancient roofs and chimney-pots to the cathedral towers . . . a satisfying Old World scene characteristic of cathedral towns (so once was Rheims). Some there are, indeed, who prefer to station themselves upon the Place Saint-Corentin beneath the beneficent shadow of the Gothic towers, in that epitome of local color the Relais Saint-Corentin.

From our elongated French windows at the Hôtel de l'Epée we looked out on tree-tops, on rooks that circled among the pepper-pot turrets of the prefecture and the medieval relics of the Hôpital Sainte-Catherine. The sound of singing caused us to step out onto our balcony and to share the delight of a joyous wedding party, youths and maidens hand in hand, marching in Breton fashion through the town. The bride and groom were scarcely more elegantly garbed than their guests, for all had come from Pont-Aven where maidens are resplendent in beribboned coifs and quilled ruffs, while swains in velvet waistcoats wear to perfection wide-brimmed hats ornamented with gorgeous buckles. Later we were to come upon this gallant group dancing a gavotte in the cathedral square.

Hardly a June day passed without the merry-making of at least one wedding party. The tiny cap of Quimper with its fluttering strings (shrunk of late years from the former suggestion of a hennin), the voluminous corseted black gowns of the Quimperoise predominated at these gatherings, enlivened by the sky-blue jackets and velvet-embellished hats of native bridegrooms. Sometimes the participants were from Pont-l'Abbé, the land of the Bigoudens, the type depicted by

Lemordant on the walls of the hotel salle-à-manger.

I have spoken of the work of Lemordant, a living victim of the World War, making to-day a no less gallant fight than on the battle-field. He it was who decorated the ceiling of the theater at Rennes. These sumptuous panels at Quimper, in Lemordant's early style, begun as they were in 1907, are the result of years of living in the country of the Bigoudens, the peninsula to the south of Quimper. The glow of rosy clouds is reflected in the luminous costumes. Tents, both white and green, gleam in the sunlight, a monumental figure of a Bigouden stands in relief against a white booth. Blowing peasants in buoyant fête-day garments scurry along the wet beach. Other panels show the toil of seaweed-gatherers and fisher-folk. The master mind has interpreted for us the entire cycle of life on the peninsula of Penmarc'h.

Feverish preparations anticipated the procession of the Fête-Dieu. We had remarked on the quantities of flowers and the sheaves of iris leaves sold at Saturday's market. The greens, we found, were used to conceal gutters and to form geometric designs. Householders worked hurriedly, draping the lower stories of their domiciles with linen sheets to which they pinned garlands of posies. From second-story windows hung festoons of red and gold, the sign of the ermine—gold on scarlet. The Rue Kéréon lent itself admirably to decoration. Its hoary gabled houses—three, four, and five centuries old—were bedecked with potted plants banked in dormer-windows. A girl outside the shop "Au Breton," where stands the wooden effigy of a youth in *bragou-braz,* was at the last minute scattering blossoms that would not be blown by wind or trampled by the waiting crowd. We took up our position. Excitement was intense.

It comes! The procession comes! The major-domo in cardinal-red garments precedes a bevy of airily clad cherubs who strew rose petals. The narrow sidewalks are packed with natives; no strangers are in evidence. Girls about to celebrate their first communion, veiled like brides, are marshaled by sedulous nuns. The throngs have closed the street to traffic now—one or two automobiles which had cut through the human cordon having turned off into a side street in response to angry mutterings. Banners, borne by Quimperoises wearing the red Cordon of Saint François, catch the sunlight: "Cœur de Jésus, Sauvez la France," reads one; another, "Sainte-Anne gardez nos Bretons fidèles."

Boys of the Ecole Saint-Yves go by, neat in blue suits and capes with hoods; young priests walk beside those lads who wear a white bow on one sleeve, signifying that they, too, are to partake of a first communion. Then come standard-bearers—*glaziks* in sky-blue—followed by bands, a motley congregation, a vested choir, acolytes with swinging thuribles from which streams of incense pour, priests too numerous to enumerate, and last, walking bareheaded beneath a beplumed canopy, the venerable Bishop of Quimper, bearing aloft the Sacrament.

So intense was the religious exaltation of the prelate, so devout and reverent the atmosphere created, that we found ourselves part of the whole and unable to disassociate ourselves. Ever since Monsieur has regretted the photograph that was never taken, but if he erred, it was on the side of good taste and his abstinence constituted the tribute of an American heretic to the spirituality of his Eminence the Bishop of Quimper.

Dramatic skies attended the procession winding, a blaze of color, to the wayside altar on the Rue Kéréon. After this sunlit climax came the whirlwind, presaged by ominous storm-clouds.

There were but few deflections from the ranks that marched unhastening to participate in high mass at the cathedral. Some mothers, indeed, threw rain-cloaks around their offspring, here and there a nun accepted a proffered umbrella, but many sisters declined and merely shook themselves like water-fowl on entering the vestibule. The banners had been rushed to cover. The bishop, unperturbed as at Rumengol, was escorted to the chancel, an attendant holding above his head an enormous parasol; the scene suggested to our lay minds the state entrance of a daimio of Old Japan.

The myriad veils, the banners, the brilliance of flaming candles, the perfume of roses, the pungence of incense, formed an amazing whole. When the clamorous chimes paused in their rejoicing, the mighty organ carried on the message with the triumphant strains of the Hallelujah Chorus. No standing-room remained in the vast edifice, but throngs still surged upon the threshold, seeking entry. In contrast to the empty cathedrals so often seen in certain parts of France and England, I remember with emotion the overflowing sanctuary at Quimper.

It was on a market-day that we visited the two museums on the cathedral square. I recollect that it was a gusty day of alternate sunshine and sudden showers, a day typically Breton. The wind had overturned a booth where silken scarfs were displayed, trailing their rainbow colors in the dust to the consternation of the saleswoman, a ponderous Quimperoise. Around the statue of Laënnec, inventor of the stethoscope and son of Quimper, the gaudy products of local potteries were stacked, while sabots were piled at the cathedral door. Our first visit was to the picture gallery famed for its canvases depicting life in the province, masterpieces by Simon, Dauchez, Royer, Guillou, and Cottet.

The art museum has one group of life-sized figures wearing ancient Breton costumes which is, I believe, to be transferred to the archæological museum. The scene represented is a wedding party outside a thatched Breton cottage from the upper window of which a bent crone leans. One might believe that a sorcerer had enchanted the entire gathering so that for ages to come neither bride nor bridegroom, guests nor musicians will wither or decay but will remain for generations yet unborn the embodiment of a Breton folk-tale.

The Musée Archéologique is consecrated to regional arts and crafts. In this respect it is almost unique in Brittany and certainly no other museum is more charmingly housed. The building, overlooking the cathedral with its garden and remnant of town walls, was up to the time of the Separation the Bishop's Palace. The most ancient portion was built from 1508 to 1540, by Claude de Rohan, at that time Bishop of Quimper. The various stories are connected by means of a superb circular stairway; following whose worn stone steps, we come, at the third and last floor, to a central column of oak, bearing the arms of the Rohans and supporting a sculptured "parasol."

Not the least of the museum's charms was the talk of its custodian, an untidy old man in black sabots which he wore when floors were of stone but otherwise left carefully at doorways. He explained, confidentially, that the reason the museum remained closed daily until one was that he had so much cleaning to do.

"Picture to yourselves, monsieur et dame, the dust, a veritable Sahara, which settles on all my furniture and especially in the lattices of the lits-clos."

It was the familiar story of an old man carrying on till the rising generation could play the part of men; of lack of funds since the catastrophe of the World War.

Hardly second in interest to the amazing display of chests of oak and chestnut, *bahuts,* and other examples of carved Breton furniture, archaic figures of saints and quaintly colored crucifixes, is the exhibit of Breton pottery.

Situated on the picturesque quay of the Odet within a few minutes' walk from the hotel are the potteries of Locmaria. Here for centuries two rather primitive establishments have turned out the quaint hand-painted *faïënce* to be seen everywhere in Brittany. Not only in Paris but even in the United States lovers of artistic ware cherish plates and platters, cups and saucers, bowls and jugs, decorated with the delightful figure of a Breton peasant in gala attire.

The Faiëncerie Henriot is the first to be reached in walking from Quimper. This was the establishment we visited, although all I shall say of it is equally applicable to the neighboring firm of H. B. Both potteries manufacture the traditional designs, but in their new mode we thought the decorative motifs of native sea-life by the noted illustrator Meheut and also the statuettes by Bachelet to be seen *chez* Henriot were vastly superior to the *grès moderne* perpetrated by H. B. It appears that Henriot now uses his entire name as trademark. Once his pieces were signed HR which led to confusion with his rival HB. The latter sued and won the day.

The establishment Henriot nestles at the foot of the linden-clad slope of Mont-Frugy. We were greeted on the day of our visit by an impeccable "buttons," with ears as protuberant as the handles of a Quimper jug. He led us past wood neatly stacked for use in the ovens and up steep steps. We found ourselves in the midst of the primitive yet flourishing industry. The only machine in use was the foot-wheel of certain potters.

We watched a dour fellow in sabots fashioning a lump of clay. He clapped it on his wheel, it whirled, water moistened it, the man clipped the edges and, presto! a perfectly molded plate. Near by pitchers were in construction, passed fresh from the wheel to a girl who tweaked out lips with the knowing turn of an implement. Other girls made handles skilfully. Buttons informed us that "the artists are the best paid, especially those who do the décor riche."

"You must know, madame," said he, "that we have three styles: the ordinaire [his tone expressed contempt], the demi-riche, the riche. The ordinaire is very common, you have seen it everywhere. Good, the riche has designs of ancient scenes taken from old tapestries."

"And the demi-riche?" I queried. "The name intrigues me."

"Well, most of this you see is demi-riche . . . the peasant figure, the bird or flower as in the ordinaire but with a more elaborate border . . . floral or geometric designs."

In the painting-room we paused beside a Bigouden in sugar-loaf coif, who explained to us that each artist does all the painting of a piece. As for herself, she usually finishes thirty small pitchers a day, for which she receives a franc each. Pots and Quimper bowls were filled with luscious-looking colors; a place to linger is the painting-room where dainty girls work side by side with stolid yokels. In fact, with windows looking out to the green forest, there is no room in the establishment where one would not wish to linger, save possibly the drying-room.

Our faithful page stood by us as we tarried for an unconscionable period in the exhibition room inaugurated in 1928 on the occasion of the one hundred and fiftieth anniversary of the foundation of the house. Nothing was for sale, but in our innocence we imagined that by jotting down numbers something would be gained on visiting one of the agencies in the town.

After our visit to the pottery we repaired to "La Civette," a tobacconist adjacent to the hotel. Here it was our pleasure to choose a dozen dozen plates and other pieces for shipment to America. We found our preference ran to the *demi-riche* rather than to the more elaborate designs, many of which are copies of old Rouen.

Imagine a minute shop crowded with the most tempting pottery of France. At the end of the narrow room a buxom dame was seated behind a counter piled with tobacco. We spread our favorite objects on the floor, the only available place for comparison. The buxom dame emerged from her lair to offer suggestions:

"Would the lady not care for a Madonna?" . . . as I walked past a row of holy-water receptacles. "Madame is not pious?"

I endeavored to explain that I am not an out-and-out atheist but merely Protestant.

Into the china-shop, with floor-space completely covered with our treasured choice, entered the traditional bull . . . a peasant in blue smock, descended from his cart to buy a sou's worth of tobacco. We hurriedly stacked our wares, to spread them again, only to be interrupted, at intervals of every two minutes, by elegant gentlemen in soft hats and farmers in blouses. How matters would be simplified if only samples were carried and those sold by number! However, the present system works, for of the two hundred pieces chosen all reached America in safety. I remember with amusement the remark of the custom official who sneered at our hand-wrought articles:

"Pottery . . . You'd better be glad it ain't porcelain, I'll say. What d'yuh see in these plates? They don't even stack."

"Where did you stay longest during your summer in Brittany?" I have been asked dozens of times. I answer, inevitably, "At Quimper," and if the interrogator's interest warrants the explanation I tell how it was done—not, as he supposes, consecutively but piecemeal.

Our first visit to Quimper was made eighteen years ago in autumn at time of the cattle-fair. Returning after so long a period, we found that Quimper in June, at time of the Fête-Dieu, ex-

The Cathedral dominates Quimper

ceeded our fondest expectations. Passing from Quimperlé to Châteaulin, and from Concarneau to Camaret, we had twice traversed Quimper. From Benodet we came to Quimper by launch on the devious Odet. On a Sunday, July twenty-second, we came again to the capital of Finistère—of that I shall straightway tell—and, lastly, Quimper was our base from which to motor in late August to the "Pardon of the Sea" at Sainte-Anne-de-la-Palue.

Quimper in July and August was a seething center for autocars overflowing with citizens of widely varied nationality, though we observed that French, English, and American predominated, with a goodly sprinkling of Dutch. (For so small a national group it has always seemed to me that the Dutch excel in spreading themselves over the entire surface of the globe!) We had noticed the erection of merry-go-rounds on the quays. We had read the flaming posters announcing the Fêtes des Reines de Cornouaille. Remembering with abhorrence the crowning of queens of beauty in our own land, we decided to avoid Quimper on the date announced. For days the local newspapers bruited abroad the doings to come. Impossible to avoid their head-lines. All the noted bards of Brittany were to participate. Never before had been assembled such a galaxy of Breton raiment as would be on the day of this coming fête. The costumes, modern and ancient, were to be judged in sunlight in the finest open-air theater in the province. Octogenarians from the interior, from the Monts d'Arrée and the Montagnes Noires had been prevailed upon to appear—the surviving few who habitually wear the *bragou-braz.* In addition to the singing of bards there would be exhibitions of local dances accompanied by the bagpipe and, moreover, a concourse of pipers.

Swallowing the scornful words which had been on my lips for weeks with regard to this coming occasion, I sounded Monsieur, whose disdain had perhaps surpassed my own. To my amazement I found that he, too, had surreptitiously been reading head-lines. Perhaps, said he, we should be making a mistake to miss the performance. (What insidious power has the daily press!) There would be no difficulty in motoring from our retreat beside the sea.

A Breton pardon is primarily a religious occasion. The Breton, though dressed in his best, is in a serious mood. It is at weddings that he is most light-hearted and gay, that his merrymaking truly surpasses similar festivities in more sophisticated lands. The fête of the Queens of Beauty of Cornouaille was on a par with one of those spectacular wedding parties sometimes found in Brittany (notably at Plougastel) where a dozen or more couples are wed at a single ceremony. Let me at once register my abject apologies to the citizens of Quimper for having harbored the thought that commercialism or vulgarity could lift their ugly heads in this peerless capital.

"We Bretons know how to stage a festival," an aged rustic remarked as we stood with the crowd outside the Hôtel de l'Epée, awaiting the cortège which would march on foot from the railway station to the Odet theater and later to the open-air "Théâtre de la Nature."

Call to mind all the most refined Celtic types of legend and romance, clothe them in resplendent garments, silks and velvets, gold-encrusted, lace-bedecked, ribbons and streamers fluttering on the breeze. Picture men in broad-brimmed hats and buckled shoes, wearing belts with golden clasps, silver-haired great-grandfathers garbed in the fashion of a century bygone, wrinkled grandmothers in towering coifs and laced into the wedding-gowns of fifty years ago . . . evoke, if you can, the setting of Quimper . . . its dominant cathedral, the sun-flecked quays, and you will realize that no canvas on the walls of its musée, no grand-operatic presentation can rival life in this pulsing, throbbing heart of Brittany.

Of all that we had seen and were to see in the province nothing excelled or could excel this exuberant pageant of young and old, high and low, marching together in utmost simplicity—for the Breton is of all men the most democratic. Jaffrenou, the poet and chief of bards, was wearing a white straw hat with fantastically long streamers;

Pastoral

Cueff of the golden voice marched with his lovely wife, who wore the queenly ruff and medieval costume of Pont-Aven. A bewitching group of children from Plougastel received a rippling applause equal to that given the blind pipers as, with mighty breath, they lifted us beyond time and space to the magical cadences of the *binous*.

Along the quays we march, a merry train, following the pipers as if in Hamelin town. Even the ships afloat on the Odet flutter flags of welcome. Past the ferry we go, hundreds, nay thousands strong, glittering with gold and silver. We mount to the beechwood of an ancient seminary, secluded as the Grande Chartreuse, once a retreat from the world for holy men. Here, in the heart of the woodland, has been cleared enough space to seat our numbers. A dais, with semicircular benches for the performers, stands against the background of a fantastic beech whose spreading branches form a stage set. The "theater" has been planned so that the audience sits in profound shadow, while those upon the stage bask in sunlight. No curtain is needed. There is no tawdry makeshift; no paint nor powder here. Naught is there to conceal. This is a festival of spontaneous song and dance, of nature's setting for bewildering beauty, of traditional rejoicing by concerted flute and bagpipe. We are in Cornouaille! This is Quimper!

Sainte-Anne-la-Palue
Patron of the Bretons of Cornouaille

CHAPTER XIV

THE PARDON OF PARDONS

Incredible as it may seem to the skeptically minded, it is believed by the devout Breton that Breton blood flowed in the veins of Jesus. The story is told in this fashion:

Sainte Anne, the grandmother of Christ, was, of course, a Bretonne. She was of royal blood and dwelt in a castle overlooking the shores of the Bay of Douarnenez. Her husband, who was a wealthy landowner, was as cruel and brutal as he was avaricious. Before the birth of her child Sainte Anne longed to escape from this tyrannical tormentor, and therefore she fled to the shore of the bay, fell on her knees, and plead to Almighty God to protect her. Immediately a boat manned by an angel put to shore and on the frail craft Sainte Anne was transported to Judea. In the town of Nazareth her daughter Mary—the Holy Virgin, likewise by inheritance a Bretonne—first saw the light.

Sainte Anne remained in the Holy Land for many years until Mary had reached a marriageable age and found in Joseph a suitable husband; then, heart-sick, as well she might be, for her native Brittany, Sainte Anne prayed that she should be allowed to return to her own country. The miraculous boat appeared, in answer to her petition, and in it she voyaged in safety to Cornouaille. Finding that her wicked husband had died, Sainte Anne divided her vast inheritance amongst her vassals and took up her abode in a humble hut beside the Bay of Douarnenez, at a place called the Anse de la Palue, which signifies the Cove of the Marshy Plain. Here it was that she was visited several times by her grandson, the boy Jesus.

On one of these occasions Jesus said to Sainte Anne: "Grandmother, what dost thou wish me to do for thy Bretons?"

To which Sainte Anne replied: "Give them a remedy for all ills."

Thereupon Jesus struck with his staff upon the ground and there welled forth the sparkling waters of a spring whose healing properties are famed until this day at what is now known as Sainte-Anne-de-la-Palue.

It is said that when Sainte Anne at last departed this life her body miraculously vanished from the earth. Some time after this occurrence fishermen of the bay, in hauling their nets, drew up a life-size stone image of the saint. This statue they planned to carry to a distant sanctuary, but so extraordinarily did the stone increase in weight as it passed the sacred fountain that the bearers were forced to put down their burden. In this manner do Breton saints express their preferences for certain localities and indicate where chapels should be erected.

Emile Souvestre has explained the origin of the word "pardon" as used in Brittany to denote the fête of the patron saint of a church or chapel. In former times the clergy granted indulgences on these occasions; therefore the word "pardon" has come to be synonymous with the fête itself. From early spring until late autumn these gatherings, great or small, enliven the entire province. Religious in character though they be—and no one who has attended a Breton pardon can question the fervor of the participants—yet after the climax of the procession, which usually is held in conjunction with vespers, there is apt to be dancing and jollity extending far into the night, if not, indeed, prolonged into a three-day festival. To the spectator who would see the best, though he attend but one, let me recommend the pardon of Sainte-Anne-de-la-Palue.

Held on the last Saturday and Sunday of August, the festival of Sainte Anne, like the pardon of Sainte-Anne-d'Auray held toward the end of July, falls at a time when Brittany is overrun with tourists. Though automobiles come from far and near, they have not, owing to the fête's unique situation, been able to mar the harmony of the whole. Unlike Auray, Sainte-Anne-de-la-Palue has no town or pretentious modern basilica. The chapel is in Gothic style and is mellowed by moss and lichen into the semblance of a greater age than it actually possesses. Near by stands the granite fountain with its venerated spring. Deserted throughout the year, this region of dunes beside the sea was all animation upon the day of our own visit.

To reach Sainte-Anne-de-la-Palue from Quimper our motor sped at twilight through gray-roofed villages where lights began to twinkle. Blowing clouds fitfully concealed or exposed the aspiring form of Ménez-Hom, yearning skyward. The breath of the sea was in our nostrils, for had we not returned to the domain of the temptress Ahès? Would we, perhaps, in the moonlight as we stood upon the shore, sense the presence of the enchantress who it is said still haunts the purlieus of the Bay of Douarnenez? Tranquil was Locronan of treasured memories, its historic *place* devoid of loafers, who were doubtless gathered about glowing hearths. Here and there rays of light escaped from shuttered casements. Jutting lanterns, of the type from which a man might swing, cast pools of golden radiance along the cobbled street. In the moonlight the sparse pines of Locronan's Hill stood stark as phalanxes of a spectral army. As we neared Plonévez-Porzay we were loath to turn away from Ménez-Hom who had bared his mighty breast for a rapturous tryst with Lady Moon. . . .

Diana, Ahès, Sainte Anne—pagan goddess, sinner, saint—your paths converge upon this fateful shore of old Armorica.

Around the isolated chapel upon the margin of the sea a village of tents had sprung into being. Camp-fires shed a fluctuating light. Savory odors arose from steaming caldrons. Entering the sanctuary, we were confronted by a sea of coifs. The statue of Sainte Anne with the youthful Virgin at her knees, typical Bretonnes both, was the focus of a seething throng. Every pilgrim bore a lighted taper. Flaring torches around the shrine sent fantastic shadows leaping and darting ceilingward. The recesses of the building were in darkness save for an occasional smoking lamp. There would, we perceived, not have been standing-room for all who wished to enter, if the worshipers had not been constantly changing to give place to newcomers. Pilgrims without the building circled the edifice and formed, as church bells boomed the hour, an undulating cortège, a stream of spluttering candles. Hundreds strong, they marched to the crest of the hill overlooking a moonlit shore, an angry wind-blown sea. The tremulous voice of a priest was lifted leading a canticle; his hand, wan and frail in the moonlight, led the fervent outpouring of a thousand souls. Bengal lights from the belfry tower flared with the lurid glare of a conflagration. Thus, swift as a dream, passed the Miraculous Even.

After a night spent on comfortable mattresses spread upon the floor of a bedroom in Quimper (no, they had not understood that there were to be four in our party and not a bed was left, but there were mattresses!) we motored once more to Sainte-Anne-de-la-Palue. The pilgrims had indulged in no such luxuries as bedrooms. Many had spent the night upon their knees within the chapel, while others had been huddled in tents which gave but meager shelter from uproarious gusts of wind.

Rain, that unwelcome accompaniment of outdoor spectacles in Little as in Great Britain, had fallen in early morning but had mercifully held off after the mass at the time when the bishops of Dara and Quimper, old friends of ours by now, issued from the church to march to the open-air auditorium. After the service we repaired to the cliffs overlooking the Bay of Douarnenez. To our right the familiar peninsula of Camaret rose stark above ominously purple water; to our left stretched the rocky ridge of the Pointe du Raz; while straight before us, across the fringe of a succession of breakers, across the surface of the foam-flecked bay, our eyes rested upon the vast reaches of the Atlantic.

All about us on the sandy dunes, seeking shelter in natural indentations in the heath or with backs to stone walls, parties had assembled. Here we recognized the fluttering cap-strings of Quimper; there the towering cones of Pont-l'Abbé; yonder the queenly ruffs, the ribbons agitated by the wind, of the "peasant princesses" of Pont-Aven; beyond, the snug starched caps of Plougastel. Lunch-baskets were opened, bread was doled out and slabs of cheese, links of sausage were drawn forth, bottles of wine or cider. Young and old settled themselves with adjusting of ample shawls and show of white embroidered petticoats. *Glaziks* in the blue jackets of Quimper, *duiks* in the black velvet of Fouessant and Quimperlé, sailors a plenty joined their women-folk. We were reminded of the groups that Simon loves to paint . . . year after year he has gathered inspiration at Sainte-Anne-de-la-Palue.

No sooner were we comfortably ensconced than my hat was lifted from my head by the rising gale and borne seaward. A half-dozen sturdy Bretons were instantly in pursuit. One, in the purple jacket of Plougastel, vaulted over a wall and captured the whirling truant before its final descent to the sea. Laughter was provoked by the incident, which served to break the ice and cause a general fusion of groups. We expressed a common resentment by turning a cold shoulder when a photographer with a moving-picture apparatus endeavored to convert our easy attitudes into a news reel. Our dignity was short-lived. After the gale, as we had

The Pardon of Sainte

Anne-de-la-Palue

hardly so soon anticipated, came the downpour. Those of us who had brought umbrellas found them instantly wrong side out, yet we had half expected this ending and fled, young and old, stout and thin, toward the distant shelter of our motor-cars. In high good humor the drenched throngs scattered, scurrying figures aiding one another over the sandy ridges of the dunes.

Vespers. Wild wind and scudding clouds. The rain had ceased. The salt tang of the sea (or was it a direct answer to their petitions?) had given new life to the very beggars. Those derelicts we had seen moaning: "Comme c'est triste! Regardez ce malheureux!" taken off guard appeared to have grown jolly between performances. Only one of their number, a blind man, remained at his post, jingling the coins in his cup and muttering, "Merci, merci tout le monde."

Multitudes have assembled for the long-heralded event. The cortège is headed by muscular *glaziks*—wearing the Breton over-jacket or *chupen*—erect despite the enormous weight of banners. The usual outpouring of Breton fête-day apparel is outdone at la Palue where gold-incrusted velvets are lavishly displayed. From family chests are drawn treasured belongings that never see the light save once a year in honor of Sainte Anne.

To the sound of drums the faithful march. A thousand voices are lifted in the familiar canticle:

Sainte Anne, ô bonne Mère,
Toi que nous implorons,
Entends notre prière,
Et bénis tes Bretons.

Pondering on this spontaneous manifestation of devotion, we wonder what the future holds in store. Was it not Anatole Le Braz who said, in speaking of this "Pardon of the Sea" at la Palue, that this festival dates from a remote period before the dawn of the Christian Era? Here, in the month of August, in those obscure pagan centuries the people annually assembled for the worship of a goddess sometimes invoked by the name of Ahès.

"She was adored yet hated. She was irresistible, and fatal. Who does not recognize in her the living personification of the sea?" Did not Sainte Anne herself sail across the sea? No wonder this is the sailors' pardon of pardons.

What vivid memories are evoked by the tarnished medal lying upon my desk on which I read the familiar inscription: "Souvenir de Saint-Anne la Palue," and, in Breton, "Santez Anna ar Palud."

Bride and Bridegroom of Pont-l'Abbé

CHAPTER XV

BIGOUDENS AT HOME

Ever since our arrival in Brittany—indeed, since the time we had set foot upon the platform of the Gare Montparnasse in Paris—we had been attracted by the bizarre costumes and pronounced racial characteristics of the Bigoudens. Those of the older generations were almost without exception short of stature, sturdy, leather-skinned, with none of the beauty and elegance to be found so frequently in other parts of Brittany, notably at Plougastel and at the Ile de Sein and, of a more sophisticated order, at Quimperlé and Pont-Aven. Yet there was something about the homely faces of these people not without its own appeal. The older women, in their stiff costumes and miter-shaped head-gear, suggested often, both as to figures and physiognomy, the Duchess of "Alice in Wonderland" fame. The fathers of families had the look of dour seamen, dogged, taciturn. It was only the younger generation, the post-war vintage, that was taller and less racially distinct. Having seen Bigoudens in numbers at the fête at Quimper, we naturally decided that we should at the first opportunity make a stay in their own section of the province, the peninsula lying to the southwest of Quimper, with capital at Pont-l'Abbé.

The usual mode of approach is to motor from Quimper to Pont-l'Abbé and Penmarc'h. Our own, as it happened, was from Audierne (unfortunately the highway does not skirt the coast and railway there is none) to the extreme tip of the Pointe de Penmarc'h, where stands the lighthouse of Eckmühl. It was here, in the modest inn, Hôtel du Phare, that we decided to stop rather than at the somewhat larger hotel at Saint-Guénolé.

As we approached our inn, late of an August afternoon, it was barely visible for the clouds of blowing smoke arising from pyres of burning seaweed. Even indoors the odor of smoldering kelp pervaded, forcing an entrance when windows were shut through invisible crevices. One of our barren rooms overlooked the lighthouse grounds with their formal planting of tamarisks; how a sprig of tamarisk in a florist's window transports me to the wind-blown coast of France! Our other bedroom at the back of the house had a view typically Breton—open fields, low-lying cottages. Here, as night fell, we watched the powerful white ray, a magic sword in brightness, pass at rhythmic intervals over the humble dwellings which, emerging from blackness, gleamed momentarily and seemed to cower as though in presence of a dread nocturnal reaper.

Minute followed minute, hour followed hour, and still the pitiless swath of light, revealing the poverty of these dwellings, alternated with abysmal blackness. To close our eyelids to shut out the blinding light was as useless as to close our casements against the insinuating smoke. We had deliberately chosen to taste the flavor of life at Penmarc'h. We had sought this source of light and found it . . . were immersed, body and soul, in brightness, purified by its cleansing baptism. Loud-voiced merrymakers passed beneath our windows. Our dreams were punctuated with silence and with song, with darkness and with light.

Dawn found us eager to explore this land so foreign to any we had yet seen. We were driven in a rickety car along the rock-strewn coast. At the Trou-de-l'Enfer, a cavern on the margin of the Bay of Audierne, our chauffeur told us had dwelt in pagan times, so runs the legend, Ar-mernoz (the Woman of the Night), druidess of the Ile de Sein. The rock of the Torch with its ominous surf was pointed out, where in the year 1870 five members of his family were swept to death before the eyes of the horrified prefect of Finistère.

A tidal wave in the sixteenth century did much to destroy the prosperity of Penmarc'h, which at that time had reached its peak. The devastated region was further scourged by the ravages of the brigand Fontenelle. Nowadays the traveler comes occasionally upon a surviving church or isolated half-ruined manor—all that remains to tell of the brilliant prosperity of Penmarc'h, once the rival of Nantes. The stretch of rocky coast-line from the point of Penmarc'h to Saint-Guénolé is rich in the "harvest of the sea." It was here that Lemordant painted his husky Bigoudens wresting their sustenance from the waves. We were shown the artist's cottage and the chapel of Notre-Dame-de-la-Joie perched on a rock beside the sea, primitive, rejoicing the heart of painters.

"It is a land of the lost," our driver, a native of Quimper, remarked, failing to comprehend our appreciation as we watched a group of barelegged women raking on the beach, their gaudy woolen skirts upturned, spreading the dripping weed upon the rocks.

Obtaining the key from an old salt among several loafers who were gazing seaward, we entered Notre-Dame-de-la-Joie, which revives its past but once a year, on the fête of the Assumption of the Virgin. Expected ex-votos of fishing-boats hung before the altar, a two-stacked steamer and—a fresh note—the model of an aëroplane presented by a surviving aviator of the World War.

Farther along the coast we reached the chapel

of Tronoan which overlooks the Bay of Audierne. Its weather-worn fifteenth-century calvary is the prototype of others in Brittany. Having a fondness for the lonely region of dunes and marshland, we penetrated as far as our car could take us and then proceeded afoot to the chapel of Saint Viaud which stands near the isolated rock whence this Irish monk, voyaging miraculously in his trough of stone, leaped ashore.

Built on the very margin of the waves, the saint's chapel by a miracle has escaped being swept to sea. The edifice is one of the smallest shrines of equal beauty in the province. Its granite spire is in the best Breton tradition, open on all sides with flamboyant decorations and the four corners carved with apocryphal beasts. On two sides of the building, stone steps lead from the ground to the belfry. Two low doors and the chancel window form the only apertures. The exterior was, on the day of our visit, incased in orange lichen which glowed in sunlight as did likewise the mellow growth on roofs of deserted cottages near by. We wandered across the marshes toward the *étang,* beyond whose still waters rose the distant spire of Tronoan.

The sun was dazzling, the heat oppressive. Quivering waves of light fluctuated over the outstretched sands. We were uncertain as to our bearings: what was water, what land, what mirage? The boom of the waves resounded in our ears, the cry of water-fowl; black and white *vanneaux*, heron-like creatures, stared us out of countenance. Who were we, mere humans, they seemed to insinuate, to force our unwanted presence upon the rightful possessors of the marsh? As once at the site of the submerged city of Ys we had beheld a lonely moorland, an isolated lake, the ever present ocean, so now again we saw a marshland, tarn, and sea through the transfiguring veil of Armorica's legendary past.

The word "Penmarc'h" signifies Horse's Head—some trace the derivation to a surmised resemblance of the Pointe de Penmarc'h to the head of a horse, while others conjecture that in primitive times the peninsula was noted for its race of wild ponies. However this may be, the name to-day connotes three things: the reef-bound point, noted for its thunderous surf; the town of Penmarc'h, once prosperous, now visited because of its church; and the solitary menhir of Penmarc'h, standing near the road to Loctudy. This menhir, a mighty monolith of granite, is formed in a manner to suggest the protruding foot (with great toe pointed skyward) of some prehistoric giant swallowed at time of cataclysm.

The Church of Saint-Nonna at Penmarc'h, a Gothic survival begun in 1308, was constructed by the wealthy privateers in the centuries before the discovery of Newfoundland, when Penmarc'h prospered as a center of cod-fishing. Those were days when Penmarc'h "could equip her 3000 men-at-arms, and shelter behind her jetties a fleet of 800 craft." The façade of the church is decorated with archaic reliefs of fishing-boats of the time of the Duchess Anne, the date of whose first marriage almost coincides with the date of the discovery of America.

The toll of the sea has always been heavy along this rock-bound shore, which has likewise been ravaged by pirates and from which Fontenelle sailed with three hundred barks of booty to his lair in the harbor of Douarnenez. In the historic tempest and tidal wave three hundred boats, each with a crew of seven men, were lost. In 1681, Colbert issued an ordinance to the people of Kerlouan on the Point of Penmarc'h that "those who light deceptive fires at night, to attract and wreck ships, will be punished with death, and their bodies attached to a mast planted at the places where they had made the fires." The other side of the picture shows the heroic sacrifice of many life-savers while rendering aid to barks in distress.

Apropos of Pont-l'Abbé the matter-of-fact Baring-Gould writes: "Here one is in the midst of the Bigouden country. Observe the curious and ugly way of wearing the hair and the coiffes. There are many folds of skirts fastened round the waists. The women are remarkably plain and have staring eyes and expose their teeth"! Those of us who

After vespers at Saint-Tual

have seen for ourselves or who know the country through the works of Lemordant and Lucien Simon beg leave to differ with this dismissal of the women and their costumes.

One of the outstanding features of the Bigoudens is that they in no way resemble other Bretons. It has been frequently said that this difference is not merely social but is indicative of a fundamentally different stock. Many writers, fancying a likeness between the Bigoudens and Mongolians or Tartars, have endeavored to prove an Oriental strain. These advocates point out the stolidity, the not infrequent almond eye, the barbaric Asiatic splendor of the costumes in which red and orange predominate in a manner to suggest a link with India. The fact that yellow (the color of dead leaves) is used for mourning also is mentioned as a Chinese characteristic. Despite the plausibility of many of the arguments brought forward, modern critical opinion seems to incline away from the Oriental or Phenician theory of the origin of the Bigoudens and toward the probability of their belonging to a primitive pre-Aryan race, which would make them the original Breton inhabitants prior to the Celtic invasion.

Whether or not the arabesques worn alike on the breasts of men and women's garments represent an endless chain, the Celtic symbol of immortality, or whether they are indeed designs dating from the age of polished stone and to be found

equaled by the gorgeous orange-red garments of the congregation. Icons, the women resembled; themselves, it might have been supposed, objects of worship.

Nothing seen on the second Sunday of August at Pont-l'Abbé compared in spontaneity, however, to what awaited us at vesper-time on driving to Saint-Tual by the sea. There had been a benediction of the fishing fleet, flags still flew from the few boats assembled on this isolated shore. Peasant carts were drawn up near booths where girls in fantastically tall lace coifs, velvets and gaudy aprons, youths in many-ribboned hats tried their luck at the clay pigeons. Crowds streamed along the lanes. Mothers, bulky as only a Bigouden can be with the aid of the round bustle worn beneath the outer skirt, trailed their innumerable offspring toward the too tempting stands of edibles. Little girls in vivid bonnets, glittering with golden paillettes, fed bonbons to bewitching babies, their faces framed in silver-beaded satin. Behind them fluttered awnings, glaring white as sails in sunlight, and above, around, dominating as do the heavens in Brittany, glowed a sky of radiant blue with cloud legions of angelic brightness—a Lemordant canvas.

Although Lemordant, deprived of sight, may no longer paint this region, Simon and Dauchez still find their inspiration here. Brothers-in-law, masters both in their chosen fields, they come annually from Paris to spend their summers . . . Dauchez to a bleak perch on the beach near Saint-Tual reached with difficulty by automobile—a means of locomotion abhorred by this painter—but ideal as a base (so he has used it for a quarter century) for yachting . . . Simon to his admirably remodeled semaphore of Combrit at Sainte-Marine.

Gay as the flower-like colors which he paints at Breton pardons are the blossoms that bedeck the garden of Lucien Simon. The master has chosen to color his steps a celestial blue like that of hydrangea hedges which form the notable approach to the sheltered house. Gardens where lovingly clipped trees stand sentinel between the charming occupants of the house and the wind-tossed pines, exposed to the ferocious tempests of the Atlantic. That Simon, by whom the Bigoudens are to-day best interpreted, is not himself of the race nor yet of Breton birth, is scarcely worthy of remark in this land of miracles.

Pont-Aven — Le Bois d'Amour

CHAPTER XVI

CONCARNEAU AND PONT-AVEN

LINKED names are those of Concarneau and Pont-Aven. The fame of Concarneau depends upon the surpassing beauty of its boats, that of Pont-Aven upon the rural scene—the fast-flowing Aven with its moss-grown mills. Both towns are renowned for the unprecedented richness of native costume. Given the picturesque setting, the wealth of appealing models, the equable climate, the moderate prices, the more than comfortable quarters, is it surprising that artists from many lands have flocked to these resorts? To the Bohemian painter they were—and to a lesser degree, since the influx of tourists in automobile days, still are—an earthly paradise.

Familiarity with other fishing ports—Camaret, Douarnenez, Audierne, even le Palais on Belle-Ile—does not prepare one for Concarneau. Many prefer the town in August, at time of regattas and the festival of Filets Bleus, but give me Concarneau in mid-June, at time of the "arming" of the boats. This ceremony consists of the renovation and outfitting of the fishing fleet and, needless to add, has no military significance. We had come to the town unprepared for the orgy of color to which we were immediately treated.

Gorgeous craft filled both the harbors. Against the old gray walls of the ancient citadel were massed the dark hulls, the multicolored sails, the delicate drying nets, blue as the sparkling sea, of the sardine boats. The outer port was jammed with larger craft, the mighty dundees of the tunny fishermen. Sails flapped in the wind, sails, freshly dyed, were spread to dry along the dock, sails of ocher, terra-cotta, ultramarine.

Fishermen, strikingly garbed in patched blue or red, swarmed among the boats. Clinging to topmasts, perched on booms, brush in hand, they added the vivid touches of color or preened the long "antennæ" of the tunny boats. Hulls glistened with fresh paint. Outside our Atlantic Hôtel, overlooking both dock and open sea, white canvas was spread, awaiting a bath of color. Seamen with bronzed and tattooed arms dipped brushes in vats of luscious pigment; and one, a hairy fellow, barefooted, with rolled trousers, poured a brick-red dye recklessly, wading in it, dancing a jig, menacing his comrades with a dripping broom.

All day and every day the dyeing of the sails went forward. We were awakened in the morning by barrows laden with white canvases being trundled from the shop of Le Rose, Volier.

One lean seaman stood out conspicuously among his comrades. His white blouse had been patched with red and his trousers were a vivid blue—a costume which would have admirably represented the tricolor of France. This sailor's companion was a lad in faded salmon. We accosted the pair as they spread their handiwork to dry upon the rocks. I had often asked, in Breton ports, the reason for the colored sails, and had invariably received the answer that the paint preserves the canvas. The lad, however, with an ingenuous stare, responded:

"Sails don't mildew as soon when they're painted, but Madame wants to know why so many different colors at Concarneau? It is that our boats shall be beautiful. There are none to equal them in all Cornouaille."

Several hundred tunny boats come to Concarneau from the island of Groix, noted for its fishermen; the backbone of the navy, these men have been called. The ships are equipped with mighty wings which give them swift flight. After the outfitting the *thonniers* depart for deeper waters, often to be gone three weeks on end. Some crews hasten back with as many as six hundred tuna fish aboard, while others, out of luck, must face a poor catch or a disastrous calm that prevents return before the spoiling of the fish. The mole at Concarneau is a lively scene during the unloading of the dundees, which—because of their size and the vivid crimson, green, blue, and yellow paint that decorates their gleaming hulls and masts—suggest junks at Hongkong. Concarneau is the center of the canning industry. The tunny boats are for the most part built at Belle-Ile but are armed at Groix or Concarneau.

War has been waged for generations over the proper kind of net for use in fishing the sardine—the picturesque blue net, the *filet droit,* or the *filet tournant,* coarser and brown in color. The fishermen, most exploited of men, have frequently been at the mercy of local syndicates, formed supposedly for their protection. A notorious example of official red tape was the fate of the petition of 1915. Sardines there were a plenty at Concarneau and Douarnenez but none in the region of Saint-Guénolé. The fishermen of the latter plead for permission to use the *filet tournant* in the pursuit of numerous schools of little mackerel. Local authorities referred the plea first to Quimper, then to Saint-Malo, and finally to Paris. Needless to say, before the answer came the schools of little mackerel had betaken themselves to parts unknown.

Disgust with the speculation by profiteers in cod roe, which is used as bait in sardine-catching, has driven many fishermen to embrace Socialism. Louis XV was so concerned with this exploitation of his Breton subjects that he arranged the purchase of the roe in Norway, whence it still comes, and had it distributed at cost.

The sardines, starting in the Mediterranean, move habitually along the coasts of Spain and Portugal, arriving with the milder temperature of summer off the coast of Brittany, and still later in the season reaching Cornwall, where they obtain a size unknown in France. In plain English, the French sardine is known as an immature pilchard, but, despite its shimmering beauty, I fear that, unlike the rose, not by that name nor any other would it smell sweet.

Individuals sensitive to horrid smells suffer at Concarneau. I place myself among their number, but, all things considered, the game is more than worth the candle. There are some, I know, like my illustrator and my artist friends of Gloucester, Massachusetts (our American Concarneau), who profess a liking for the odor of drying fish. But at Concarneau the canneries are not the worst offenders. The most breath-stopping stench is that which emanates from the harbor, noisome at low tide. You may, however, escape this evil moment by retirement to the Atlantic Hôtel where seabreezes prevail. Those who prefer their local color at a still greater distance may put up at the beach or across the bay of la Forêt at Beg-Meil, whose hotels on the dunes are frequented by members of the Comédie-Française.

Artists, however, will unfalteringly remain at their posts in Concarneau. Which one of us at the Atlantic, for all the fragrant roses of Beg-Meil, would have relinquished our glimpses of the sardine fleet's departure before the dawn? its return at sunset? The latter ceremony seemed staged for our dinner-hour. As we reveled in *sardines frites* the boats, drifting like gulls before the wind, would float harborward. As the buoy was reached, topsails would drop out of sight. The distant beach of le Cabellou with its low-lying trees and smoking seaweed pyres made fitting background, while appropriate foreground was not lacking—groups of aged seamen puffing reminiscent pipes.

The Ville-Close, or walled town, covering an islet in the harbor and washed by the waves at high tide, resembles a miniature Saint-Malo. The oldest portions of the ramparts, which have been much restored, date from the fourteenth century. In 1373 the English, then in possession of the isle, were besieged by du Guesclin. In 1576 its governor was surprised and overcome by a party of Calvinists, who were, however, not long able to hold the town against the outraged population. For centuries the Ville-Close was considered one of the four strongest fortified places of Brittany.

Concarneau was one of the five Breton towns held by Louis XII until he obtained a promise from Anne de Bretagne that she would be his wife. Anne formally pledged herself (on August 19, 1498, less than five months after the death of her husband Charles VIII) on condition that he could obtain the necessary dispensations and the annulment of his marriage to Charles' sister, Jeanne de France. Louis thereupon relinquished Saint-Malo, Brest, and Concarneau, retaining Fougères and Nantes for surety until the accomplishment of his marriage. It seems unlikely that Anne ever visited her subjects at Concarneau, but on her triumphant tour of Brittany in 1506, when she journeyed from Nantes to Folgoët and to Vitré, many of them probably turned out to welcome her as she passed with her queenly train from Quimperlé to Quimper. The main bastion of the Ville-Close bears her name.

My chief remembrance of our walk through the one thoroughfare of the Ville-Close, now occupied by fishermen, is that an eccentric dealer in ancient furniture used every wile to prevail upon Monsieur to barter his sketches for certain antiques . . . a subtle flattery.

Amusing incidents were the rule at Concarneau. Feeling that we should see from the water the Ville-Close, the docks, the myriad boats, we set about to find the owner of a rowboat. Having interrogated a ruddy mariner, we understood that he would be willing to forgo his tinkering to take us. We were, however, shifted to a friend who proved to be a mute.

"He will not understand you," so spoke the

The fame of Concarneau

depends upon the beauty of its boats

mariner of our choice, "unless you speak to him in Breton."

Speak to him in Breton indeed! We longed miraculously to receive the gift of the Breton tongue —a gift bestowed on the missionary Père Maunoir, according to the fresco in the cathedral at Quimper.

We had, unfortunately, made a pretext of going fishing, and now, with lines and bait procured, we felt ourselves committed, though the excursion with our mute companion boded ill. The man was pock-marked, and wind-blown as to hair. Noxious whiffs blew from his pipe and he muttered inarticulate sounds. His reeking rowboat was propelled from the stern, in the Breton way. Under the chains of anchored boats we glided, narrowly avoiding now a bow, now a stern of the countless craft whose bare masts formed a leafless forest. We noted names on sterns: *Jean-Jaurès, Yves-Marie-Yvonne, Gars de Groix, Ange Gardien, Etoile de la Nativité, Humanité,* according to whether the owners were devout or Socialist . . . the ancient quarrel which divides the French.

We anchored off the shore of le Cabellou. Of luck we had none, the hour being neither early enough nor late enough to entice a fish to nibble. Suddenly, on a distant pier at Concarneau, we observed a youth performing antics, waving arms in mad gesticulations. Our bear of a fellow mumbled guttural sounds. There was, it dawned upon us, a connection between this performance on the dock and our own length of stay. Our anchor was abruptly pulled. With no knowledge of why or wherefore (a knowledge which was, indeed, consistently withheld) we made for the shore, in order, we surmised, that our gruff companion should find a more congenial occupation.

Days of tempest followed. We watched the fleet making for port, even the two-masters scurrying into the foam-flecked harbor. Combers broke on the rocks. Pools of rain-water took color from the newly dyed sails. Seamen in slickers, consulting the barometer of the Laboratoire Maritime, wagged their heads and muttered:

"Stormy. Always bad weather!"

When at last the sun emerged with splendor, the choppy water of the bay gleamed blue as the Mediterranean. We felt moved to seek a sail-boat. Setting out on our errand along the docks, we passed the shop Au Sabot d'Or. At the threshold red blouses were buoyant in the wind. We went by the wine-shops where old salts congregate. One *buvette* had a caged parrot, taking the air, which shrieked at us in the Breton tongue. The owner of the place, a piratical-looking fellow with a peg leg, emerged to leer at us with a sinister grin. Passing seamen carrying floats and pots of odorous tar were convulsed with laughter.

The artists from our hotel had set up easels on the docks. Here we observed the lank girl with shingled hair and the accent of Montana. She painted bareheaded, wearing tortoise-shell goggles. Her friends (so she had confided in us during the period of rain) had told her, when she won the traveling scholarship, that English is understood everywhere in France.

"But you know," she had complained, "I can't afford to go to the hotels where they speak it, and I don't know one word of French. You watch me, though; I'll learn their lingo."

There was Smythe of Maine, in red trousers and blue blouse, at his post, progressing famously on his study of the *Tante-Titine,* a black-hulled bark with sails of Venetian red and a mist of blue nets hanging from her masthead. The canvas would be exhibited at this painter's one-man show in Paris. He and his vivacious wife, with sparkling black eyes and silvery bobbed hair, had unburdened their hearts to us on the superiority of Boston brown bread and blueberry cakes to anything to be found at a French pastry shop.

There were the amateurs from San Francisco, elderly sisters, who had divulged to us that they drank unboiled water and milk everywhere, yes, even in Spain; the bearded Scotchman with his collie; the dainty Parisian, standing to work, in modish hat and scarf, wearing gauntlets. But why go on? Their number was legion.

The sloop *Amazon* at last secured, we set off with the wind, scuppers in water, spray in faces. Heading toward the Glenan Isles, the open sea, we looked back on Beg-Meil, a shimmering beach above which piled billowy clouds. When we returned, a shining white Concarneau gleamed across the water. Even the crude sardine houses assumed a silvery hue. How often had we, at this twilight hour, watched home-coming sails glide harborward.

"Now if we were only at our windows, we could see our boat come in!" exclaimed Monsieur, with rare detachment.

Pont-Aven, renowned of old as the town of fourteen mills and fifteen houses, owes its fame chiefly to one woman. When Julia Guillou came to the Hôtel des Voyageurs not a dozen painters had found their way to Pont-Aven. Julia was, appropriately, a miller's daughter. At a tender age she was sent as a maid to an inn at Concarneau. As there were no roads, the journey was made afoot by the lanes. Her astonishment was great on her return after ten years to behold a highway. It was soon after Julia had come back that the owner of the Hôtel des Voyageurs was called from home on secret business and, knowing the girl's worth, prevailed upon Julia to take her place. The tragic event of the owner, on her return, hanging herself in the courtyard of the hotel, led to uncertainty as to the fate of the inn.

The artists and writers who had profited by

Julia's régime offered to lend her money for marketing, and with the aid of an elderly farmer this peasant girl of twenty-three bought the hotel. This was in 1871. Up to the time of the World War (in 1914 Julia was stricken by illness from which she never recovered, although she was not released by death until 1927) her inn, generally known as the Hôtel Julia, had made Pont-Aven the most popular resort for artists in all Brittany. Here in 1913–14 Lemordant painted his ceiling for the theater of Rennes. Here the English author Vachell stayed and, in 1906, published "The Face of Clay" with its delightful dedication to Mademoiselle Julia Guillou. Here came Blanche Willis Howard, who described Mademoiselle as having "the air of a Roman matron in a Breton coif." The result of her visit was "Guenn" with its account of life at Pont-Aven and Concarneau. Here came painters innumerable, English, American, French: Wylie, Harrison, Swift, Guillou, Gaugin, Le Blant, Renoir, to name but a few.

Julia, it is said—she was rarely called "Mademoiselle" in those days—was ever the last to bed and the first to rise. Her forceful personality, her vision, her kindness of heart endeared her to all her pensionnaires. She nursed them when they fell ill, lent them money to pay their debts, and on occasion was known even to bury them in her own lot in the cemetery.

In the beginning her artists paid fifty francs a month, and the cuisine at the Hôtel Julia has always been famous. In 1900 the large building known as the annex was constructed, with its spacious summer dining-room, bedrooms, and artists' studios. Port-Manech, a ruined fort on the coast some two miles to the southeast of Pont-Aven, was bought in 1904 and made into a retreat for those who preferred a quieter life than that of Pont-Aven. In 1903, Botrel came to sing in the salle-à-manger of the annex—an event which was to have far-reaching consequences.

Théodore Botrel had perhaps as picturesque a career as any modern Breton. Born in Dinan in the year 1868, Botrel was the son of a humble blacksmith. He was taken to Paris at an early age, and at eleven received a certificate for having accomplished his primary studies. Ground down by poverty in his youth, Botrel was never to be awarded any other diploma. He was, indeed, the first of his family to read and write. His father apprenticed him to a locksmith, but he showed no aptitude for the calling. At the age of fifteen the boy recited to his astonished parents a poem of his own composition:

Ma plume qui n'est pas à vendre
  Gardera toujours sa fierté,
Toujours la première à défendre
  Et le Peuple et sa liberté.

Le cœur joyeux, l'âme ravie,
Pour l'opprimé, pour le sans-pain,
Je veux lutter toute ma vie,
La plume en main.

True to the sentiments expressed in the poem, Botrel was all his life an ardent advocate and friend of the poor, the oppressed. "The workers had more than his pity, they had his admiration."

At the age of twenty-eight Botrel made his début at a cabaret in the faubourg Saint-Honoré. He received some applause. A few days later—when he sang his original poems the "Round of the Chestnuts," "Fanchette," the "Paimpolaise"—the entire audience rose and acclaimed him. Two years later, in 1898, his "Chansons de Chez Nous" was crowned by the French Academy. In rapid succession volume followed volume—poems of his native province written in the French tongue and set to popular airs. Returning to Brittany, partly out of preference and partly for his health, Botrel settled at Port-Blanc, where he became the pupil and friend of Anatole Le Braz. Botrel's verses spread like wild-fire, carried by deep-sea fishermen to Iceland and to the banks of Newfoundland. The poet awoke to find himself the most popular of the bards.

The coming of Botrel to Pont-Aven was a happy occurrence. Charmed by the warmth and color of the place, in striking contrast to the bleak Port-Blanc on the north coast, and by the heartiness of his reception, Botrel decided to return the following summer . . . later he made Pont-Aven his home. He it was who organized the first fête of the Fleurs d'Ajoncs, held at the time of the blossoming gorse. This was the first of the regional fêtes (not to be confused with the religious pardons), and, partly because of the personality and golden voice of its founder, during his lifetime the festival drew enormous crowds to Pont-Aven.

The author of a brochure on Botrel at Pont-Aven (the poet's Ker Botrel is still the summer home of Madame Botrel and her two bewitching daughters) has called the bard "an apostle of Patriotism and Faith." Botrel expended his health and energy without stint—one year giving three hundred concerts—in order to spread his message of idealism and for the financial benefit of the causes in which he believed. His tours carried him beyond the boundaries of France, to Canada, Tunis, Belgium and Holland, and Switzerland—wherever the French tongue is understood. Everywhere he was acclaimed, and nowhere more than by the soldiers at the front during the World War. Botrel's career came to an end in 1926, when the poet, worn out by his labors, died and was buried in the cemetery at Pont-Aven. Here, a few months later, Julia Guillou was laid to rest.

After a lapse of eighteen years my illustrator and I were destined to return to Pont-Aven. The dominant figure of Mademoiselle Julia, a very general for efficiency, was indeed lacking (Botrel we had never known), but a welcome awaited us in the hospitality of the present owner—Julia's capable niece, Madame Jacob. It was, luckily, early in the season. We were therefore permitted to linger over our lobster *à l'américaine* in the old salle-à manger, whose walls are crowded with paintings given to Julia by her beloved "anciens." We were told the studios had mostly been abandoned. The artists, we surmised, had fled before the influx of chars-à-bancs—for the Hôtel Julia lies on a pulsing highway.

The Aven, the Avon of Brittany, rushed foaming as of old over its rock-strewn bed, turning the moss-grown wheels of romantic mills. Our footsteps sought involuntarily the Bois d'Amour—the grove beside the river, the scene of so many sentimental meetings. In this leafy allée of beeches overlooking the Aven may be found on any fair afternoon—and are not all days fair at Pont-Aven?—maids wearing sumptuous velvets, quilled medieval ruffs, lace-winged caps with fluttering gay ribbons, lads likewise picturesquely garbed and coming of a handsome race. Keeping at a discreet distance from the refreshingly shy young couples, we crossed the stile and mounted through a grander allée of splendid chestnuts to a gate of newly hewn branches.

Ascending farther, we came upon the hoary chapel of Trémalo. Quiet prevailed, the hush of the forest primeval which still hangs over rural Brittany. Above this sacred relic of Christian piety two druidic oaks outstretched their arms in blessing. Children peered at us from the threshold of a thatched cottage, then scurried to cover. The foliage of the Bois, on which we now looked down, had become a blur of tender green . . . the subtle semblance of a summer sea. From far below was lifted a haunting tenor, caroling with the abandon of a bird of the forest the familiar refrain:

Par le petit doigt
Loula, loulaire . . .
Par le petit doigt
Loula!

As we listened, enthralled, the singer was drawing nearer to our vantage-point, and now a woman's voice, spontaneous as the song of the lark, alternated with that of her lover as he led her, we had no cause to doubt, in the modest Breton fashion through the Bois d'Amour.

Quimperlé the Picturesque

HENNEBONT ✣ The CHÂTEAU

CHAPTER XVII

QUIMPERLÉ THE PICTURESQUE

"PONT-AVEN is advertised even on the boats going to Egypt, but who ever mentions Quimperlé?" So spoke an aggrieved native of the latter town with whom we fraternized on the terrace of the Lion d'Or.

"You see my coif," continued the Quimperloise. "It's as fine as Pont-Aven's. The quilled collar ["The queenly ruff," said I] is the same, the aprons are equally gay, the dresses of richer velvet. There are more excursions to be made from Quimperlé. We have two rivers to their one, flowing through the fields and orchards which poets compare to Arcady, and look at our town, look at it!" and she waved a dainty hand in the direction of the amazing medieval conglomeration mounting from the farther bank of the river and reaching its culmination in the Church of Saint-Michel.

"Pont-Aven—bah! it makes me tired! 'Fourteen houses, fifteen mills'—it makes me sick! There is nothing to see at Pont-Aven. A bare place, a dusty road, tourists and chars-à-bancs."

"It is true," I said, "that they have killed the very thing they come to seek, rusticity, once the charm of Pont-Aven . . . and Julia is dead. Tell me about Quimperlé."

"Our costume is the equal of any hereabout. Bannalec, Rosporden, Scaër—they are all much the same. The cider of Clohars, near by, is the equal of that of Fouessant, and our women—judge for yourself—are the match of Fouessant's much extolled lasses."

We were seated beneath clipped lindens at a marble-topped table, one of thirty or forty, at each of which family parties sipped *sirops* or *apéritifs*. The sound of music came from the allée beside the banks of Laïta, for it was Pentecost, a high day at Quimperlé. Many of the patrons of the hotel and all of the waitresses, scurrying to frequent calls of "Mademoiselle!" were garbed in the apparel of the region.

"Pont-Aven offers no such setting as this," I agreed. "From now on I intend to sing the praises of Quimperlé."

The feminine touch, everywhere so much in evidence in the inns of France, is what is chiefly lacking in our own man-made caravansaries. Rarely in American hotels of any pretension does one deal with a woman. Now, in Brittany quite the opposite is the case. Take, for example, the Lion d'Or, an old establishment, the recognized rendezvous in this town of nine thousand inhabitants. The inn is run by sisters. The younger one, with chic bobbed hair, a black dress brightened by pearls, and white sandals, occupied herself with superintending the waitresses. The elder sister was hostess, room-clerk, cashier.

"In France," said she, "it is only the large city establishments that are managed by men. In Brittany we have men chefs, men to make purchases at the market, to choose the wines; but it is the women who occupy themselves with the management of our hotels."

"And a good thing for the hotels," Monsieur gallantly and, I must admit, truthfully interposed.

To those who would revel in front windows on the place at Quimperlé let me recommend a suite *au troisième*. The *second* was not available at the time of our visit and was, we gathered from stolen glimpses, rankly inferior. *Au premier,* with obvious advantages in the liftless reaches of this high-ceilinged hostelry, is not to be considered, because its outlook is a wall of close-cropped branches. We used to linger in the rambling corridors to gaze gardenward, where untrimmed lindens swept the waters of the Ellé racing to its tryst, off-scene,

with Isolé (Quimper Ellé, the junction of the Ellé) to form the discreet, slower-flowing Laïta. In our garden—for our building was once the priory of Sainte-Croix, the ghosts of whose former inmates are still said to roam—stood an ivy-clad half-ruined tower of masonry, a pigeonry of dreams. Yonder the Ellé was spanned by that artist's model the Pont Fleuri, the rough-hewn bridge invaded by moss and wallflowers and valerian.

The more I attempt to paint a picture of Quimperlé the more brilliant, as I seek to capture them, do the colors grow. There is a mellow brightness about the place which is perhaps unique in Brittany. In vivid contrast to the colder coast towns, a former aristocratic and religious center—rivaling the feudal sites in the neighborhood of Rennes, possessing the wealth of costume to be found only in Finistère, yet basking in sunlight as warm as that of Morbihan, many of whose citizens pour to its pardons—among inland towns Quimperlé is indeed unparalleled.

To understand the former importance of the place it is well to know something of its history. The upper town or Ville-Haute with its fourteenth-century church is considered quite an upstart. The lower town boasts the Abbey of Sainte-Croix founded in the sixth century, burnt by Norman invaders, and rebuilt in 1029. The Romanesque crypt of the abbey church with its tomb of Gurloës (popularly known as Saint Urlou) is still frequented by sufferers from gout. The basilica has been restored in modern times to conform with its first plan—an imitation of the Church of the Holy Sepulcher in Jerusalem.

Sainte-Croix was known as the Black Abbey because of the dress of its Benedictine monks. Near by the establishment of the Dominicans, founded in 1255 by Blanche de Campagne, was known as the White Abbey, or Abbaye Blanche. In the chapel of the latter may be seen the tomb of Jean de Montfort, who died in the year 1345.

Jean III, Duke of Brittany, died in 1341 without issue. His half-brother, Jean de Montfort, whose tomb we have just visited, claimed the succession while Jeanne de Penthièvre, niece of the late duke and wife of Charles de Blois, insisted that she had been chosen by her uncle as his successor. Charles de Blois in supporting his wife's claim was upheld by the forces of his uncle, Philippe le Bel, King of France, while de Montfort's claim was backed by Edward III, King of England. Quimperlé, a hotbed of Breton aristocracy—relics of whose mansions remain on the Rue de Bremond d'Ars—whole-heartedly supported de Montfort. Thus it was that for a period of years the town came to be garrisoned by the English; indeed, it was not taken by the French until du Guesclin's entrance in 1373. We shall hear more of the rival claimants when we reach Hennebont, and of de Montfort's firebrand spouse, Jeanne la Flamme.

The abbots of Sainte-Croix were men of distinction. Anne de Bretagne on her famed pilgrimage to Saint-Jean-du-Doigt stopped at Quimperlé and was entertained by watching, from a balcony of Sainte-Croix, gavottes danced in her honor. After Anne's death the abbot of Sainte-Croix was one of the bearers of the golden pall at the time when the heart of the queen was carried in a heart-shaped vessel to its resting-place upon the tomb of her father, François II, at Nantes.

An abbot of Sainte-Croix, the Cardinal de Chatillon (Odet de Coligny), was brother to Admiral de Coligny. Like his brother embracing Protestanttism, he died in 1571 in England. "He would have been worthy of a better destiny if the libertines of the times had not drawn him away from the Catholic faith. The apostate Cardinal makes a blot on the history of our abbey, after more than five centuries of holiness, honor, and piety." So writes the chronicler.

A Queen of England, Marie-Henriette, daughter of Henri IV and wife of Charles I, fleeing in 1644 with her seventeen-day-old infant, was cordially received at Quimper and at Quimperlé on her way to Vannes and Auray, where she gave thanks at the shrine of Sainte-Anne for a safe voyage. A year later she was to hear of her husband's execution.

The Dukes of Brittany used frequently to hunt in the forest of Carnoët, a woodland which endures to our own day. We had, indeed, come to Quimperlé to participate in its most popular fête, held at Whitsuntide near Toulfoën in the forest of Clohars-Carnoët. This fête is known as "The Pardon of the Birds"—in honor of a local legend. The ruined Abbey of Saint-Maurice is to be found in another part of the forest. It is recounted of Maurice, a monk of Langonnet and later in charge of the abbey, that in his childhood his parents, humble peasants, kept him away from school to guard their fields against an onslaught of crows. The birds had come in hosts and were destroying the crops. The child Maurice began his work by freeing crows which had been captured and caged. Calling the birds about him, he reproached them for their misdoings. The crows straightway allowed themselves to be locked in the barn and Maurice went blithely on to school.

In memory of this episode in the life of the Saint Francis of Cornouaille a fête is held yearly in mid-forest. Until a short time ago caged finches were for sale, but nowadays the birds are merely feathered toys that flutter on strings, not to mention the invisible songsters which warble in tree-tops.

All day Sunday the crowds had made their pilgrimage to Toulfoën, but Monday the throng was tenfold. A motley company marched to the forest, a long and dusty way from Quimperlé, following the lead of the bagpipes. As for ourselves, we jumped into an autocar already overflowing with peasants. Private cars were at a premium and used as dangerously laden jitneys.

We observed that many of the girls who attended the festival were neither peasants nor gentry but of a lower bourgeoisie, sophisticated enough to indulge in rouge, and feather boas, and frizzed pompadours . . . incongruous with the medieval cut of brocaded velvet costumes. Yet, seen en masse, even these self-conscious worldlings made vivid pictures in the sunlight which flecked the forest paths.

There were more serious folk who visited the

tiny chapel of Lothéa, but for most the affair was one of jollification, merry-go-rounds, dancing, lunch in the open air. The venders of artificial birds, pinwheels, and balloons did a lively trade. Lured by the skirling of bagpipes, we wandered to a grassy spot beneath the shade of oaks whose spreading branches filtered the sunlight. Here, surrounded with leafage, moss, and ivy, the people danced. Of sailors from Lorient there was a sprinkling, of lads in snug-buttoned velvet jackets quite a few, and some—the first we had seen—with many-streamered hats of the Morbihan. For the first time we saw girls from Pontivy, Baud, and Guémené who charmed us no less by their fresh young faces than by the originality of their costumes.

The musicians, seated on barrels in this forest glade, were two, in accordance with tradition—he of the *binious,* or bagpipes, blowing till he was nigh to bursting, his face scarlet, the other performing upon the *bombarde,* or flute, staring before him with wan Celtic eyes. The sounds which were conjured forth by these wizened men, whose strangeness was accentuated by their bizarre buckled hats, could well have drawn forth from their lairs a host of dancing Corrigans.

To cap the climax, as we wandered through the woodland we came to a sign "To Bluebeard's Castle." The way was long, the day was hot, but

The Foire: Place Saint-Michel

we beguiled the time to this mystery-wrapt ruin with memories of its legend which we had been reading in Souvestre.

The local Bluebeard (for there were several in Brittany!) was one Comorre. He was a man of ill repute, but, in order to avert a bloody warfare, and on the recommendation of Saint Gildas, the King of Vannes gave the Count Comorre his daughter Tréphine in marriage.

Tréphine was the fifth of Comorre's wives. For the first months of marriage the terrible count was a model husband, but no sooner had Tréphine whispered to him the news of an expected heir than his manner changed, and, moreover, the magic ring that Saint Gildas had given Tréphine to warn her of danger turned black. In her grief Tréphine sought the solace of prayer. She visited the chapel and knelt till midnight before the tombs of Comorre's former wives. To the distracted Tréphine their shades appeared.

The first spoke: "Haste, doomed princess! Flee to your father. Comorre plans to kill you to-night as he killed me."

"But how shall I pass the ferocious dog?" Tréphine demurred.

"Poison him with this which poisoned me," quoth the first wife.

"How shall I escape?" asked the princess.

"Take this rope with which the count hanged me and let yourself down from the tower," commanded the second phantom.

"How shall I find my way in the darkness?" queried Tréphine.

"By the light of this fire which burnt me," said the third specter.

"But how shall I have strength for the journey?" said Tréphine.

Whereupon the fourth wife spoke: "Take this staff with which Comorre killed me."

Thus aided, Tréphine fled from the castle and rested a while in a shepherd's hut, deserted save for a magpie.

Comorre, searching for his spouse, gazed after a raven on the wing.

"No," said he, "she has not taken that road," and toward the sunrise he followed with his eyes the flight of the swallow. "No, she has not taken that path; she loved her home too well to follow the swallow." He noted listlessly the course of the sea-gull, but when he noticed a white dove flying toward the setting sun he muttered, "Yes, that is the road the gentle Tréphine has taken." Then Comorre followed the dove to the hut, where he heard a magpie lamenting (copying the words uttered by the princess), "Poor Tréphine, poor Tréphine!" Soon after the time that Tréphine had hidden her newborn babe in the forest Comorre came upon her and with one blow of his sword severed her head from her body.

The King of Vannes, warned by his falcon of what had taken place in the forest, carried his complaint to Saint Gildas, who said:

"It is not for long. I shall command Tréphine to take her head in her arms and to walk with her babe to the castle of Comorre."

Tréphine, accompanied by the saint, the king her father, and his retinue, obeyed the holy man's instructions. No sooner had the company reached the castle of Comorre than the child threw a handful of pebbles against its mighty walls, which immediately collapsed, killing the wicked Comorre. Thus a prediction was fulfilled that Comorre should be destroyed by the hand of his first-born.

Tréphine, placing her head in its proper position, retired to end her days in a convent. Her son, Trémeur, became a saint. In some versions of the tale he too had his head severed by his unnatural parent. A representation of Trémeur holding his head in his hands, like a veritable Saint Denis, may be seen at the portal of the Church of Saint-Trémeur at Carhaix, once the capital of the notorious Comorre.

Next to the Pardon des Oiseaux our interest centered in the Friday market held in the Place Saint-Michel. Although the congested Rue Saint-Maurice with its wealth of fifteenth-century houses was adjoining our hotel, yet the Quimperlé which to me most nearly coincided with my ideal of an Old World town was the quarter of Saint Michael's Church, whose rugged tower so adequately topped the hill. The picture which the historic edifice formed from our windows at the Lion d'Or, with its foreground of tree-tops, river, steeply mounting streets, and ancient houses, the summer clouds and circling swallows which so frequently formed a part, was not more pleasing than a nearer view at time of cattle-fair. The black-and-white cows bred in the environs were marshaled by country girls much more winsome than the bourgeoisie at the fête. The older women, matronly and loquacious, almost without exception wore a delectable head-dress of stiffly starched muslin with refractory streamers. Never had I known the meaning of "pigs in clover" till I saw the cart-loads of red trefoil and the feasting hogs of Quimperlé. And the carts! What beauty here! equal in spirit of decoration, if not in color, to the Sicilian.

Many are the excursions to be made from Quimperlé: Pont-Aven and Concarneau are near by; there is Arzano with memories of the poet Brizeux who studied here, and, too, his beloved bridge of Kerlo, boundary between the Morbihan and Finistère. There is Hennebont—the hen-pont, or old bridge on the Blavet—whose history is so intimately bound with the war of the two Jeannes . . . Jeanne de Penthièvre who claimed the province (wife of Charles de Blois) and Jeanne de Flandre (wife of the other claimant, de Montfort), the Jeanne d'Arc of Brittany.

When Jean de Montfort, fourth of the name and recognized by Parliament as the Duke of Brittany, was taken prisoner at Nantes by the brother of the

King of France (ally of Charles de Blois), de Montfort's wife, Jeanne de Flandre, who was at Rennes, presented herself before the barons, carrying her infant son.

"Montfort is taken," said she, "but nothing is lost. It was only one man; here is my son who will be, if it please God, his restorer."

Thereupon Jeanne rode on horseback through lower Brittany, inspiring the people to resist the enemy. When Charles de Blois reached Hennebont (the year was 1342) he was astonished to find how strong was its defense. Jeanne had laid aside her hennin for a helmet and put herself at the head of her troops—"a woman," it was said, "with courage of a man and the heart of a lion."

Day and night the walls were manned by young and old, noble and peasant, Jeanne's ardent supporters. Froissart gives a stirring account of the events, but it is above all to the popular song, rendered from Celtic to French by H. de la Villemarqué of Quimperlé, that we know the tale.

Armed in a corset of steel and coifed in a black helmet, carrying in her hand a flaming torch, Jeanne set out one night from a gate of the town. To the four corners of the French camp she went, setting fire to the tents of her enemies—three thousand of whom, according to the song, were consumed.

"What a splendid tillage! For every grain of barley we shall have ten. The Romans said, 'There

Bertrand Du Guesclin
Constable of France

is nothing so good as the bones of Gauls, ground fine, for making the barley grow,' " . . . thus spoke Jeanne la Flamme.

Issuing by stealth from her stronghold, Jeanne threw herself into Auray, whence she brought fresh troops to her beleaguered garrison. But, as time wore on and starvation loomed, her advisers insisted upon capitulation. Jeanne, however, plead for a two-day deferment. At the eleventh hour from her tower at Hennebont were sighted the sails of an English fleet, sent by her ally Edward III of England. Twenty-two years later Jeanne's son was to obtain the dukedom of Brittany after the decisive Battle of Auray, and still later he was to become the son-in-law of King Edward III.

The Porte Prison, portal of the Ville-Close, intact as when Jeanne made her entry after setting afire the camp of her enemies, has power to transport us to the tempestuous century of Jeanne la Flamme.

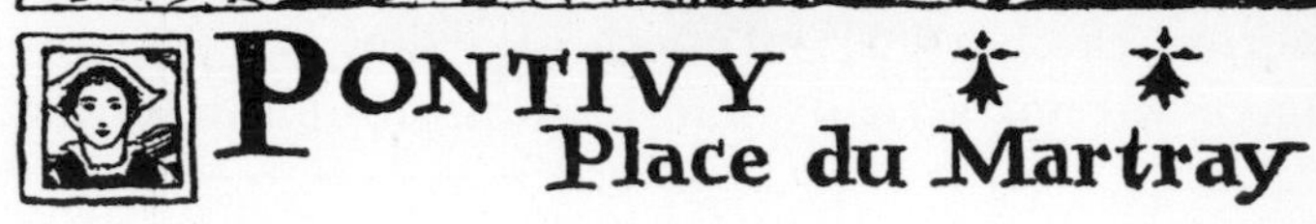

PONTIVY
Place du Martray

CHAPTER XVIII

THE HEART OF BRITTANY

THE greater part of this book has had its scene laid in the department of Finistère. We began, it is true, with Ille-et-Vilaine, followed shortly by the Côtes-du-Nord; but ever since our arrival at Morlaix, twelve chapters back, Finistère has been our setting; and most often, for the last ten chapters, that section which coincides with the ancient province of Cornouaille. Two of the five departments of Brittany remain to be visited. In due time we shall come to Nantes, situated in Loire-Inférieure, but for the nonce let us make merry in the glamorous province once known as Vannetais, with Vannes as its capital; now the department of the Morbihan.

At Quimperlé we were still in Finistère, although the excursion to Hennebont carried us across the border, but at the Pardon des Oiseaux have we not already had a glimpse of the varied costumes of the Morbihan worn by natives of Guémené, Pontivy, and Baud? So much were we attracted by the gay plumage of their ambassadors that we resolved at the time to visit all three of these towns. This resolution we shall now carry out, taking the route which leads through le Faouët (not to be confused with le Faou in Finistère), a quaint town lying directly to the north of Quimperlé.

Our dapper chauffeur assured us that he had driven a car since he was fifteen. He had been old enough to serve during the last two years of the war and had been one of a hundred chauffeurs employed at the War Office in Paris. He mentioned with awe that he had driven Foch.

"I never dared look at him, and of course the general must speak first. Foch never did. He would give orders to the lieutenant sitting beside me."

Making up for past silences, this native of Quimperlé chattered on. He told us of the dislike Bretons bear to Italians, who, said he, commit most of the murders that take place in France. He told of his brother, a mariner who had been around the world and always everywhere he had found Bretons. Born in Quimperlé, our young man spoke Breton, but when we questioned him about the meaning of a poster in his native tongue—

Potred
broiou Gourin ar Guémené hagar Faouët!

he remarked: "Something from a deputy about elections. I speak Breton, yes, but to read it is another matter!"

I remember that we made a detour to see a horse-fair at Gourin. Our car had difficulty in pushing its way through the narrow streets, where horses were wandering at will or champing at ropes. Owners and prospective buyers thronged the highway. As we sped under the fragrant apple blossoms which embowered the road to le Faouët we passed many carts from outlying districts and peasants leading sleek horses tied heads to tails—or do I win if I call it tails to heads? Almost without exception the animals shied at our automobile. Refreshing, we thought, in these days of sophistication.

Of le Faouët my impressions are meager. Its picturesque market-house was deserted. The only diversion at the inn was the unwelcome one of sticking to newly painted chairs of emerald hue.

"We *are* green!" Monsieur exclaimed with forced levity, busying himself with gasoline and miscellaneous rags.

Overlooking a wild ravine to the northwest of le Faouët stands the chapel of Sainte Barbe. A more unlikely spot for the building of a church could hardly be conceived. The explanation is that a Sire of Toulbodou, hunting in this valley of the Ellé, was overtaken by a thunderstorm. As he reached the site of the present chapel a bolt of lightning struck a gigantic boulder. About to be crushed by the severed rock, the sire invoked the aid of Sainte Barbe, promising a chapel if she would save his life. (The saint is still called on for aid by the imperiled in Provence, Gascony, Poitou, Champagne, and Flanders.)

A steep ascent leads over scarred rocks to the hilltop of Sainte-Barbe. The day was sultry as we stumbled along the trail, catching our clothing upon the thorns of gorse bushes, pausing to get our breath beneath the shade of beeches. Higher and higher we mounted, until the platform where hung a mammoth bell was gained at last. With its twisted pines and gigantic bell, tolled by each arriving pilgrim who possesses the force to accomplish the act, this place reminded us of similar shrines in far Japan. A dwarfish guardian appeared, dangling a key, and led us past the rock-perched chapel of Saint Michel to the lichen-incrusted edifice dedicated to Sainte Barbe. The panorama from this favored site includes open country, the sinuous Ellé embroidering a silver strand across a far-flung mantle of green. Although so much of Brittany is moorland—one fourth of Finistère and perhaps an equal proportion of Morbihan—yet my predominant remembrance of the interior is of trees, if not, indeed, of forests, then of woodlands, of orchards, of fields and lanes bordered with distorted oaks.

Nearer to le Faouët than Sainte-Barbe, and

placed upon the plain, is the hardly less noteworthy chapel of Saint Fiacre. The saint is the patron of horticulturists. I am told that an Irishman, Savage by name, introduced many rare plants into Paris. Saint Fiacre was his chosen patron. A fellow-countryman and owner of cabs, out of compliment to Savage, had the face of the saint painted on a number of his landaus. In the course of time these vehicles came to be known as fiacres.

The chapel of Saint Fiacre was built by the founder of the chapel at Kernascléden, which we visited on the road to Guémené-sur-Scorff. It is recounted that, the number of tools in the region being insufficient, angels carried the mallets back and forth as the builders had need of them.

Guémené is the town where women's heads turn as if on pivots to stare at strangers. Monsieur and I were forced to walk in different directions to divide attention, in order to catch fleeting glimpses of the backs of the most intriguing head-dresses in Brittany. Perhaps because of the very difficulty of approaching the vivid ribbon-bound hair, protruding from lacy wings like butterfly tails, the chase became as fascinating as if we had indeed been naturalists with nets. The older women wore head-gear equally to our liking, fashioned of black broadcloth lined with Chinese blue. The form of this enveloping bonnet, suggesting that of an advocate, reminded us of the Pyrenean *capulet*. The Breton hood is called *capoten* and in winter is worn alike by young and old of this region and—with scarlet lining—at Pontivy.

Monsieur, with true collector's mania, instantly made up his mind that he must possess one. Our

visit to the woman who sells coifs resulted in her guiding us to the house of "my aunt who makes *capotens.*" We passed along the main street—a sixteenth-century survival—and plunged down a dark alley which came out upon a court with stone fountain where water dribbled from a pursed mouth of a moss-grown cherub. "My aunt" proved to be a gracious specialist who showed us examples of her millinery, *capotens* in all stages of completion. Each stiff-lined crown—the crowning glory!—takes a day to quill by hand. On looking back I believe it is the presence of numbers of these medieval head-dresses that contributes more than any other one thing to the undoubted fairy-tale feeling of gatherings at Guémené and Pontivy. The stream of life in these towns still flows in ruts worn in the Middle Ages.

Pontivy is situated in the valley of the Blavet, no less famous than the idyllic valley of the Scorff. The name "Pontivy" is derived from that of its founder, Saint Yvy. During the First and Second Empires the place was called Napoléonville. Lying as it does almost in the geographical center, and popularly known as the heart of Brittany, Pontivy, had Napoleon's vision been carried out, would have become the military center of the province. With this end in view the river Blavet was canalized in 1802 to connect the town with Lorient and the sea. The modern quarter with its barracks and Place Nationale looks indeed as if its name were Napoléonville, but, probably because of this distinct division of the town, old Pontivy has remained unharmed.

The Republican movement in Brittany centered in Pontivy. Indeed, one of the reasons for the construction of the canal was for the protection of the urban citizens, isolated in the midst of an insurgent peasantry. A pact concluded at Pontivy in 1790 by the Jeunes Citoyens Actifs of Brittany and Anjou was said to have been a prelude to the Federation of the Champs-de-Mars. Opposite to the church stands a statue dedicated to the "Rights of Man and of the Citizen."

Our arrival at Pontivy coincided with the Sunday races. A bewildering wealth of youth and beauty gorgeously arrayed passed our windows giving on the Place Nationale. Coifs of exquisite lace—the machine-made variety has not invaded Pontivy—framed innocent young faces; skirts were short, bouffant; aprons richly embroidered, of turquoise, salmon, apple-green, lavender, old-gold. Above the promenade horse-chestnuts were in bloom, shedding rosy petals upon the passing multitude. As we watched, a chic motor drew up at our door. A prosperous citizen in white sport cap and wearing gloves helped his wife to alight. We noted this Bretonne's coif of superlative quality and apron of resplendent crimson. She was a handsome swarthy woman of the type more often associated with Provence—a Divonne stepped from the pages of "Sapho." Once more we saw the couple. They were ushered into the smoke-filled salle-à-manger where pandemonium reigned. Threading their way between convivial citizens of Pontivy, Guémené, and Baud, blue-bloused drovers, beribboned spectators come to the races, they were shown to a reserved table. A wine-card was instantly procured and Divonne and her prosperous *mari* mastered its intricacies at a glance. Were they, in keeping with the rôles we had assigned them, wine-growers of repute? No love-lorn nephew marred their equanimity.

The old town of Pontivy has two settings of inestimable worth. One is the Place du Martray, the other the squat château constructed by Jean de Rohan in 1485. (After the creation of the duchy of Rohan, in 1663, Pontivy became its capital.) It is in front of this captivating castle of dreams that, of a Monday, the cattle-fair is held. Picture men in blouses, assisted by their women-folk, busied with recalcitrant pigs and heifers. Jeers arise at paltry bids. When buyers are forced to capitulate, bargains are concluded not by mere grasps of the hand but by violent percussions.

The naïveté of the citizens of Pontivy is one of their charms. Mathurine, our chambermaid, found us curious beings, as she never before had heard the English tongue. When I attempted to purchase *meta,* the foreign form of solid alcohol, the shopkeeper's wife regarded me as if I were asking for the moon until her husband broke in, telling her, "Yes, that does exist, but we have it not in Pontivy." At the market we looked for cut flowers but found only seeds. Who would buy flowers when all may have gardens? Simple are the townsfolk of Pontivy even as the barker put it to the gaping crowd upon the *place:*

"You are such hardheads here you don't know the latest vogue when you see it," said he, holding up a hook-handled horror of an umbrella. "Look! it will turn wrong side out without harm," and he suited the action to the word. "Now you have a basket for eggs and solid enough to hang the sausage inside! Marguerite," he pointed to a shy young girl, "with her Breton bonnet and one of these umbrellas would make a sensation in Paris."

On the Place du Martray stands a mansion with corbeled turret, the one-time hunting lodge of the Dukes of Rohan. Other ancient buildings, with stone pilasters and fantastic gabled roofs, become an equally appropriate background for scores of hooded wives of Pontivy lined up with poultry and pats of golden butter. Hardly another open-air market in Brittany so combines perfection of costume and of architectural surroundings.

On the first Monday in March is held one of the most curious fairs of the region, the Foire des Gages. Boys and girls, from twelve to fourteen years, are brought by their parents and are hired as farm-hands or servants by landowners from the Côtes-du-Nord. Many of these young people become accustomed to a different scale of living and to the French tongue and therefore do not return to their own firesides.

Our return to Pontivy on August fifteenth, to

take part in the pardon at Quelven, was at the suggestion of Elsie Masson, collector of folk-tales and widow of Emile Masson, the distinguished Breton scholar and friend of Lemordant. With Madame Masson for comrade and guide we had scoured the lanes for miles around, braving wind and showers. We had walked for hours between hedges of hawthorn or moss-grown scrub-oaks, coming out often to open moorland but seldom to a road. When I praised these byways, commenting on the lack of consideration shown the pedestrian in America, Madame exclaimed, "To make them has taken thousands of years!"

The chapel of Quelven is situated upon a plateau near Pontivy. The image of Notre-Dame de Quelven is one of the most popular in Brittany. During the Revolution the key to this statue was lost, but an oral tradition persisted to the effect that the Madonna of Quelven opened. To-day the lost has been found. The Madonna is one of those curious figures constructed like a cabinet and filled with bas-reliefs. On August fifteenth, from all the outlying towns—Guémené, Baud, and even Hennebont—the people flock to Quelven to celebrate this day sacred to the blessed Virgin.

On the assembled multitude the sun lavished its golden light as if in benediction. Many motorists had come from a distance. Old men of Pontivy had donned their elaborate white-cloth jackets. Around the church swarmed representatives from

Quelven

Guémené, the costumes of men and women embellished with rows of gleaming buttons. The girls of Baud caught our attention with lace headdresses drooping low upon the shoulder. Everywhere were *capotens,* lined with blue or vivid red.

The Bishop of Port au Prince was escorted from the presbytery to the portal of the church. Banners were in readiness for the procession. Above the chanted vespers, competing for a hearing, rose the endless blare of mechanical music. The raucous sound issued from a merry-go-round in full swing beside the church. Expectation was at its highest flood when church doors were flung wide. A prolonged wait followed and then a rumor spread that there would be no procession; the bishop would not officiate unless the carrousel could be stopped; the owner, who had leased the ground, had refused, for he was coining money. No procession! At first all were incredulous, but at sight of the bishop without his robes of office, escorted from the church, the consternation grew.

"C'est bête!" a man near by exclaimed. "They might have stopped the infernal thing for half an hour. People have come from Brussels, others from England. France should be ashamed to have foreigners see this everlasting wrangle of politician and priest."

A nun elucidated: "There is an old feud," said she, "between the curé and the mayor. The latter once sold a house which before the Separation had belonged to the church. The mayor, I take it, has rented this site to the owner of the carrousel to spite the curé, who objected to the sale."

"And next year," I asked, thinking that for once my sympathies were with the Church of Rome, "will public opinion discipline the mayor or will the pardon languish?"

A shrug of the shoulders was the only answer.

The road from Pontivy to Vannes runs through the town of Baud. We had come in order to behold the idol, the "Witch of la Couarde," known as the Venus of Quinipily. Hewn from a block of stone, perhaps in pagan centuries first worshiped as a formless menhir, this idol possesses a curious history. It was unearthed at the hill of Castennec, near the site of a camp of Moorish soldiers in the armies of Rome. That a ruined temple discovered at this spot by Saint Gildas was dedicated to Isis seems not improbable. The "Venus" has undoubtedly many of the characteristics of the Egyptian goddess. From time immemorial the women of the region have had the curious habit of bathing in a granite trough beside the statue—an act which it was said insured safety in pregnancy and childbirth.

At the prayer of Christian missionaries Claude II, Count of Lannion and Seigneur of Quinipily, had the idol rolled into the Blavet. Belief in the magic power of Groac'h er Couard, as the Bretons called her, was so strong that the peasants raised the statue from its watery grave and laid it on the river bank, whereupon the Bishop of Vannes demanded its destruction. Superstitious masons, ordered by Count Claude to demolish the idol, merely chipped off an arm and rolled the stone back again into the river. In 1696, Pierre de Lannion rescued the statue from oblivion and had it put up in its present situation, the granite trough at its feet. Forty oxen were employed to drag it to the quiet retreat where it still stands beside the now ruined château.

Guide-books may reiterate, at the instigation of zealous priests, that the image of Groac'h er Couard is not the original but merely a copy. Old wives and antiquarians know the truth. Despite the anathema of Holy Church, Isis, Mother of Horus, reigns in the fruitful orchards of Quinipily.

The Towers and Bastions of Vannes

CHAPTER XIX

ROMANTIC MORBIHAN

THE history of the Morbihan and in particular of Vannes, its capital, is steeped in romance. The ancient inhabitants of the region were known as Veneti—a maritime people for whom it is claimed that they colonized the Adriatic and gave their name to the Venetians. Traders with Cornwall, undisputed masters of the Northern seas, the Veneti were forced with the other peoples of Armorica to give hostages to Cæsar in the year 57 B. C. The following year, however, they refused to pay a still greater tribute to the Romans unless their demand for the return of hostages were granted. Cæsar appeared in person on the scene. He found, to his astonishment, that without the aid of his fleet he was powerless against the uprising of the Armoricans who had migrated to the countless islands of the Morbihan—the Breton for "little sea"—from which the province takes its name.

Cæsar wrote in his Commentaries, "Of all the

people of Gaul the inhabitants of Morbihan made the most determined resistance."

The great oak ships of the Veneti, driven by leathern sails, bore down like avalanches on the galleys of Rome, dwarfing with their gigantic size the enemy's boats. Brutus, in command of the Roman fleets, was considering how best to retreat, when the wind fell, the wind without which the mighty hulks of the Veneti were deprived of power and unable to hasten to one another's aid. One by one the mammoth winged craft, forerunners of a type long to be master of the sea, were despatched, until not a hull of the two hundred and twenty remained. As for the Veneti, deprived forever of their maritime power, they were unmercifully slaughtered, the few survivors sold as slaves.

Our thoughts were stirred by memories of these tales of holocaust as we set foot on the tiny craft which would carry us from the Promenade de la Rabine at Vannes for a tour among the islands of the Morbihan. There had been a downpour before seven, but there was still enough uncertainty about the weather to add zest. Clouds were banked low on the horizon as our steamer chugged its way across conflicting currents. The beauties of the cruise—Gravinis with its prehistoric tumulus, the lesser islands, the view of sunlit Quiberon, for blue sky had broken through the mists of morning—were overshadowed by our enjoyment of the Ile aux Moines. One of the few regrets of our Breton experience is that we had but a meager seven hours to give to this unique island.

It was a Sunday; the words are significant to those in search of gala costume. The cove where we landed had the leisured look unknown save upon bucolic islands. A cart drawn by a pair of lazy red-and-white oxen was in waiting for passengers' bags. Women jogged by in creaking donkey carts. Was the place more reminiscent of Spain or Portugal? Monsieur and I asked each other, our thoughts reverting to the cloud-caressed Azores. We chose to walk along the lanes, edged with hawthorn, to the pines of the Bois d'Amour (with memories of Pont-Aven) and to the sheltered beach beyond. We lingered at the cypress-guarded cemetery; we found our way across the island to the church, a rugged mass of masonry whose sturdy columns speak its age. Ever and anon we came upon glimpses of the sea.

"I have the soul of a Celt!" exclaimed a radiant young person with an aureole of golden hair who claimed us as fellow-countrymen at the Hôtel du Golfe. "My sister is prosaic. She writes, 'Why have you gone again to that forsaken island?' Is it the spell of Merlin? I know that two summers here is all too short for me! Good Americans are said to go to Paris when they die, but this is my foretaste of Elysian Fields."

Quality is stressed at the Hôtel du Golfe, whether it be of guests, cuisine, or floral setting. Our eyes ran over the habitués assembled at déjeuner. The variety and brilliancy of color in frocks and parasols, the gay ties of the men suggested a country club, but the faces were subtle, not mundane. There was the Gallic poet whose graying hair waved back from a high forehead. He wore a tight black coat and Byronic shirt open at the throat. His willowy companion hung on his every word. There was a debonair matron—with exuberant children—who greeted friends with an ecstatic "*You* here!" There were chic actors from Paris. Aloof in one corner sat a brown-robed monk with shining tonsured head and silvery beard; an appropriate figure on this Ile aux Moines, although nowadays the monks, those early settlers of the place, are naught but a name.

After luncheon we took the road to Kergonan, a village where white-, buff-, or salmon-plaster houses were topped by thatched roofs curled delectably over dormers. Shaggy eaves cast fringed shadows on gleaming walls. Stone stairways led to second-story windows, tempting Romeos! Magnolias shed their fragrance; mimosa was out of bloom, but its delicate foliage enhanced the bowers of these gardens. Figs flourished, twisted pines, and here and there a palm. Roses and fuchsias, spreading grape-vines were trained fantastically. Pigeons cooed and fluttered. Glints of brass and copper could be seen through open doorways and—the soul of this Arcady—women of gracious mien, tall and languorous, their coiled hair crowned with coronets of lace, gave the clue to the mysterious charm. These people are descended from the early settlers of the island, who were natives of Spain. The race has taken root and thriven on this semitropical isle.

Had we not already known Saint-Brieuc, Morlaix, Quimper, perhaps the town of Vannes would have impressed us more. A painter friend of ours says that Vannes is his favorite town in Europe. He must have started his tour from Nantes, rather than from Saint-Malo, in which case the indisputably charming costumes of the place would have been his first initiation to unspoiled Brittany. There is undoubted allurement in the remnants of Vannes's feudal walls, and more especially did we admire the towers and bastions which rise above the insignificant river of Rohan and the Promenade de la Garenne. The quaintly roofed *lavoir,* where laundresses are wont to enliven the river bank with wag of tongues and sunning of gaudy garments, is one of Vannes's attractions. Having traversed so many Breton towns, I can no longer expatiate upon timbered dwellings and romantic keeps. Had we started here, rather than at Dinan, perhaps I should be better able to do Vannes justice.

In the Palais de l'Ermine at Vannes, Jean de Montfort (son of Jeanne la Flamme), on pretext of showing a tower of the stronghold, imprisoned Olivier de Clisson, Constable of France, with whom he had differed as to the fate of the sons of de Montfort's slain rival, Charles de Blois. De Clisson was not set at liberty until after the payment of a heavy ransom.

Between the Gulf of Morbihan and the Atlantic runs the narrow peninsula of Rhuis—its chief town Sarzeau, birthplace of Le Sage, the author of "Gil Blas." Near Sarzeau stands the ruined château-fort of Sucinio, constructed in 1250 by Jean le Roux. The erection of this fastness is said to have stretched over a period of one hundred and one years. No structure is more intimately associated with the Dukes of Brittany. Taken by Charles de Blois in 1324, it was retaken by Jean de Montfort in 1364. In 1474 the earls of Pembroke and Richmond were imprisoned within its mighty walls. Sucinio was given by Anne de Bretagne to John of Chalons, Prince of Orange, from whom it was wrested by Anne's son-in-law François Ier and presented to his favorite Françoise de Foix, Comtesse de Chateaubriand.

We found Sucinio the picture of desolation. Once surrounded with a forest, the château now stands upon a plain invaded by gorse and bracken. The moat—flooded in former times by the sea which possibly rises to these heights nowadays during the storms of winter—was overgrown with rushes. Remote from man's dwellings as of yore, save for a few miserable hovels, Sucinio retained even in ruin the semblance of power and majesty.

Henry Adams writes: "As the west portal of Chartres is the door through which one must of necessity enter the Gothic architecture of the thirteenth century, so Abélard is the portal of approach to the Gothic thought and philosophy within. Neither art nor thought has a modern equivalent; only Héloïse, like Isolde, unites the ages."

Born in 1079 at le Pallet, near Nantes, the eldest son of Bérenger, Sieur du Pallet, Pierre du Pallet—known as Abélard—went to Paris at the beginning of the twelfth century "with as much faith in logic as Bernard had in prayer or Godfrey of Bouillon in arms, and led an equal or even greater number of combatants to the conquest of heaven by force of pure reason." After studying dialectics with Guillaume de Champeaux, Abélard became a lecturer of note. He is said to have had a following of three thousand students. Remembered to-day chiefly because of his love for Héloïse—the house where they sojourned, on the left bank of the Seine, is marked by a tablet—Abélard and also the youthful Héloïse retired into religious orders shortly after their secret marriage.

Abélard had a passion, second only to his passion for Héloïse, which was for the discussion of the third person of the Trinity. In vain the Church tried to silence him. It may, indeed, have been at a hint from Paris that the monks of Saint-Gildas-de-Rhuis on the peninsula of Sarzeau called Abélard to be their abbot. During the ten years of his exile at Saint-Gildas, Abélard's voice was not heard. Héloïse, meanwhile, had become abbess at the monastery of the Paraclet, near Fontainebleau, built and named by Abélard.

The monks at the Abbey of Saint-Gildas were prejudiced against their abbot because of the strictness of his régime. Commenting on conditions at Saint-Gildas, Abélard wrote: "The life of the monks was undisciplined. The abbey gates were decorated with the feet of stags, bears, and boars. The monks were roused from their slumbers by no other signal than the hunter's horn and the baying of hounds. The natives were barbarous and disorderly."

Fearing for his life, the abbot fled at last, in the year 1138. In 1140 he was judged by a council of kings and bishops in session at Sens, and their verdict was confirmed by the pope. Abélard was condemned to silence. No longer might he publicly analyze the persons of the Trinity. Still in name Abbot of Saint-Gildas, Abélard sought refuge at the monastery of Cluny, and here he died in 1142. The Abbot of Cluny, Peter the Venerable, sent an epistle to Héloïse "on the loss of a husband who was the Socrates, the Aristotle, the Plato,

Auray

of France and the West, who, if among logicians he had rivals, had no master; who was the prince of study, learned, eloquent, subtle, and was never so great as when he passed to true philosophy, that of Christ."

Hardly less desolate in situation than Sucinio, the Abbey of Saint-Gildas-de-Rhuis is exposed to the winds of the Atlantic. Saint Gildas, coming from Glastonbury in the sixth century and settling on the peninsula, is said to have taken Trémeur to this monastery. It was, therefore, startling to us, as we approached the buildings, to behold a man apparently without head, marching along the road before us. On nearer view, however, the individual proved to be so bent with age that his head was actually not visible from the rear.

Although the cloisters do not date to the time of Saint Gildas—still popular in the region—they are the same where Abélard paced, his mind in ferment, the same from which he penned his distraught letters to Héloïse. A straight-lipped nun conducted us over the premises and, to our questionings, showed us plainly that at Saint-Gildas, Abélard is remembered as one who strayed from the fold—and no saint.

Auray is noted for three dissimilar events. The first was the decisive battle waged on September 29, 1364, which resulted in the death of Charles de Blois and the acclamation of Jean de Montfort as Jean V, Duke of Brittany. The second was the shooting, in July, 1795, of nine hundred and fifty-two Royalist émigrés (returning from England) who had disembarked on the peninsula of Quiberon under the protection of the English fleet and of Cadoudal, leader of the Chouans, but who were seized by the Revolutionists and executed at Auray. The place of the holocaust is known as the Martyrs' Field. The third event was, happily, not of a sanguinary nature.

In December, 1776, the American war-ship *Reprisal,* bound for Nantes, was unable to enter the Loire, owing to contrary winds. Aboard, chafing at the delay, was Benjamin Franklin, who had been delegated by Congress to negotiate "a treaty of commerce and friendship with the Court of France." Having been at sea since October 26, the date of his sailing from Philadelphia, Franklin was all impatience to go ashore. Leaving the becalmed vessel in the bay of Quiberon, the American landed at Auray. Letters in his hand were written from the town of Auray, under date of December 4, telling that he would proceed to his destination, Nantes, by land. The quay at Auray bears his name.

It is a curious fact that many of the volunteers who came from France to Washington's aid in the darkest days of his country's need (and especially is this true of enlistments in the navy) were Bretons. La Fayette was not born in Brittany and yet it should be remembered in this connec-

All Brittany unites to celebrate

tion that his mother was a Bretonne (this is authentic, though the incredulous may doubt the Breton origin of Sainte Anne). Marie Louise Julie de la Rivière was her name. She was the daughter of the Marquis de la Rivière—scion of an ancient Breton family. Her son, born in Haute-Loire in 1757, was christened with a name which tells of his Breton connection—Marie Joseph Paul Roch *Yves* Gilbert Motier, Marquis de La Fayette. (To his own son, born in Paris in 1779, La Fayette gave the name Georges Washington.)

It was from Brest that Rochambeau embarked

the Festival of Sainte Anne d'Auray

in 1780, accompanied by five thousand men. Twenty-five Bretons were members of the Sons of the Cincinnati; and over three hundred Breton officers served in the American navy.

"The least little Gothic chapel, lost in the *lande*, moves us more than all this architecture erected in days of modernity and lack of faith." So writes the author of "Un Mois en Bretagne." "In no wise does it [Auray] compare with Rumengol, Sainte-Anne-de-la-Palue, Locronan nor yet Guingamp or Plougastel." Having attended all these pardons, I can add my word of acquiescence in this opinion; and yet, and yet . . . There is fervor even in modern Catholicism.

All Brittany pours into Sainte-Anne-d'Auray to attend the pardon of the Virgin's mother. No other fête compares to this in popularity. The groups which we have seen individually celebrating in other localities meet here for the one festival which unites dwellers in all the parishes of la Bretagne *bretonnante*. From Plougastel, Châteaulin, and Brest; from Carhaix and Huelgoat; from Morlaix and Guingamp; from Quimper and Pont-l'Abbé; from Pontivy, Guémené and Baud; from Quimperlé and Pont-Aven; from Lorient and Vannes; indeed, from every town where costumes are still worn the people pour on this last Sunday of July, to the pardon of Sainte-Anne-d'Auray. The trains disgorge their thousands, the highways are congested. Some of the devout, in fulfilment of vows, march barefooted, carrying their shoes. We were told that many soldiers who returned in safety from the war performed this act of piety, walking with bare feet from far-distant towns.

The sun shone pitilessly on that afternoon of July 26, when, mass and vespers having been duly celebrated, the multitude surged toward the axis of a carefully planted avenue where stands the oratory. The bishops took their places, gleaming amid satellites. Twinkling with gold and silver, the gala-costumed multitude, dazzling to the eye as a river of light, flowed through the allées. Beneath tall trees, courting the all-inadequate shade, pilgrims stood in reverent throngs or sought precarious perches upon walls. The mercury had soared, the blaze of sunlight on aged heads had caused prostrations, but pictorially we had no complaint about the dramatic performance at Auray.

Belle-Ile-en-Mer: The Port of Le Palais.

CHAPTER XX

MEGALITHIC MONUMENTS

CARNAC takes its name, some say, from the Breton word *karn,* signifying the "place of bones," but others, among them the Scotch archæologist Miln, founder of the museum at Carnac, maintain that the word is derived from *carn,* a Celtic word denoting an elevation or cairn. A like difference of opinion now obtains as to the origin and purpose of the mighty monuments of stone which in the region of Carnac and Locmariaquer rear their hoary heads above the plain.

Formerly the stones were known as "Celtic monuments," and it was thought that they were erected by the druids as memorials to their dead. Nowadays, however, many think the monoliths were set up to serve the living at a period long antedating the druids, going back beyond the historic to the Neolithic Age. The priest was in those days, it is believed, an astronomer. What more natural than that he should have observed the return of the sun to its same point of rising, after the absence of a year? He would therefore be qualified to announce to the people the season to sow the harvest.

Monsieur le Rouzic, curator of the museum at Carnac, has said that "the stones were astronomically arranged to indicate the direction of sunrise at the solstices and the equinoxes and thus to fix the periods for the festivals or ceremonies of a very ancient solar worship." A comparison has been drawn between the erection of certain menhirs and the "stretching of the cord" which fixed the axes of Egyptian temples . . . as the temple of Memphis with its axis directed to the May sun. Is there perhaps a connection between the names Carnac and the Egyptian Karnak?

Still another way of accounting for these unaccountable monsters is to accept tradition, which has named them the Soldiers of Saint Cornély. According to the legend, Saint Cornély was a pope driven from Rome by the barbarians. Taking with him his two faithful oxen, the holy man had come as far as the spot now known as Carnac when his flight was cut off by the sea. He found himself overtaken by the legions of the pagans, but in answer to his prayer his enemies were transformed into blocks of stone. In the story of Saint Cornély and his oxen we find the probable survival of the Celtic deity Hu-Gadarn, whose two oxen brought about the cessation of the deluge by dragging ashore a monstrous crocodile. One valiant beast died from the exertion, while the other pined away, lamenting his yoke-mate.

Then, again, it is said that these blocks of stone were the tombs of the warriors slain at the legendary Battle of Carnac, celebrated in song and story, which some say was a battle fought on this barren plain (and not at Dol) between Chramne and his father Clotaire I, King of the Franks.

It is supposed that at one time there were at Carnac alone as many as fifteen thousand menhirs. Of these, somewhat more than two thousand have survived the wilful inroads made upon them by local builders. The State to-day owns, preserves, and where necessary reërects what the vandalism of man has spared. The Church, indeed, has had much to do with the destruction of these prehistoric monoliths. In 658 a Council of Nantes was outspoken against the "false worship of stones in ruined and woody places, where the people make offerings and pay vows." The bishops were commanded to see to the overthrow and concealment of the offending stones. This is conclusive evidence of a late survival in Brittany of the *Cultus Lapidum*—prohibited in England by Canute—which at Carnac, the Stonehenge of Little Britain, one hesitates even in the twentieth century to call dead.

Stone-worship seems to have been common to all peoples in prehistoric times. What more enduring monument could man erect to symbolize his unknown creator? . . . As the Kaffirs say, in speaking of their sacred stones, "This stands for God, but we do not know His shape, therefore we leave the rock untouched by the chisel."

In the opinion of Jubanville of the Sorbonne, an authority in such matters, the stones of Carnac, although employed by the druids in practising their ceremonies, were placed in their present positions thousands of years before the druids came to Gaul. It is with the druids, however, that the menhirs of Carnac are most intimately associated in the popular mind—neolithic man being, perhaps, harder to visualize to-day. It is undoubtedly true that the Celts accepted many of the deities of the mysterious race which preceded them. Celtic ritual centered around the worship of the Sun-god. Although human sacrifices were probably offered at times to propitiate the gods, yet many precepts attributed to the druids are admirable.

Cæsar wrote, "It is a law of the druids that no man shall be richer than his neighbor." Other rules were: "The druid shall be pure and chaste" . . . "Women may be judges and arbiters" . . . "Foreign merchants are forbidden to import luxuries among us" . . . "No children shall be brought up in cities. The child shall be brought up in villages" . . . a law that would seem to be even more commendable if applied to the cities of to-day.

Sir James Frazer in his classic opus "The

Golden Bough" throws much light on the druids' reverence for mistletoe. (He calls attention to the fact that in the Morbihan dried boughs of mistletoe are still hung at stable doors to protect cattle from witchcraft.) Is not the golden bough, gathered at solstices, he asks, an emanation of the sun's fire? Perhaps, he elucidates, instead of saying that the mistletoe was an emanation of the sun's fire, it might be more correct to say that the sun's fire was regarded as an emanation of the mistletoe. To the ancient Aryan the sun was periodically recruited from the fire which dwelt in the oak and which could be drawn out by friction or combustion. The evergreen mistletoe was looked upon as the heart of the oak, containing the seed of fire.

According to Pliny:

> The druids esteem nothing more sacred than the mistletoe and the tree on which it grows, provided only that the tree is an oak. But apart from this they choose oak-woods for their sacred groves and perform no sacred rites without oak-leaves, so that the very name of druids may be regarded as a Greek appellation derived from their worship of the oak. For they believe that whatever grows on these trees is sent from heaven and is a sign that the tree has been chosen by God himself.

Mistletoe was regarded among the druids, in much the same manner that the fountain of Sainte-Anne-de-la-Palue is regarded by their successors, as all-healing. On the sixth day of the

moon, and after the sacrifice of bulls, a festival was held. A priest clad in robes symbolic of purity would climb the oak and cut with his golden sickle the treasured mistletoe, which would be caught in a snow-white cloth.

Carnac, it appears, was the Mecca, the Rome of the druidic faith. The rows of vast menhirs formed a gathering-place—a temple, shall we call it, open to the sky—where pilgrims congregated long ages before the foundation of Auray. The cromlechs may have corresponded to the chancels of our churches. Judging from the evident importance of the occupants of these prehistoric mausoleums, archæologists believe it likely that notables were brought from a distance for burial at Carnac. Although some tombs have been found beside menhirs, the most important burials were made beneath the dolmens, which in turn were, according to high authorities, always covered with mounds or tumuli. Mont-Saint-Michel at Carnac reaches a height of forty feet and has yielded innumerable treasures of the age of polished stone and bronze.

Zacharie le Rouzic, a native of Carnac and formerly Miln's assistant in his excavations, is curator of the museum and himself an authority. In a preface to Monsieur le Rouzic's enlightening volume entitled "Carnac," Anatole Le Braz has written, apropos of a visit to the Musée Miln, "It is no longer a museum when you do the honors, my dear le Rouzic, but a room of your palace of long ago, ornamented with relics and trophies of your family . . . of your distant past."

The heat was oppressive on the day of our visit, and yet the frail curator, barely recovered from illness, not only autographed his books for us but expended energy in showing his recent discoveries and in recounting the conclusions to be drawn from them. A menhir is, of course, of unfashioned stone, a primitive obelisk: an alignment is a group of these stones in one or more lines. A dolmen consists of uprights topped with roof or "tables" of stone; these uprights are of ogival form and to the quickened imagination of Monsieur le Rouzic represent the goddess of the fruitful earth.

With loving fingers our expounder of wonders showed us the sun-symbols, the hieroglyphic representing a beard of wheat, symbolic of life and immortality—found, said he, at Locmariaquer, on both the dolmen of the Table des Marchands and the fallen monster menhir the Men-er-H'roëck. Necklaces of turquoise and jasper, trinkets of gold, buried with the dead and evidently intended for use in a future life, were among the finds dating from the Gallic centuries. What more natural than that these may yet prove to be the long undiscovered tombs of the Veneti?

Coins of Tiberius and Trajan have been found at Locmariaquer; however, these do not interest our curator, who scorns the Roman but turns with radiance to the contemplation of thunder-stones—votive axes known as "celts" and still considered efficacious by the peasants, who build them into their chimneys in lieu of lightning-rods.

Superstitions are still rife among the peasantry. The menhirs are said to go to the water to drink on Christmas Eve, and crushed would be he who stood in their path or who (during their absence) robbed the revealed pits of gleaming gold. Buried treasure is sure to be found beneath the "singing" rocks—for of course you must know that in Brittany there are rocks that sing at rising or setting of the sun. At Ploumanac'h the people say 'tis the prayer of the Holy Virgin, pleading for her Bretons.

"Strong as a Kerion!" The saying is still in use in the Morbihan.

"A Kerion?" we queried, and were told:

"There was once a race of strong dark little men who lived in this region; some call them Corrigans or fairies. The dolmens were their dwellings."

The finest dolmens are to be found near Carnac at Locmariaquer, which lies at the juncture of the river of Auray with the inland sea of the Morbihan, here narrowing to a strait between the peninsula of Locmariaquer and the peninsula of Rhuis. It is said that these curious structures, some of them with several chambers, have entrances so placed as to face an imaginary line drawn between the rising and setting midsummer sun. Here is the famous Table des Marchands, second in my affection only to the Roche-aux-Fées so romantically placed near Retiers, on the old road from Vitré to Rennes, so overshadowed by secular oaks, the foot-path leading to it so little worn, wrapt in the silence of the past.

It is supposed that an earthquake once shook this peninsula of Locmariaquer, forming the gulf of the Morbihan, destroying the low-lying Roman town on the site where Locmariaquer now stands, shattering into four parts the mightiest menhir in the world. Impressive even in impotence, its remains rest to-day amid the heather—this Mener-H'roëck, or Fairy Stone.

The menhirs of Carnac consist of three distinct fields or groups, each with its own orientation—those of Menec (sacred stone), Kermario (house of the dead), and Kerlescan (house of burning). The granite blocks which form the monuments

The Stones of Carnac

are thought to be erratics of the glacial age. Many approximate the height of a man, others are not so tall, while many loom like giants. It is by the light of the moon that menhirs live again their past. Carnac seen in my youth, amid the rush and babel of tourists, had proved a disappointment. Carnac as seen with my artist husband proved a revelation. The plain was deserted, unillumined save by a watery moon, which toward midnight had risen high above the dusky grove of pines. Daylight had faded slowly, but it had, one might have thought, irrevocably gone . . . so cut off we seemed from earth itself. Cries of wild birds, souls in pain, rose from the direction of the

beach. We stood alone among the crowding monsters—towering ghost-white presences which cast about us, like some sinister spell, their phalanxes of Stygian shadows. As we neared the alignments of Kermario the blackness that enveloped us was uncannily dispelled, periodically pierced by the pitiless regard of ruby-eyed guardians of the shore . . . high gods with jeweled eyes whose glare turned to blood-red ourselves and then (with horrid suggestion) dyed crimson the sacrificial stone—as once it was reddened with the warm blood of human sacrifice.

Dunes and stunted pines characterize the spit of land which terminates at Quiberon. From this popular resort daily sailings are made to Belle-Ile, largest of the Breton islands. Lying at a distance of nine miles from the shore, Belle-Ile consists of a wind-swept plateau ten miles in length, cut by fertile valleys. Even in a region of rocks and waves Belle-Ile is, according to the Guide Bleu, "one of the most grandiose sites of Brittany." Two islets, Houat and Hœdic (duck and duckling), lie to landward from Belle-Ile. It was off Houat, in the Passage de Teignoure, on the night of August 27, 1922, that the ironclad *France* gutted itself upon a submerged and uncharted reef.

Belle-Ile has had a somewhat checkered career. It was known to prehistoric man, if we may judge from the wealth of megalithic monuments once found there—of which but two menhirs have survived the rapacity of the road-makers. The mass of the plateau, not being granite like the stone of the mainland but slate, has caused certain geologists to play with the idea that Belle-Ile, with its neighboring isles, the island of Groix, and the Glénans, may be the survivor of a lost continent.

During the Middle Ages, Belle-Ile belonged to the Counts of Cornouaille and was given by one of their number to the Abbey of Sainte-Croix at Quimperlé, in whose possession it remained from the tenth to the sixteenth centuries. At this time forts were constructed to protect the monks who had settled on the island, from the frequent ravages of pirates—Normans, Basques, and even Saracens . . . the latter have given their name to Sauzon and Bor-Sarrazin. During the Wars of Religion the island was taken by Montgomery, the chief of the Protestants; later it was given by Charles IX to the Duc de Retz, a native of la Vendée. (The Vendean head-dress was introduced at this time.) The Cardinal de Retz, compromised during the Fronde, escaping from his prison in the Château of Nantes, sought but did not find refuge on the island. The impoverished cardinal finally sold his patrimony to Fouguet, Minister of Finance under Louis XIV.

Fouguet's destiny likewise was clouded. Excoriated by all but Madame de Sévigné, who defended him, he spent his last days imprisoned upon the Isle of Sainte-Marguerite. Once more Belle-Ile reverted to the crown. In 1761, after a siege of thirty-eight days, Belle-Ile was taken by the English, who occupied it for two years. The island was restored to France in 1763, by the Treaty of Paris, which gave Acadia (Nova Scotia) to England. Two years later seventy-eight French families from Acadia landed at Saint-Malo and were supplied by Louis XV with farms at Belle-Ile. The colonists brought the potato with them from the New World; this was prior to its introduction into France by Parmentier.

A homespun known as *acadie* is still woven on the island, where much of the enterprise of the inhabitants is attributed to the vitality of this Canadian stock. The population speaks French and not Breton. Songs are sung here which had their origin across the Atlantic, in Quebec.

On the boat to le Palais, the chief harbor and capital of Belle-Ile, we encountered the bard Emile Cueff, Botrel's successor at Pont-Aven. He was on his way to sing on the island, but had left his regional hat at Quiberon, fearing to lose it in the wind. His tossed brown locks made him more than ever the picture of a bard.

We complimented the singer on his spirited performance of "Matilin an Dall," which we had heard both at Paimpol and at Quimper.

"The song was composed," said he, "by a blind bard and first given at the court of François Ier. . . .

"I love to sing the old songs, the Breton songs," he said. "I was asked to sing in opera in Paris, but I refused."

We asked him to tell us about the Gorsedd (the college of bards), which corresponds to the Welsh Eisteddfod.

"It is," said Cueff, "a society all of whose members write in Breton. The head of it is called the archdruid, the officers are known as druids . . . Jaffrenou is a 'druid' . . . the rest of us singers are bards. All must have written something in Breton. Each bard is given a Breton name; mine is Kaner-Léon, 'the singer from Léon.'

"Since my marriage two years ago I have lived in Pont-Aven. I speak the Léon tongue, my wife that of Cornouaille. The speech of the Morbihan is harder to understand. The people of the Morbihan mumble and eat their words; but the best singers to-day are found in the Morbihan."

He spoke of Gourvil, the bard of Morlaix: "*There* is a man who speaks Breton—a true *diseur!*"

We mentioned the good time we had had at Gourvil's book-shop and how Gourvil had shown us a rare copy of "Ar Bibl Santel"—the Bible published in Breton, which he told us could be read by any users of the tongue. There is a chapel in central Brittany, near Pontivy, where the parish priest holds services in each of the three major dialects!

Exhilarated by wind and spray, by pleasant converse—apropos of a passing cruiser Cueff had reminisced about his wartime experiences at the Dardenelles—we found ourselves nearing the port of le Palais before we realized that an hour could have passed. The rough crossing, which, fortunately for the rusticity of Belle-Ile, deters many tourists, had had no terrors.

Le Palais is dominated by an ancient citadel, built by the Maréchal de Retz in the sixteenth century and augmented by Vauban. A reformatory school is housed in a building once intended for political prisoners. Its several hundred inmates are taught to be sailors or farmers according to inclination, the latter being housed inland. The harbor is filled with ruddy-sailed boats, the adjacent shipyards teem with activity. Fishermen in striking costumes promenade along the quays. From the dining-room of the Hôtel de Bretagne, whether looking seaward or in reflecting mirrors, one may watch sails slip to port as one may from the windows of the Atlantic at Concarneau. Indeed, it was of Concarneau that Belle-Ile reminded us, and more especially the inner port of le Palais with blue nets drying against a background of gleaming buff or salmon house walls. Other comparisons which came to mind were with the Isle of Bréhat and with Camaret. The more visited part of the island—chauffeurs are insistent upon taking the traveler for the *Grande Tournée:* Sauzon, the Pointe des Poulains, the Apothicairerie—resembles Bréhat; but the wild moorland, the hamlets, the absence of villas (which the local guide-books deplore!), the many windmills around Locmaria suggest the wind-swept region of Camaret's rock-bound coast.

Contrary to precedent, we made our way first to the wilder end of the island—to the lighthouse on the Côte Sauvage, to Port Coton, and, via the road built by German prisoners, to Bangor and Locmaria. (German submarines are said to have girdled Belle-Ile with sunken shipping.) Horses were turning threshing wheels. Golden stocks of grain towered in the barnyards. Women were out with flails, singing rhythmically as upon the Ile de Sein. A funeral issued from the church at Locmaria; we remarked the dignity of these erect, coifed daughters of Canadian ancestors. We saw the grotto of Locmaria, near the stone pylon surrounded by the sea, chosen by Dumas for the scene of the tragic death of Porthos. We passed the Pointe de Kerdonis with its lighthouse renowned for the heroism of a woman and child who kept the light from failing in wartime during the mortal illness of the guardian. We paused for refreshment with friends who own the little fort, now a château, of la Biche, and found our way home to le Palais by a rural hilly road over which our islander chauffeur had never before traveled!

The grotto of the Apothicairerie with its natural arch of stone is overshadowed in my memory by the climax of Belle-Ile—the Pointe des Poulains. Dramatic as its late owner, Sarah Bernhardt, the point with its rock-bound cliffs defies the force of the Atlantic to overwhelm it . . . even as the divine Sarah defied age or the amputation of a limb to subdue her dauntless spirit.

"Quand Même"! Well chosen was the motto which adorned your curtain, O Bernhardt, that night when I heard you utter the deathless lamentation of Phèdre.

"You called her, in America, 'the divine Sarah'!" exclaimed our red-clad chauffeur, who had just completed his military service at Vannes and whose mother sells fishermen's garments in the shop beside the Hôtel de Ville at le Palais.

"I have often spoken with Madame Bernhardt; she was adored on the island. She came first to the Villa Simone, then she bought this *fortin déclassé,*" and he pointed to one of the little forts which formerly protected the island's coast. "She gave the Government only a few thousand francs for it, but I know she hated to leave it to move to the large house which she purchased later; it was less damp there. She had these avenues of tamarisks planted and the labyrinth that you so much admire. She had her farm-house, the Villa l'Aiglon for her friends, and another villa where her artist who painted the portrait lived; it was he whom she loved the best. You see the little house beside the fort? That was for her son, Maurice. Its name is 'Cinq Parties du Monde'; her love embraced the universe.

"She came to Belle-Ile for thirty-five years—yes, the very summer before her death. There is the rock where she wished to be buried. No, the one where the waves dash and the cormorants circle . . . a bizarre idea. There you have it: she was bizarre, the divine Sarah, bizarre but yet divine.''

Alas, that fate has deprived you of your storm-racked tomb, O indomitable Bernhardt!

The Fort of Sarah Bernhardt

ROHAN SUIS

Second to none in Brittany is the Château of Josselin.

CHAPTER XXI

THE FOREST OF BROCÉLIANDE

The very antithesis of the capital of Belle-Ile-en-Mer is Rochefort-en-Terre. While le Palais, cut off from the mainland by the sea, depends upon waters and shipping for its never ending animation, Rochefort, no less completely shut off from the outside world by that desolate moorland the Landes de Lanvaux, relies upon its own innate rusticity for its unfailing charm. One point these two have in common—that artists are drawn to them as sardines to bait of codfish roe. No railroad leads to Rochefort—which circumstance adds to its allure—but the town may be reached from the station of Malansac, some five kilometers away, or by motor from Vannes from which it lies about twenty-five miles to eastward. That a place of such inconsiderable extent as Rochefort-en-Terre should ever have been called a town is explained by the former importance of its castle, once an almost impregnable fortress.

To the discerning traveler ardently in quest of the individual, the picturesque Rochefort offers a unique opportunity. It possesses an inn, of the type of the Hôtel Julia at Pont-Aven in its halcyon days before the addition of the annex; a wealth of ancient houses calculated to delight the soul of an artist; a château of intrinsic merit; a situation unequaled in central Brittany. It forms a convenient center for some of the most fascinating inland excursions to be made in the province—those to the historic Towers of Elven; to the Castle of Josselin, the seat of the Duc de Rohan and incomparably the finest habitable château in the province; and, via the delectable towns of Malestroit and Ploërmel, to the Fôret de Paimpoint, known to lovers of Arthurian romance as the Forest of Brocéliande.

The site of Rochefort was colonized by the Romans. The first Christian missionaries, judging from the statues which have been unearthed, substituted the cult of the Virgin for that of Venus. In the tenth century the place was stormed by the Normans. At this time the sacred image of Mary was concealed in a tree trunk. According to the curé of Notre-Dame-de-la-Tronchaye, the figure of the Virgin was discovered in the twelfth century and reinstated in the edifice which bears her name. In this church many of the Counts of Rochefort have been interred. Among them was Pierre de Rochefort, Marshal of France, who fought with

Jeanne d'Arc and regained Dieppe and Harfleur from the English. In 1438, de Rochefort was taken prisoner before Compiègne and was starved to death by his captors. A nephew was allowed to carry out his uncle's last wish, burying him at the feet of Our Lady of la Tronchaye.

Monsieur le Curé waxes eloquent on the subject of the outrageous conduct of the daughters of another Marshal of France, Claude de Rochefort, who died before his children had been educated. The elder, known as Guyonne la Folle because of her scandalous conduct, was excommunicated by the pope and, to spite his Holiness, turned Protestant. The younger, Claude, was held by the good rector in equal disfavor because she had become a Protestant and actually had married one of the arch Huguenots—François de Coligny, brother of the illustrious admiral. Calvinist services (what a blot on the scutcheon!) were held in the chapel of the château.

This stronghold of the powerful Counts of Rochefort was destroyed for the first time by men-at-arms of Anne de Beaujeu, who wished to chastise the Marshal Jean IV de Rieux et Rochefort (grandson of the heiress Jeanne and Jeane II de Rieux) for his persistent opposition to the marriage of his pupil Anne de Bretagne with Charles VIII. After she had become Queen of France, Anne de Bretagne made a present to her former tutor of one hundred thousand golden crowns. With this tidy fortune the aggrieved count was able to construct a still more formidable fortress.

High-perched above the barren valley of the Arz and overlooking arid rock-ribbed hills, the château-fort withstood attack by the Prince de Conti, who tried to take it for Henri IV and the League. After hurling two thousand five hundred cannon-balls against its impregnable ramparts the prince withdrew in high dudgeon. Two years later, however, the castle was burnt by the Governor of Redon; thus was secured a victory for the Catholic Leaguers.

Jean de Rieux-Rochefort, lieutenant of the king in Brittany, was deprived of his fastness in 1589, following the defeat of his armed forces. An old record of the year 1633, written during the life of the last count of the family of Rochefort, tells, "Of the château, there remain only the ruins."

About 1658, one Exupère de Tarlan reconstructed the Castle of Rochefort, which was to be again destroyed, after over a century of peace, by disaffected peasants. Fifteen thousand strong, these revolutionists stormed the place, the year being 1793. "Volunteers," as they were called, were permitted to invade the haughty château of the counts, carrying away its stones piecemeal to further their own building operations. When Mr. Klots, American artist and present owner, set himself the congenial task of reconstructing the château (a task for which he was well fitted by taste and fortune) he found five half-ruined towers and the crumbling walls of the ancient keep.

Not the least of the benefactions of the present lord of the manor (his château was used as a convalescent home for American soldiers during the war) is the initiative he has shown in giving window-boxes and plants to the villagers and in offering prizes for the most beautifully decorated houses. In 1926, Rochefort was awarded one of the Touring Club prizes, given annually to *villes fleuries.* An article in "L'Illustration" suggests that as Harlem is noted for its tulips, so Rochefort is noted for its geraniums. Its name, the writer goes on to say, should be "Rochefort-les-Fleurs."

One of our happiest memories of the town was our charming reception by Mr. and Mrs. Klots, who showed us their treasure-house with its carefully acquired antiques, a primitive Madonna probably from the château chapel but found in an attic at Rochefort; the master's striking portrait of Cardinal Gibbons in the "Ecclesiastic Room," an apartment gorgeous with crimson damask. In his guest-book the owner pointed out the names of Anatole Le Braz and Mary D. Le Braz—acclaimed alike in peasant cottage and lordly château.

As Julia was responsible for the popularity of Pont-Aven, so the late Madame le Cadre and the daughters who worthily follow in her footsteps have made the reputation of Rochefort-en-Terre.

ROCHEFORT-EN-TERRE

The Hôtel le Cadre is known to the initiated throughout the length and breadth of Brittany. The simple wayside inn accommodates a very moderate number of guests. Riotously blooming window-boxes are the only feature of the exterior of the inn—placed as it is directly upon the street, without benefit of garden—which foretells its charm. Pelouze the landscape painter, I believe, started the vogue for Rochefort. Pierre Emile Cornillier, distinguished Parisian, spends his summers here. Upon the paneled walls of the inn innumerable other artists have left souvenirs of their passing. Let those who relish the idea of lighting themselves to bed with a *bougie* (what gleaming candlesticks bedeck the chimneypiece!) and who can with equanimity forgo the morning tub, flock to as yet unspoiled Rochefort. Nevertheless a word of caution: it is not wise to tarry unduly on excursions; Mademoiselle is strict as to the hours of meals, and late-comers win disfavor and cold victuals in lieu of confections cooked to perfection by

Mademoiselle Marie-Françoise and served, with equal distinction, by her sister, Mademoiselle Anastasie. It must be remembered that these two darlings (becoifed after the fashion of Rochefort) have reached years when most ladies of their refinement would have retired to enjoy the fruits of labor, but to the sisters le Cadre the administration of their inn is as necessary as breath to their nostrils.

"Has Madame seen the terrace?" was one of the first questions Mademoiselle Anastasie asked me, and—getting a negative reply, for I had not so much as guessed the existence of a terrace—she led me through the court, past the garage, to the most bewitching spot to be found in Rochefort, with few rivals in midland Brittany. Here, on the terrace, Monsieur and I were wont to linger at tea-time; sitting in welcome shade amidst twining tendrils and fragrant blossoms; remote from the town; overlooking, from our hillside, the meager stream of Arz, the opposite ridge of the Roches Noires, the heath-purpled hills. I remember the intrusion of sophisticated Parisians and their patronizing "Un pays perdu!"

Another day—it was the dinner hour, but Mademoiselle Anastasie could not round up her *pensionnaires*—we were startled by the trumpet of the town crier and shouts of "Fire! Fire on the hills!"

Knowing the dryness of the heather, the inflammability of the pines, the townspeople turned out pellmell. It was on the slopes opposite our terrace that the fire was raging. We looked across the valley, to the assembling throngs. From the river to the blaze women formed a hurrying brigade. Buckets and watering-pots leaped from hand to hand. Smoke rolled up in billows. Men savagely beat the flames. Darkness fell before the conflagration was extinguished.

On August 19 we assisted at the *fête fleurie,* held in the allées. After this our stay was prolonged to take the excursions which form so important a reason for a stay at Rochefort. Long before the time of departure the place had taken a hold upon me which I should little have thought possible, remembering my first impressions. It was, I think, a mark of especial favor which prompted Mademoiselle Anastasie to lead me, on that last morning (as she had done upon the first), to the terrace and to gather for me the seeds of what she called *paquerettes*, the tall bushy marguerites found in every Breton garden and known to seedsmen as Leucanthemum. After she had shaken the dry seeds into an envelop of the Hôtel le Cadre she turned to me and, with a beautiful smile illuminating her spiritual face, she said:

"Now when you gather paquerettes in your American garden you will send a thought to Rochefort, n'est-ce pas, madame?" . . . This very summer, I am resolved, Mademoiselle Anastasie shall

Elven ⚜

receive photographic proof of my success as a gardener.

Since the destruction by the Germans of Coucy in the Aisne, the Tour d'Elven is the largest donjon to be found in France. Reached from Rochefort-en-Terre by a drive through undulating uplands, desolate moors strewn with megalithic remains almost equal to those of Carnac, the two surviving towers of the Castle of Largouët take the name of a neighboring village and are known as the Tours d'Elven. It is still possible to mount the worn steps of the massive octagonal keep—la Grosse Tour, built in 1460—to where young Henry Richmond (afterward Henry VII of England) and his uncle the Earl of Pembroke were confined from 1474 to 1476. Fleeing after the Battle of Tewkesbury, the noblemen sought refuge in Brittany but were held as hostages by François II, Duke of Brittany, and did not regain their freedom until after fourteen years in captivity.

Octave Feuillet has used the setting of the Great Tower for a daring scene in the "Romance of a Poor Young Man." The slit of a window and the oak to which the leap was made are shown quite as though the affair had actually taken place. Indeed, the episode is more alive in our time than the unchronicled events of Elven's dead yesterdays.

Second to none in Brittany is the Château of Josselin, half-way from Rochefort-en-Terre to Pontivy and to-day the seat of the Duc de Rohan, as once was Pontivy. Second to none, too, is the noble family, proudest in Brittany—as is shown by its oft-quoted device:

Roi ne puis,
Prince ne daigne,
Rohan suis!

The original castle was begun by the Vicomte de Porhoët and named for his son Josselin . . .

this in the eleventh century. In the next century it was besieged and destroyed by Henry II of England. Rebuilt by the de Porhoëts, the stronghold of Josselin was owned successively by the houses of Fougères, Lusignan, and France.

During the Hundred Years' War, on March 27, 1351, Jean de Beaumanoir, who was governor for the Countess of Penthièvre and in possession of Josselin, set out to right the wrongs perpetrated by the English (in league with the widow and son of de Montfort), established at Ploërmel. It was decided that Beaumanoir and Bembro—appointed by Edward III Governor of Ploërmel, leader of the English forces—should each choose thirty supporters, champions to meet in deadly combat. The conflict was held half-way between the two towns, at the Chêne de Mi-Voie. Wounded, de Beaumanoir plead for water, but an enemy cried, "Drink thine own blood!" Eventually the French forces were triumphant. With sprigs of broom in their helmets and singing to the glory of the warriors' patron Saint Cado, as since minstrels have sung the fame of "the Thirty," they led their surviving opponents prisoners to Josselin.

Olivier de Clisson, valiant Constable of France, trading lands, came into possession of Josselin in the year 1370 and made the stronghold an impregnable nucleus of the French in Brittany. Three feudal towers of the *fier castel* date from this epoch. De Clisson took for his second bride the widow of de Beaumanoir, Marguerite de Rohan. . . . Recumbent statues of the pair dignify their tombs in Notre-Dame-du-Roncier at Josselin. . . . History records that the constable's daughter Margot, Comtesse de Penthièvre, when the news of the death of Jean V of Brittany reached her, ran to her father's bedroom and addressed him in this wise:

"It rests now with you to help my husband recover his inheritance!" insinuating that the late duke's children, de Clisson's wards, should be put out of the way. The constable seized a javelin and his unworthy offspring fled for her life.

It was in this chamber overlooking the hills that the "très haut et très puissant seigneur Monseigneur Olivier de Clisson, jadis connétable de France," died in 1407. His eldest daughter, Béatrix de Clisson, wife of Alain VIII, Vicomte de Rohan, inherited the Castle of Josselin. Over five hundred years later it was another Duc Alain de Rohan—in whose family the château had always remained—who undertook the restoration of the abandoned castle, and to-day his grandson, young Alain de Rohan, the present duke, spends his summers at Josselin. The late Duke Josselin de Rohan—gallant descendant of Olivier de Clisson—wounded at Verdun, was killed in action in the Somme at the age of thirty-six.

That the illustrious name of Rohan was not without its enemies is proved by the fact that in parts of Brittany pigs are called *mab-rohan,* that is to say, "sons of Rohan"! . . . an expression doubtless coined by an Anglo-Breton or by an anti-Huguenot. The Rohans were the first to introduce the Protestant faith into the province. The massive table on which the Edict of Nantes was signed now stands in the salon of the Château of Josselin.

Josselin, unlike its noble owners, presents two faces to the public. The one frowns menacingly from the cliff bank of the river Oust, the other smiles upon the gardens that blossom in the castle's ancient moat. The frowning Josselin is that of Olivier de Clisson; the smiling Josselin or *logis seigneurial,* flowering with late Gothic ornament, the arms of Rohan, France, and Brittany, dates from the time of Jean II de Rohan. It is this creation of John the Builder that, because of similarity of style and decoration, has been compared with three of the world's acclaimed buildings: the Palais de Justice at Rouen, the Hôtel de Cluny at Paris, and the Château de Blois.

The forest of Paimpont, the Brocéliande of Arthurian romance, may be visited by motor from Rochefort. It is wise to make an early start, in order to pause at Malestroit (with memories of its sire and the "New Arabian Nights"!) and at Ploërmel, scene of Meyerbeer's opera "Le Pardon de Ploërmel," both of which towns are justly

famed for examples of the domestic architecture of long-gone centuries.

Approach the forest via Trécesson; at Beauvais venture afoot to the Val sans Retour; when and *if* you return, lunch at Paimpont, where sun-time reigns, man not having tampered with the clock; after lunch drive back to the Haute Fôret and on to the Etang des Forges and the Etang-Neuf, where you will find Arthurian oaks, with mighty trunks and spread of limbs, mantled with moss, ferns growing in crotches; then hasten home by way of Guer to Rochefort-en-Terre. These instructions are for the romantically minded, to whom this privately owned and exploited remnant can by aid of imagination's magic once more become the vast forest haunt of druids and knights of the Round Table—the Armorican Brocéliande where, having withdrawn from Arthur's court, the enchanter Merlin

to this day lies spellbound by the incantations of Vivian.

The witchery of Brocéliande began for us without the forest's borders, at the Château of Trécesson. Even as I write the word I wonder if Trécesson can actually exist in this twentieth century in this our workaday world. Trécesson would seem to be the creation of a dream did not my guide-book clearly state "Château de Trécesson, 15th century, owner the Comte de Prunelaie"! The exquisite residence of Monsieur le Comte rises, as might a fairy castle, from the quiet surface of a lake. I see again in memory the ivy-clad turrets mirrored in still waters, the drifting white water-fowl—ducks, geese, and swans—the bucolic pastures with grazing cattle, the magnificent allées of Breton oaks.

It was at Beauvais, an insignificant hamlet, that

we secured a guide (for so he styled himself) to Merlin's prison, the Val sans Retour. This guileless youth wore ragged woolen socks and ill-fitting sabots which slipped on the dry grass. At regular intervals he was forced to remove his foot-gear in order to extract thorns from his horny toes. Following his lead, we passed a deserted manor where the path narrowed, climbed over a bristling hedge, and, to our amazement, plunged into an almost impenetrable thicket. After floundering amid gorse, brambles, and holly, stopping often to save eyes and disentangle clothing, hoping always to regain a path, we came upon a trail of sufficient height for a wild boar but so choked with briars as to necessitate our bending double. Having completely lost faith in the ability of our witless youth, and possessing no magic by which to reduce in size, we thought at one juncture that we might stick head-foremost in a blackberry bramble, repeating the misfortune of Merlin shut spell-bound in a hawthorn bush.

"The Valley whence None Return; why came we hither?" So spoke Monsieur.

"The spell is powerless," I replied, "save in the case of false lovers. Have no fear."

After a stubborn uphill climb, torn and tousled, we did at last arrive at a vantage-point. From the rocky ridge our eyes wandered over the desolate moor to the mysterious Bois Guillaume. At our feet lay the silent valley which told no tales of how many faithless lovers it held enthralled.

That we did not encounter a wild boar on this expedition was a bit of good fortune, for a forester's wife, with whom we chatted at Haute Fôret, told us there are many about. Frightened by the huntsmen and their dogs, the boars often become ferocious; one had killed a woman only the month before. We had driven through a part of the forest where men were felling firs, to the woody Carrefour de Haute Fôret; here five routes converge. This was the culminating altitude. As we looked over undulating country which rolled away to the horizon, we were startled by the apricot hue of the sky.

Yes, the forester's mate informed us, the toll of trees lost by fire is heavy; the foresters, her husband among them, were fighting flames at that very moment in the direction of Roche-Plate . . . pray God that the monster beech be spared. Often, she told us, fires have started with the charcoal-burners.

Have you ever, O gentle reader, known the joy of coming, after days of fruitless search, upon the clearing of a charcoal-burner? Such was our luck in the forest of Camors, near Baud. Two smoldering mounds, formed like mammonth ant-hills, showed gleaming signs of hidden fire. The charcoal-burner told us of the work's routine. His

A charcoal-burner in the Forest of Camors

patron would buy a grove of oaks; yes, always oaks—oh, the pity of it! After the wood-choppers have held their sway, come the tanners with hides, to use the bark, and, last, the charcoal-burners.

And should we like to see his *loge?* and, as we beamed our pleasure, "It is not forbidden to enter," said he, pointing a sooty finger at a larger mound with earth-covered roof festooned with ivy. The young wife received us graciously, offering cider and displaying the bairns. She, too, loved the forest life. Oh yes, the fires must be tended during the night.

At Paimpont the genial keeper of the inn queried with quizzical interrogation:

"You found the Val sans Retour somewhat invaded by vegetation?"

"Somewhat!"

He told us that in this canton of Brécilien, and indeed elsewhere in Brittany, it is not unusual to hear a peasant remark in Breton when the wind blows, "King Arthur is riding through the forest with his men."

No time had we to regain youth at the Fountain of Jouvence; nor yet to test the magic powers of Merlin's spring of Barenton, once haunted by a black-mailed chevalier; nor yet to visit all of the fourteen lakes or tarns, nor the rough dolmen known as Merlin's tomb—but we know better, for at time of the Saint-Jean does not Merlin still meet his Vivian?

"Alas!" writes the chronicler, "he [Merlin, son of a nun and a demon] met near Barenton the gentle Vivian, daughter of the Seigneur de Comper, to whom he taught his art of sorcery. . . . Shut he lies in the Valley without Return till Judgment Day."

Let him who would sleep beneath a hawthorn tree beware the snare of that fay Vivian!

Château de Trécesson

Anne: Duchess of Brittany.

CHAPTER XXII

NANTES, BIRTHPLACE OF BRIAND

To THE Englishman or American, Nantes is first and foremost the birthplace of the famous Edict. It was here in the château, most probably, though some insist that it was in the Maison des Tourelles, that Henri IV signed the document which accorded liberty of conscience to his Protestant subjects, the Huguenots. The ninety-five general articles were signed on April 13, 1598, the fifty-six particular ones on May 2 of the same year.

In order to appreciate this hard-won victory of the Huguenots, one should know something of the history of Protestantism in the region. Following the Massacre of Saint Bartholomew in 1572, the Duc de Montpensier, Governor of Nantes, wrote officially from Paris, where he was staying, advocating a like murder of Huguenots in the city of Nantes. Thanks to the refusal of the mayor, however, the proposed slaughter did not take place.

Ever since the visit of Dandelot, brother of

Admiral Coligny, to Nantes, in 1559, interest in Protestantism had been growing. The Catholics having burnt the meeting-place of the Protestants, the latter retaliated by molesting the Catholics at worship in the cathedral—some of the Huguenots going so far as to enter the sanctuary on horseback. After this episode the Protestants and their pastors took refuge at the suburb of Blain. On the whole, the citizens of Nantes did not take kindly to Protestantism but joined the League under the leadership of the Duc de Mercœur, Governor of Brittany, who installed himself in the château and was loath to allow entrance to Henri IV even after Henri had turned Catholic.

In the year 1622 the Protestants la Muce and le Noir were ordered to make amends for their heresy, before the altar of the cathedral; after which they were to be dragged by four horses, their bodies quartered, and placed in the four principal avenues of the town. Fortunately the two, a nobleman and a pastor, escaped to La Rochelle and the sentence was carried out only in effigy. A château owned by la Muce was demolished, however—that it would be torn to the ground he had been forewarned—and the wood of his forests cut "to the height of a man."

A month after the revocation of the Edict of Nantes, in 1685, the parliament of Brittany ordered the destruction of the church at Sucé, where the Huguenots of Nantes had worshiped in comparative safety. The Protestants in great numbers now left the country, emigrating to Holland, Brandenburg, and England.

Although Nantes, as I have said, has been associated chiefly with the birth of the noted Edict, yet the city is likewise the birthplace of many distinguished figures, among them—to choose my oddly assorted favorites!—Anne de Bretagne, Jules Verne, and Aristide Briand.

Jules Verne was one of the first to appreciate the qualities of Briand, and honored this youthful admirer by making him the hero of one of his tales. As a young man Briand was, like so many who have become good Republicans, a revolutionary Socialist. His biographer remarks that in the penniless youth, the barrister quick to defend innocent though moneyless clients, the revolutionary journalist, few could have seen the future first statesman of Europe.

"Poincaré knows everything and understands nothing," Clemenceau is reported to have said. "Briand knows nothing, but he has antennæ through which he understands everything."

Expelled from the Socialist party because of its dogmatic lack of vision, Briand is at heart a true Socialist in his idealism and belief in human solidarity.

"Peace," says Briand, "is an exacting mistress, still more exacting than war."

It was our good fortune to be in Nantes at the

time of the signing, in Paris, of the Kellogg-Briand anti-war pact. The provincial city was ablaze with bunting. Pride was exhibited on every hand at the doings of "the deputy from Nantes," as they liked to call him at the Hôtel de France.

"Briand used to stay here when he came to Nantes," said our host, "but now he must stay at the prefecture. He lives in an apartment in the Foreign Office in Paris; he says the wind in the trees reminds him of Brittany."

The house on the Place de Bretagne where the premier of a dozen cabinets was born is no longer standing, but Aristide Briand is to-day acclaimed in his native city. Of humble origin, possessing, like Ramsay MacDonald, an innate refinement and Celtic beauty, a mystic and yet a man of action, the hero of Locarno is assured a high place in the history of his time.

Capital of the department of the Loire-Inférieure, chief city of Brittany, Nantes has won at least numerically over its long-time rival the city of Rennes. In the tenth century the dispute for sovereignty ran high between the Counts of Rennes and Nantes. Pierre de Dreux, declared duke by Philippe Auguste, made Nantes his capital. It was, indeed, the preferred residence of many of the dukes. The number of its inhabitants is to-day more than double that of Rennes. Nantes, an impetus to whose shipping was received during the World War, has become a center of maritime commerce and industrialism.

Souvestre has compared Nantes to an Italian city, a "Venice without sun or gondoliers." Situated on the right bank of the Loire—whose five branches one is always crossing—some thirty-five miles from its mouth, Nantes is a city of bridges. Here, also, the river Erdre, forming a lap of the Nantes to Brest Canal, throws itself into the Loire.

Nantes has been called a trading port second only to Marseilles, but was not the writer unmindful of Bordeaux? Indeed, it is with Bordeaux that comparisons leap to mind. Both have handsome monuments in Neo-Greek taste, both have been enriched by the fortunes of eighteenth-century ship-owners. (The merchants of Nantes grew fabulously wealthy carrying on a slave-trade with the West Indies.) At Nantes, however, the natives do not mouth their French nor roll their "r's" as at neighboring Bordeaux!

The ancient quays of the Loire have sinister associations. The citizens of Nantes, ever loyal to the Revolution and offering a stalwart resistance to Vendean uprisings, were, many of them, victims of the Terror. During four long months the guillotine performed its bloody task on the Place du Bouffay. During the unspeakable régime of Carrier, sent from Paris, dark deeds were done the memory of which haunts the stranger to-day as he

wanders along the river bank. The dying groans of the drowning seem to echo down the centuries as thoughts turn to the notorious noyades.

Associations with Anne de Bretagne are of a happier nature. Anne was born in the Château of Nantes; the room is still shown to visitors. After her husband's death it was to the Château of Nantes, rebuilt by her father, that the youthful widowed queen retired. In 1499 it was in the castle's chapel (since destroyed by an explosion) that the marriage which was to restore to her the crown of France took place. Although she died in the Château of Blois (on January 9, 1514) and was interred with ceremony in the burial-place of the kings at Saint-Denis, Anne bequeathed her heart to her "good town of Nantes," with the request that it should be placed in the tomb of her father, Duc François II.

Three massive towers of the fastness at Nantes date from the reign of the Duchess Anne, while the north bastion was an addition erected by the Duc de Mercœur. The castle was once washed by the waters of the Loire. The Grand-Logis, in the style of the Renaissance, now houses a collection of Breton art.

We were particularly interested in the native pottery. One plate of the Revolutionary period represents a sturdy Breton peasant with a cross over one shoulder and a sword over the other, the motto being:

Je suis las de les porter . . .

That was in 1791. A Socialist friend of ours remarked that the Breton is still weary of carrying his double burden—but thinks, when entering a battle for Church or State, that he is fighting for his God and his Liberty.

The famous "Book of Hours" of Anne of Brittany—with forty-eight full-page miniatures, twenty-four illuminated calendar pages, the Latin text bordered with designs of fruits, flowers, insects, and reptiles—is to be seen to-day in the Bibliothèque Nationale. Nantes possesses, at the fascinating Musée Dobrée (where, too, is an engraving of Henri IV signing the Edict), a facsimile of the only known manuscript letter by Anne, the original of which is in the British Museum, and several letters signed by the duchess. Here, too, may be seen the golden heart-shaped casket which up to the time of the Revolution contained that "precious jewel the heart of the queen."

"The golden vessel," says the chronicler, "was carried through the streets with great pomp. The houses were hung with white draperies and candles blazed in every window. A crier in black velvet opened the march. At every cross-road he rang the bells which he carried in each hand and demanded prayers for the dead queen. A hundred men followed, clad in black, carrying massive torches. Then came all the notables of the town. The chancellor of Brittany bore the heart of the *bonne duchesse* which was deposited in a magnificent chapel." . . . Four thousand candles were lighted at Notre-Dame in Paris for the Queen of France, but Nantes offered five thousand for the beloved Duchess of Brittany.

The tomb in the chapel of the Carmelites (the chef-d'œuvre of the Breton sculptor Michel Colombe which had been erected by Anne in memory of her parents, François II and Marguerite de Foix), having been violated at the time of the Revolution, was later transferred to the cathedral. The two marble effigies may be seen there to-day, still guarded by representations of the cardinal virtues, that of Justice, it is said, being a portrait of the Duchess Anne.

The Château of Goulaine, rising above the marshes of the Loire southeast of Nantes, still remains the property of the Comte de Goulaine, who also owns a château near Hennebont. It was at the Castle of Goulaine that Henri IV stayed on his way to sign the Edict of Nantes. Louis XIV is said to have ridden on horseback up the broad stone stairway. Since the war Goulaine has been classed as an historic monument and its exterior has been put into repair by the State. The count is in the act of restoring the interior. Ivy-clad, approached by a long allée, surrounded with majestic chestnuts, Goulaine has preserved the spirit of its illustrious past. Here—more, indeed, than at Nantes—may be recaptured the glamorous days of Henry of Navarre.

Clisson—still farther southward, on the river Sèvre—is now but a mere shell, a ruin which speaks of former grandeur. Here, in this castle erected in the thirteenth century by an ancestor of Olivier de Clisson, François II, Duke of Brittany, was married to Marguerite de Foix. Near by is the grotto sacred to the memory of Héloïse and Abélard. It was at the hamlet of le Pallet, a few kilometers away, that, in 1079, Abélard first saw the light. His ancestral château has fallen to dust, but the interior of a tiny sanctuary dedicated to

Sainte Anne remains intact. It was to le Pallet that Héloïse and Abélard fled from Paris. At le Pallet their child, Astrolabe, was born, and christened in this very chapel of Sainte-Anne that is to-day overgrown with luxuriant ivy, guarded by age-old cypresses. Time has swept away all other souvenirs of Abélard.

Westward from Nantes, at the mouth of the Loire, lies the modern ship-building town of Saint-Nazaire. Here the svelte *Paris, France,* and *Ile-de-France* have glided from the ways. Near the boulevard bordering the Atlantic, on a rock in the water, an effective statue of a young American crusader borne by a gigantic eagle was erected in 1926 to commemorate the landing in France of the first American troops, on June 26, 1917. The road continues to fashionable la Baule, and the sardine-fishing port of le Croisic.

Like le Croisic, the Bourg-de-Batz was once surrounded by the sea. To-day all but stranded amid marshes, the inhabitants earn their livelihood by harvesting the ocean's salt. Six thousand tons, I am told, is amassed annually. Although the fantastic dress of the *paludier* or salt-worker is rarely worn nowadays except for festivals, the region of the Bourg-de-Batz is not without an individual charm. The marshland is divided into rectangular basins which at high tide mirror the sky. To us the scene recalled the paddy fields of

Japan—the cone-shaped hillocks of salt reflecting in the still waters like the distant Fujiyamas of Hokusai.

No less curious than the salt-marshes of the Bourg-de-Batz is the neighboring peat-bog of la Grande-Brière. Throughout the winter the morass is covered by the Loire save for a few granite islets, on which the inhabitants dwell; the better-drained portions are used in summer as pasturage. The Briérons of one village communicate with the natives of other settlements by means of a network of canals. Once the Brière, like the marsh at Dol, was a vast forest; ebonized oaks are occasionally disgorged. During only nine days in the year are the inhabitants allowed to cut the peat.

If the Bourg-de-Batz had reminded us of Japan, the Grande-Brière, we thought, was still more suggestive of China. There was a strange un-European desolation about the place. Rude shaggy-thatched, almost Asiatic huts bordered the canals. I remember an especial hamlet beyond Marland, overgrown with rushes; Breca is, I think, its name. Beyond it no road leads. It sits upon the very edge of the drear and untraversable bog. Trignac, its canal dotted with white ducks, transported us in memory to the populous duck-farms along the West River above Canton.

Picturesque salt-workers from the marshes of the Bourg-de-Batz, natives of the isolated villages scattered on islets in the peat-bog of la Brière, gather of a Saturday at the market of Guérande. . . . I have left Guérande to the end of my narrative, for anything coming after would be an anti-climax. It is true that we had seen Vitré, Monsieur and I; we had known Aigues-Mortes and Avignon in Provence, to which Guérande has been compared; yet, barring Carcassonne, we had never before come upon so satisfying a medieval conglomeration. Guérande is complete. Ten towers punctuate its girdling ramparts. The town was once surrounded with water, but to-day its approaches and its moats have submitted to a peaceful invasion of grass blades, where once blades of steel flashed bright in the sun. The drawbridges of Guérande were lowered to receive du Guesclin. De Clisson was needs forced to abandon his attempted siege. The mighty gates of Guérande are four—facing, it has been said, the four winds.

A Paludier on the salt fields of Batz

To the north lies the road to Vannes, to the south that to le Croisic; the road to the west leads to Piriac, while that to the east, beginning at the portal of Saint-Michel, ends shortly at Saint-Nazaire.

Capital of Brittany for a time, Guérande, hardly known beyond the borders of the province, slumbers as peacefully as if no stirring historic events had ever been transacted within its walls. Indeed, the town rarely awakens, but on occasion may be seen such animation as marked the Fête of August 26, 1928, when Duke Jean V received, as of old, the homage of his loyal *paludiers*. It was at Guérande that, in 1365, the treaty of peace was signed between Charles V, King of France, and Jean de Montfort, the ally of England.

Thus even the seemingly never-ending War of the Breton Succession, an integral part of the Hundred Years' War, drew at last to its close . . . and this at Guérande. So likewise, O patient reader, at Guérande must end this journey we have made together. Starting with the walled town of Saint-Malo, we have wandered near and far through the fair forests, moors, and meadows of Brittany. Together we have tarried in her orchards, visited her ancient cities, assisted at her pardons, tramped along her beaches, sailed her seas, ventured to her islands. With eager eyes we have scanned the open pages of her past, we have looked full in the faces of her people, we have listened to their glamorous tales, and, if I mistake not, we have discovered for ourselves—what any of her native sons could have told us in the beginning—the province's true name . . . "Enchanted Brittany."